The Jew and Human Sacrifice

The Jew and Human Sacrifice

[Human Blood and Jewish Ritual]

An historical and sociological inquiry

Hermann L. Strack

Dev Publishers
New Delhi

Published by:
Dev Publishers & Distributors
Second Floor, Prakash Deep,
22, Delhi Medical Association Road,
Darya Ganj,
New Delhi-110002

www.devbooks.co.in

ISBN 978-93-5944-645-5
This edition 2025

Printed in India

CONTENTS

ABBREVIATIONS IN BOOK TITLES

BE = Berlin L = Leipsic

FROM THE PREFACE TO THE FIRST THREE EDITIONS

EVERY year, especially about Easter-time, there is a revival of the accusation that the Jews, or, if not all the Jews, certain Jews, make use of the blood of Christians for purposes of ritual. The charge is bound to be often repeated, so long as the replies to it are limited to the contradiction and exposure of the falsity of the reasons brought forward. . . . . . That is why I discuss the accusation in connection with the *significance of blood as regards religious belief*, and particularly as regards the *superstitions of humanity at large*.

I expressed my opinion on the question, whether the Jews use Christian blood for ritual purposes, as far back as 1882, the year of the Tisza-Eszlar trial, in the *Evangelische Kirchen-Zeitung* (12th August, No. 32). . . . . . . Further investigations (apropos of the Bernstein case, v.p. *144 sq.*) convinced me more than two years ago, that, whilst I was correct in my negative answer to the charge, it was possible, and even necessary, to base it upon a deeper foundation. I am now compelled to publish the results of my fresh researches by the renewal of the controversy about ritual murder in consequence of the assassination of an eight year old girl in Corfu during the night of the 12th to 13th April this year (v.p. *213 sq.*) . . . I have made it my special business to let the facts speak for themselves, and have . . . . . . almost confined myself to quoting, without alteration, the actual statements in the sources of information I have utilised: so anybody who wishes can arrive at an unbiassed judgment for himself.

The facts I have had to bring forward are, for the greater part, of a very loathsome kind. But, in order to cure the terrible disease of superstition, we must first of all *know* the disease. . . My exhortation to our Christian priesthood, to our whole Christian people is: Up and gird yourself for battle, not only against unbelief, but also against superstition! When German Christendom, free from superstition, stands firm in true belief in the crucified Saviour, risen from the dead, the question, so far as concerns Germany, whether Christian blood is ritually employed by Jews, will be exploded and futile, for more reasons than one.

2 July, 1891. *H. L. Strack.*

FROM THE PREFACE TO THE FOURTH EDITION

I have occasion to be thankful for the success of this volume. Most of the journals which used formerly to talk about "Jewish blood-ritual" and "Jewish ritual murder," have been for several months gradually exchanging those phrases for "Jewish blood-murder," "Jewish blood-superstition," avoiding direct reference to *ritual.* However, they still try to prove to their readers, that blood-murder and cases of blood-superstition are peculiar to *Judaism,* and so they keep alive the idea that there must be something ritual behind it all.

Still, the charge against the Jews of using human blood is considerably less effective than it was up till now. Accordingly, those persons who formerly employed it with great success as a means of getting up an agitation, have abundantly emptied the vials of their wrath over me, who, if I have not yet killed it, have yet deadened its effect a great deal. In particular, O. Bachler (of the *Staatsbürger-Zeitung*), Balla (of *Das Volk*), and E. Bauer (of the *Neue Deutsche Zeitung*), have dared shamelessly to *calumniate* me as a scholar, as a man and as a Christian, although they knew the truth, or could have ascertained it without any trouble. Nor did it suffice them to utter the falsehood that Prof. Strack was hardly acquainted with the elements of Hebrew grammar, and only knew about the Talmud what the Rabbis had stuffed him with; they had actually the effrontery to presume that I was receiving money from Jewish quarters for my writings. Attempts are even made to alienate from me the trust of my students, to influence whom, for the benefit of our Evangelical Church and our German fatherland, is both a heartfelt need and a consolation to me in a life full of cares. Were I descended from Abraham on my father's or my mother's side, I should not have to blush. However, as it has been tried to fasten suspicion on me in that respect also, I here affirm that all my ancestors were of pure "Christian-German" descent, the men mostly clergymen or teachers. . . . . .

In order to render the calumniations of myself and the continuance of the blood-accusation extremely impressive, the three persons named (together with Carl Paasch and Normann-Schumann), after exalting the *Osservatore Cattolico,* a paper which appears in Milan, to the dignity of a "universal organ of the Vatican," sent the stuff that suited their purposes to Milan, and transferred it thence into their papers! As the statements had been published in such a "highly esteemed foreign journal," readers must be at once convinced of their truth! . . .

If, on the discovery of a crime, distinct external indications do not point to the perpetrator, inquiries must be made into the possible motive for the deed. Avarice, lust, revenge, jealousy, are motives known to every coroner, and about which, in any given case, he inquires in due course. But he ought likewise not to omit to ask whether the motive might not have been a *superstitious* one. On pp. *89 sq.* I have given numerous examples proving that blood-superstition has often been a cause of crime. An accurate knowledge of superstitions will not seldom lead to the discovery of the criminal, and in other cases prevent following up a false scent. I may therefore recommend this work to the attention of *lawyers.*

It is yet more requisite for *clergymen* and *teachers* to pay heed to the truths propounded in this book. He who has had the good fortune to grow up in a God-fearing family, very often learns nothing about either the barbarity and vices or the superstitions of other social strata, and therefore readily believes it to be all harmless or even denies its existence. . . . . I have now therefore pointed out, even more emphatically than in the original edition, that superstition, especially the "*blood-superstition*," is even nowadays *very wide-spread*, and that it has had in the past, as it has in the present, deplorable, yes and horrible, consequences.

18th Oct., 1892. *H. L. Strack.*

PREFACE TO THE RE-WRITTEN RE-MODELLED WORK (5TH—8TH EDITIONS)

Untruth does not become truth by frequent repetition. But as long as it is repeated, it is a duty incumbent on him who claims to be a champion of truth, knowledge, and justice, to be continually exposing the falsehood of his opponents' assertions, and to state the real truth of the matter. Silence cannot be refuted, and the endeavour to kill the defender of truth by its adoption is only too general. If then the protagonist of truth were actually silent and did not show his power at all, how much more would not conclusions be drawn therefrom against the cause championed by him! For my part I shall not keep silent, so long as I can still wield the sword of mind, and I am also taking measures that my words may be known to those whom they are intended to influence.

I had indeed hoped, after my exposure of the "blood-falsehood" in 1892, to be able to devote myself entirely to different duties: what an enormous task the last decades have imposed upon those investigators of the Old Testament who, rightly, consider the essence of the old faith reconcilable with serious scientific work! and how important it is to show that a knowledge of Jewish literature can be acquired not only by Jewish scholars, but also by at least a few Christians! And my hope seemed to be well-founded, since Aug. Rohling thought it best to answer by silence my crushing attack on him (ch. 17)! Whilst those who had till then calumniated me, viz., Bachler, Balla, and Bauer, made, so far as I was aware, no further attempt to besmirch my good name. Albertario's *Osservatore Cattolico* (v. *pp. 170 seq.*) had whimperingly appealed for help in the *Neue Deutsche Zeitung*,* and got none, because the few German scholars, who had till then assumed the possibility of ritual murders, recognised that they would put their honour in the pillory if they attempted to give such assistance. Bauer's *Neue Deutsche Zeitung* collapsed in Leipsic, and the *Volk*, unfit for the struggle of life in Berlin, fled into a corner. Abbé David Albertario was condemned in 1898 to three years' loss of liberty on account of revolutionary disturbances. Carl Paasch, the author of "Eine jüdisch-deutsche Gesandtschaft und ihre Helfer," L. 1891 (965 pp.) was recognised, also by a Court of Law, as being no longer responsible for his actions. Robert Normann-Schumann, who tried to press himself upon me in 1885, and who, later on, taking pay simultaneously both from Anti-semites and Jews, deceived both of them, thought it advisable, when he was prosecuted for *lèse-majesté*, and feared the discovery of other inci-

* 15 Oct. 1892, No. 241: "The following appeal from the editor of the *Osservatore Cattolico* in Milan reaches us, with the request to publish it:—'As soon as Prof. H. Strack shall have published the brochure announced by him, we intend to reply to it by a comprehensive refutation. Thanks to the kindness of some readers and the ardour which our co-workers have displayed in this campaign, we already possess considerable material for proving the existence of Jewish ritual murder—in cases, which can be attested by witnesses who are still *living* (Alb. refers, e.g., to the Eisleben case! v.p. 218). Nevertheless it would be very useful if readers in foreign parts, by contributing fresh evidence, were to prove their interest in these highly-important polemics. In all cases they may certainly rely upon the strictest discretion (!). We know that there are still in private libraries and other collections important MSS. on the subject, which should no longer be withheld from publicity. Any contribution, any suggestion, any explanation is welcome. . . . We also beg all Christian editors to make this appeal known.'"

The *Neue Deutsche Zeitung*, the *Staatsbürger-Zeitung*, Berlin, 16 Oct., No. 485, the *Neue Preussische Zeitung* (at that time still the organ of the ill-reputed Freiherr v. Hammerstein), 18 Oct., No. 487, and other papers did their best to circulate the appeal.

dents in his career, to go and live quietly in hiding in free Switzerland. Paulus Meyer (*v.p. 148 and pp. 224 sq.*) who was hired to traduce me, had to undergo severe terms of imprisonment owing to libels and insults he had uttered. O. Bachler alone was in a position publicly to continue to deviate consciously from the truth (*v.p. 218*).

My hope, however, proved to be mistaken. The "blood-accusation" appeared such an effective means of exciting the populace that the anti-semites were constantly tempted to make misuse of the word. At the end of March, 1899, a favourable opportunity was afforded by the murder of Agnes Hruza, at Polna (*v. pp. 228 sq.*). It did not matter to the un-Christian people, who called themselves Christians, whether the murderer were discovered or the suspicion resting on Hilsner were seriously probed; but Dr. Baxa, who was nominally counsel for the murdered girl's mother, was to assume and prove ritual murder. But he only proved his disgraceful ignorance. For example, according to an abstract of the shorthand report, which reached me a few days ago, he made, besides other falsehoods, the following statement: "And I ask whether Dr. Aurednišek (Hilsner's counsel) knows the declaration of the Rabbi Vital, that the coming of the Messiah will be hastened by the blood of sacrificed Gentile virgins, or whether he knows it is stated in the first book of the Sohar, that the fourth, the best palace shall be inhabited by those who have killed Akums, i.e., Christians; whether he knows the assertion of the Rabbi Eliken (read: 'Elieser'), that all Gentile nations are mere brute beasts."*

* Baxa got this rubbish out of Rohling's "Polemik u. Menschenopfer," Paderborn, 1883, 58, 72, 75; Cf. in my book p. 157, pp. 161 sq. As to the description of Gentiles as beasts v. J. Kopp, "Zur Judenfrage," 107-118; Bloch, "Acten" I., 253-263. That the expression "Akum" is entirely an invention of the critics is shown in my "Einleitung in den Talmud," 4th Edition, Leipsic 1908, p. 51.

The unrest caused by this trial, especially in Austria and South Germany, has compelled me to postpone the revised edition of my "Einleitung in den Talmud," which has been out of print for a long time, and to expose anew the "blood-falsehood." My book in its present form will be convincing to all who have not, out of racial hatred, made up their minds to maintain the truth of the "blood-accusation" against the Jews, despite all refutation. It is in great part a new book. Most of the contents of chapters 18—20 have been re-written; it was important to show that history affords us no evidence of "Jewish ritual-murder," and that the most eminent Popes and temporal rulers have emphatically declared against the "blood-charge," that no single Pope has countenanced it. The first part, too, has been considerably augmented. I am certain that now, besides ecclesiastics, teachers, and state attorneys, even professional Folklorists will be able to learn and get stimulus from it.

I have had to include in my purview very varied domains of human knowledge, and the procuring of the material has cost much time and labour; e.g., in order to be in a position to make a trustworthy statement with regard to J. E. Veith's oath (*pp. 245 sq.*), I had to write some fifteen letters. I am the more heartily grateful to Professors Dr. Ludwig Freytag, Dr. Otto Hirschfeld, Dr. med. J. L. Pagel, who are all in Berlin, and others, in that they have answered several questions of mine, and have suggested many improvements in this work. To this expression of thanks I add the request that those who are in a position to complete, to corroborate, or to confirm by their own experience the statements here made public, may not shrink from the trouble of sending me in that connection as precisely accurate a communication as may be possible. Even a paragraph that appears unimportant in itself may acquire value by its context.

My publicly entering the lists on behalf of my conviction, and particularly my refutation of the calumnies against the *Jewish religion*,* has procured me not only abuse in the daily Press, but also serious material damage. But I am none the less assured that it is my duty to go on as before. During the last months, I had to contend against the feelings of pain and disgust occasioned by all the horrors and deeds of horror, about which I had to write even more in the fifth edition than in the preceding. But I then reflected that the esteem in which both the Christian religion and our Lord and Saviour Jesus Christ are held among the Jews, had suffered severely, owing to the aforesaid calumnies, and especially owing to the "blood-accusation" against them. I knew it to be my sacred duty as a Christian theologian to do everything in my power to compass the conviction in Israel that Jesus does not desire falsehood but truth, not hatred but love: He makes them just who truly believe in Him, and He is worthy that mankind should bend their knees in His name.

May my fight against untruthfulness and superstition at any rate help towards the furthering of peace and a purer knowledge of God upon earth!

Gross-Lichterfelde, nr. Berlin, 18 Feb., 1900.

* I emphasise the word "religion," and refer to my brochure, "Die Juden dürfen sie 'Verbrecher von Religionswegen' genannt werden?" L. 1893 (30 pp.) J. C. Hinrichs. I add with satisfaction that several German courts of justice later on gave decisions in accord with my demand in the pamphlet, and above all, the spreading of the "Talmud-campaign" in Bavaria has been made punishable at law.

PREFACE TO THE ENGLISH TRANSLATION

This translation, which is the work of Mr. H. F. E. Blanchamp, is in many respects superior to the German original. I have not only cancelled many paragraphs of only temporary or local importance, but carefully revised the whole, and added a good deal of new material—*vide* especially chapters xviii and xx. So I hope my book will make its way in English-speaking lands, and help to discredit the propagation of the abominable blood-accusation. The work of remodelling went greatly against the grain, but "to him that knoweth to do good, and doeth it not, to him it is sin" (James iv, 17).

I am not a "Philo-semite" in the now generally accepted sense of the word. I have even been slandered as an "Anti-semite." As a Christian theologian, I wish simply to serve the truth, for the sake of my Lord, who is "the way, the truth, and the life."

Hermann L. Strack.

Grosslichterfelde West, near Berlin,
March 7th, 1909.

I INTRODUCTION

BIBLIOGRAPHY

The exceeding importance of blood in life has doubtless been evident to mankind from remotest times, seeing that it was inculcated by frequently recurring experiences, e.g., in butchering and in hunting. Man himself has a feeling of weakness after losing much blood, and if he loses more than a certain quantity of blood, life itself ceases.

The knowledge of this high value of blood gave rise, firstly, to bloody sacrifices (a living being is the greatest sacrifice), especially human sacrifices (Ch. 2); secondly, to symbolical* acts (Ch. 3); thirdly, to the conviction that extraordinary effects are procured by blood, particularly the humàn, but also animal blood (Chas. 4-7, 9). Closely connected with this conviction is the other, that wonderful powers belong to the human body, also to the corpse, and its parts (Ch. 8); especially to the body of one who has died a violent death, e.g. of an executed person and a suicide (Ch. 7); and, further, to that of an innocent human being, e.g., a little child, especially an unborn, and a virgin (Chas. 11-12). Therewith is connected the use of the bodies, bodily parts and evacuations of animals for healing and other purposes (Ch. 10). Another first element, especially when there is blood adhering, is the fatal knife or sword.

To what results, often hideously outrageous to

* Cf. J. B. Friedreich, "Die Symbolik und Mythologie der Natur," Würzburg, 1859, 676-684; P. Cassel, "Die Symbolik des Blutes und Der arme Heinrich von Hartmaun von Aue," Be. 1882 (265).

present-day reasoning and feelings of decorum, such ideas have led, is shown in the "Curieuse, Neue . . . *Hauss-Apothec*, Wie man durch seine eigne bey sich habende Mittel, als dem Blut, dem Urin, Hinter-und Ohren-Dreck, Speichel und andren natürlichen geringen Mitteln, seine Gesundheit erhalten, fast alle selbst vor incurabel gehaltene Kranckheiten . . . . heilen, und sein Leben, vermittelst Gottes Gnade . . . conserviren möge und könne . . . . Von einem Liebhaber der Medicin. Frankfurth am Mayn, 1699" (316), p. 33:—

"*Der Mensch, das Ebenbild, ist Gott selbst angenehm,*
Hat vierundzwanzig Stück zur Arzenei bequem,
Bein,[1] *Mark,*[2] *die Hirnschal*[3] *samt derselben Moos*[4] *ist gut,*
Das Fleisch[5] *und Fett,*[6] *die Haut,*[7] *Haar,*[8] *Harn,*[9] *Hirn,*[10] *Herz*[11] *und Blut,*[12]
Die Gall,[13] *die Milch,*[14] *der Kot,*[15] *der Schweiss*[16] *und auch der Stein,*[17]
Das gelbe Schmalz,[18] *so in den Ohren pflegt zu sein,*
Die Nägel,[19] *Speichel,*[20] *auch die Nachgeburt*[21] *ist gut,*
Der Helm,[22] *der Samen*[23] *und menstruosisches*[24] *Blut.*"*

Much of the contents of the book forms even now matter for popular belief in most parts of Germany, Cf. especially:

A. WUTTKE, "*Der Deutsche Volksaberglaube der Gegenwart,*" *Third Edition, by E. H. Meyer. Be. 1900 (536).*

E. L. ROCHHOLZ, "*Deutscher Glaube und Brauch im Spiegel der heidnischen Vorzeit, I. (Deutscher Unsterblichkeitsglaube.)*" *Be., 1867 (335).*

* Roughly translated as follows:
"Now man, God's likeness, pleasing to His sight,
Hath four and twenty items for med'cine suited quite,
Bone, marrow, skull, and eke its pulp are good,
The flesh and fat, the skin, hair, urine, brain, heart, blood,
The gall, the milk, the dung, the sweat, and eke the stone,
The yellow wax, which in the ears doth find a home,
The nails, the spittle, and the after-birth are good,
The caul, the semen, and the menstrual blood."

U. JAHN, "*Zauber mit Menschenblut und anderen Teilen des menschlichen Körpers" (in "Verhandlungen der Berliner anthropologischen Gesellschaft," 1888, 130-140).*

M. R. BUCK, "*Medicinischer Volksglauben und Volksaberglauben aus Schwaben." Ravensberg, 1865 (72).*

FLÜGEL, "*Volksmedizin und Aberglaube im Frankenwalde." Munich, 1863 (81).*

G. LAMMERT, "*Volksmedizin und medizinischer Aberglaube in Bayern und den angrenzenden Bezirken." Würzburg, 1869 (274).*

M. HÖFLER, "*Volksmedizin und Aberglaube in Oberbayerns Gegenwart und Vergangenheit." Munich, 1888. A new edition in 1893 (244). "Das Jahr im oberbayerischen Volksleben mit besonderer Berücksichtigung der Volksmedicin." Munich, 1899 (48), 4°.*

V. FOSSEL, "*Volksmedicin und medicinischer Aberglaube in Steiermark*[2]." *Graz, 1886 (172).*

J. GOLDSCHMIDT, "*Skizzen aus der Mappe eines Arztes. Volksmedicin im Nordwestlichen Deutschland" (Oldenburg). Bremen, 1854 (157).*

L. STRACKERJAN, "*Aberglaube und Sagen aus dem Herzogthum Oldenburg." Two vols. Oldenburg, 1867 (422 and 366).*

U. JAHN, "*Hexenwesen und Zauberei in Pommern." Breslau, 1886 (196).*

W. J. A. v. TETTAU AND J. D. H. TEMME, "*Die Volkssagen Ostpreussens, Litthauens und Westpreussens." Be., 1837 (255-286: "Meinungen und Gebräuche.")*

M. TÖPPEN, "*Aberglauben aus Masuren.*[2]" *Dantzig, 1867 (168).*

H. FRISCHBIER, "*Hexenspruch und Zauberbann. Ein Beitrag zur Geschichte des Aberglaubens in der Provinz Preussen." Be., 1870 (167).*

E. LEMKE, "*Volksthümliches in Ostpreussen." Three volumes. Mohrungen, 1884, 1887 (190 and 203). Allenstein, 1899 (184).*

W. MANNHARDT, "*Die praktischen Folgen des Aberglaubens, mit besonderer Berücksichtigung der Provinz Preussen.*" *Be., 1878 (88).*

The following should not remain without mention in this connection:—

ALBERTUS MAGNUS [!], "*Bewährte und approbirte sympathetische und natürliche Geheimnisse für Menschen und Vieh.*" *Reutlingen, 1874. (Cf.* AM URDS-BRUNNEN *II., 88-90, 96-8, 175-7, 222; III., 134-5, 141-3;* UR-QUELL, *1893, 279).*

"*Das 6 und 7. Buch Mosis, d. i. Mosis magische Geisterkunst. . . . nach einer alten Handschrift*" [!]. *Often, e.g. Philadelphia* [?], *1888 (79).*

"*Geheim- und Sympathiemittel des alten Schäfer Thomas,*" *14 parts, Altona, 1858-76.*—"*Des alten Schäfer Thomas enthüllte Geheim- und Sympathiemittel,*"[4] *Reutlingen, 1875 (64).*—"*91 Geheim- und Sympathiemittel des alten Schäfer Thomas,*" *new, revised edition. Magdeburg, 1867.*

See for the period of the middle ages, *H. B. Schindler*, "Der Aberglaube des Mittelalters. Ein Beitrag zur Culturgeschichte." Breslau, 1858 (379). Espcly. 163-193, 129, 130, 225; pp. xi. to xxii. contain a detailed bibliography.

An abundance of relevant material taken from different nations and periods is contained in *Am Ur-Quell. Monatschrift für Volkkunde*, Hamburg, 1890-5; later *Der Urquell*, Leiden, 1897-8, published by *F. S. Krauss* (during 1881-9 the title was *Am Urds-Brunnen*).

The more important articles in Volume III. (1892): H. F. FEILBERG, "*Totenfetische im Glauben nordgermanischer Völker*" *(blood-magic, blood of executed persons as cure for epilepsy, love-magic, blood as a remedy. Spittle, sweat, skulls, the thieves' candle. Bones; hearts, especially of unborn children; human skin. Human flesh, after-birth, etc.).*—B. W.

SCHIFFER, "*Totenfetische bei den Polen*" *(healing and magic power of corpses, of their parts, of blood as well as of animal bones; blood of living people, blood of the Saviour and consecrated wafers, thieves' superstitions, coffin and other things pertaining to corpses; cloth connected with corpse, rope of a hanged person, straw connected with corpse; snakes and other animals).*—H. v. WLISLOCKI, "*Menschenblut im Glauben der Zigeuner*" *(love-magic, thieves' superstitions, healing of diseases, Jews. There are also described well-attested occurrences in the most recent times). P. 93: "The South-Hungarian gypsies believe that Jews and Greek-Oriental priests smear their beards with human blood, to make them long and thick."*—TH. ACHELIS, "*Ueber den Zauber mit Blut u. Körperteilen von Menschen und Tieren.*"—J. SEMBRZYCKI, "*Ostpreussische Haus- und Zaubermittel.*" *(Cf. I., 136-8, and* ALTPREUSSISCHE MONATSSCHRIFT, *1889, 491-501).*—K. ED. HAASE, "*Volksmedizin*" *(Mark of Brandenburg c. 1598).*—O. SCHELL, "*Ueber den Zauber mit dem menschlichen Körper u. dessen einzelnen Teilen im Bergischen.*"—A. F. DÖRFLER, "*Das Blut im magyarischen Volksglauben.*"—*Vol. iv. (1893):* A. F. CHAMBERLAIN, "*Zauber mit menschlichem Blut u. dessen Ceremonialgebrauch bei den Indianern Amerikas*"; *v. also V., 90-2.*—O. SCHELL, "*Volksmedizin im Bergischen.*"—H. VOLKSMANN, "*Schleswig-Holsteinische Haus- u. Zaubermittel.*—*Vols. V. and VI.:* A. HAAS, "*Das Kind im Glauben u. Brauch der Pommern.*"—URQUELL *I. (1897):* VUKASOVIĆ *u.* DRAGIČEVIĆ, "*Südslavische Volksmedizin.*"—J. BÖCK, "*Volksmedizin aus Niederösterreich.*"

"Mélusine, Recueil de mythologie, littérature populaire, traditions et usages, publié par *H. Gaidoz* and *E. Rolland,*" Paris 4°. I. (1878); II. (1884-5); III. (1886-7), etc. Here may be mentioned the very long essay, "La fascination," by J. Tuchmann, vol. II-IX.

F. S. Krauss, "Sitte und Brauch der Südslaven," Vienna, 1885 (681); "Volksglaube und religiöser Brauch der Südslaven," Münster, 1890 (176).

H. v. Wlislocki, "Aus dem inneren Leben der Zigeuner," Be. 1892, 75-98; "Blutzauber." (It would be worth the trouble closely to compare what has been testified in regard to the gypsies with what has been deposed about the Jews. There have presumably been plagiarisms on the part of both classes of "globe-trotters"); "Volksglaube u. religiöser Brauch der Zigeuner," Münster, 1892 (184). "Aus dem Volksleben der Magyaren," Munich, 1893 (183); "Volksglaube u. relig. Brauch der Magyaren," Munich, 1893 (171); "Volksglaube u. Volksbrauch der Siebenbürger Sachsen," Weimar-Be., 1893 (212) (Cf. *Urquell*, 1893, 69 sq.; 98-100).

J. Haltrich, "Zur Volkskunde der Siebenbürger Sachsen." A new edition revised by J. Wolff, Vienna, 1885 (535).

Nicholas Lémery, "Traité universel des drogues," Paris, 1714.—*L. F. Sauyé*, "Remèdes populaires et superstitieux des montagnards vosgiens," in "Mélusine," III., 278 sq.

A. de Cock, "Volksgeneeskunde in Vlaanderen," Ghent, 1891.

M. Bartels, "Die Medizin der Naturvölker," L., 1893 (361).

A. Löwenstimm, "Aberglaube und Strafrecht. Ein Beitrag zur Erforschung des Einflusses der Volksanschauungen auf die Verübung von Verbrechen," Be., 1897 (232). 136-147: "Die Volksmedizin." (From the Russian. The author brings forward a large amount of material, especially for Chapters 11, 12 of the present book, but does not quite sufficiently examine into the causes of the phenomena.)

According to the reports of recent travellers, there would be no difficulty in collecting, particularly from Africa, parallels and complements of the contents of the first part of this work.

C. v. Hovorka and A. Kronfeld, "Vergleichende Volksmedizin. Eine Darstellung volksmedizinischer Sitten und Gebräuche, Anschauungen und Heilfaktoren, des Aberglaubens und der Zaubermedizin," Stuttgart, 1908. 2 vols.

The "popular medicine" notions enumerated in these books and essays, and similar ones elsewhere, go back to very ancient times. Cf. in the first place the Ebers papyrus, which was written in the sixteenth century B.C., but is far older in its contents. "Papyrus Ebers. Das hermetische Buch über die Arzneimittel. Published by *G. Ebers*" (L., 1875; done into German by H. Joachim, Be., 1890). It names as ingredients of Egyptian medicaments: (a) blood; dried blood; the blood of the ox, the ass, the dog, the pig, and of other animals, but not of man. (b) Flesh; living flesh; fresh flesh; putrid flesh; flesh of a living ox. (c) Milk; human milk; women's milk; milk of a woman who has borne a boy. (d) Semen; semen of the 'm'm: and of the 'm'mt (?), 88, 7. (e) Ordure; ordure of man, crocodile, cat, dog, ass, gazelle, etc. Menstrual blood was not used; the same is probably true of the urine (but Cf. *Erman's* "Aegypten und ägypt. Leben im Altertum," Tübingen, 1887, 486).—Cf. as well *A. Wiedemann*, "Das Blut im Glauben der alten Aegypter" (*Ur-Quell*, 1892, 113-6).

Cf. especially the commencement of Book 28 of the important Natural History of C. Plinius Secundus, who perished in 79 A.D. at the eruption of Vesuvius. A contemporary of his was the physician Xenocrates of Aphrodisias, about whom the renowned Claudius Galenus of Pergamos (131-200 A.D.) gives the following account*:—"He described, as from personal experience, with much boldness, what ills could be cured by the use of human brain, flesh and liver; or, again, the bones of the human skull, fibula, and fingers, some burnt, some unburnt; or, lastly, by the use of blood. . . . He writes also what effect dung may have, if it is smeared on wounds and into the œsophagus, and is swallowed. He speaks also of the internal use of ear-wax. . . . The most nauseous, however, is the dung and the drinking of the menses. . . . Less abominable is the outward application of excrement or of sperma. Xenocrates distinguishes with great nicety the potential effects of sperma by itself, or of the sperma which flows out of the vagina after coitus." Galen goes on to relate that doctors employ the blood of pigeons, owls, cocks, lambs, and goats, but declares that these and many other remedies taken from the animal kingdom are partly directly rejectable, partly superflous, since there are numerous well-tested remedies.

I was at first of the opinion that the anonymous "Hauss-Apothec" was merely the expression of the beliefs which at that time obtained in popular medicine; but in 1892 I convinced myself that *its contents were believed in among wide circles of PHYSICIANS even after the middle of the eighteenth century.*

Take such a book as the "Neu-Vermehrte, Heilsame *Dreck-Apotheke*, wie nemlich mit Koth und Urin Fast alle, ja auch die schwerste gifftigste Kranckheiten, und bezauberte Schaden, vom Haupt bis zun Füssen, inn- und äusserlich, glücklich curiret worden; Durch und durch mit allerhand curieusen, so nütz- als ergetzlichen Historien und Anmerckungen,

* "Περὶ τῶν ἁπλῶν φαρμάκων κράσεως καὶ δυνάμεως," xi, 1. Opera ed. *C. G. Kühn* XII. (L. 1826), 249 sq.; done into German in *L. Israelson*, "Die 'materia medica' des Klaudios Galenos," Juryew (Dorpat), 1894, 176.

auch andern Feinen Denckwürdigkeiten, Abermals bewährt, und üm ein merckliches vermehrt, und verbessert. Von *Kristian Frantz Paullini. Franckfurt am Mayn*, 1697" (420 and 207 pp.).* This work is now regarded almost exclusively as a characteristic example of a dirty and ridiculous superstition which died out two centuries ago. But the assumption is wrong. For the author, who was born 25th February, 1643, received, after prolonged medical studies and much travelling, an honourable invitation to a professorship at Pisa, which only illness obliged him to decline. Later, after he had practised in Hamburg and in Holstein, he became body physician and historiographer to Bishop Christoph Bernhard in Münster, and remained in that position till the death of his patron in 1678. He then stayed in Wolfenbüttel and Hameln, till in 1689 he was appointed physician to his native town, Eisenach; he died as such on 10th June, 1712. As regards his busy literary activity in the domains of poetic art, natural science and medicine, and also historical research, I refer to *J. Moller*, "Cimbria literata II.," (Copenhagen, 1744), 622-633, and *K. F. H. Marx*, "Zur Beurtheilung des Arztes Christian Franz Paullini," Göttingen, 1872 (39). ("Abhandlungen der Göttinger Gesellschaft der Wissenschaften, vol. 18.") Among other things, the latter says: "Medicine takes a different shape with almost every century; so the remains of the past, however fantastic, should not be regarded as contemptible," and P.'s name deserved to be mentioned "as that of a thinking, learned, well-meaning doctor, and one of the most industrious men of his time."

Joh. Chr. Schröder (1600-1664, Cf. Poggendorf,

* The first edition: "Heilsame Dreck-Apotheke" (Frankfort a.M. 1696) is not within my reach. A third edition appeared in 1713.

"Biographisch-litter. Wörterbuch zur Geschichte der exakten Wissenschaften," II., 843), a physician of Westphalian origin, who practised in Frankfort a. Main, compiled a thesaurus of drugs, which was commented on by Friedr. Hoffmann, the elder, a physician in Halle (d. 1675): "Clavis pharmaceutica Joh. Schroederi cum thesauro pharmaceutico (Halle, 1681)." A German translation first appeared in Nuremberg, 1685. Its second edition consists of a folio covering more than 1,500 pages: "Vollständige und Nutzreiche Apotheke. Das ist: *D. Johannis Schroederi* treflich-versehener Medicin-Chymischer höchstkostbahrer Artzney-Schatz Nebst *D. Friderici Hoffmanni* darüber verfassete herrliche Anmerckungen als eine Grund-Feste beybehalten: So nun aber . . . aus denen itziger Zeit Fürtrefflichen und Berühmtesten Medicorum und anderer Gelahrtesten . . . Schrifften . . . . Zusammengetragen und vermehret. . . . Auf vieles und unablässiges Verlangen Teutscher Nation zu sonderem Nutzen eröffnet von *G. D. Koschwitz, M.D.S.P.*," Nuremberg, 1693 (Koschwitz is presumably the Georg Daniel Koschwitz who died in Halle, 1729, Professor of Medicine).—Ch. 33 of Book II. (pp. 82 sq.), which treats of the chemist's shops, is headed: "On the blood." The text observes: "In the chemist's shops one certainly finds no blood; yet it is customary at times to use them (bloods), especially when they are still fresh," and there follows an enumeration of various bloods: of ducks, geese, asses, dogs, pigeons, horses, goats, men, menstruating women, hares, partridges, oxen and turtle-doves.—In Book V., the "Animal science," is a 20-page section devoted to man. It begins p. 31: "The natural apothecary articles. These are taken either from the still living body, and are: [1]The hairs, [2]the nails, [3]the spittle, [4]the ear-wax, [5]the sweat, [6]the milk, [7]the menstrual blood, [8]the after-birth, [9]the urine, [10]the excrement, [11]the semen, [12]the blood, [13]testicles, [14]worms, [15]the lice, [16]the skin that surrounds the head of the fœtus. Or from parts of the dead body, such are: [1]The whole corpse, [2]the skin, [3]the fat, [4]the bones, [5]skulls, [6]the pulp of skulls, [7]the brain, [8]the gall, [9]the heart."—P. 33: "If you then ask, whether one can safely use inwardly the menstrual blood? This we can answer with a Yes. Take a cloth, steep it well in the menstrual blood, let it dry; when you wish to use it, draw the same with squill vinegar out of the cloth which one can fitly employ to promote the woman's monthly flux. The linen cloth soaked in such blood and dried is laid externally on erysipelas or also on other swellings and pains; pre-eminently it quiets the pains of Podagra. It has cured tertian fever when such a cloth has been merely hung on the neck. The maidens prepare their love-potions from it, after which commonly ensues delirium or madness."

Even in *D. W. Triller's* "Thesaurus medicamentorum," which appeared in 1764 at Frankfort a. M., the following drugs are still mentioned: Stercus caninum album (album graecum), pavonum stercus, vaccae stercus et urina, bufones exsiccati, cervi priapus, equi testes, etc.—In respect of the prescription book of the Ettenheim municipal surgeon, *Joh. Conr. Machleid*, which embraces the period from 1730 to 1790, Cf. "Anzeiger des Germanichen Nationalmuseums" (Nuremberg), 1895, 89 seq., and *Ur-Quell*, 1897, 167-9. "To cure colic: Take three living lice from the patient; should he have none, from another person. Give it him to eat in a bit of bread. A sure and approved medicine; but you must not tell that patient, else he won't take it."

Much that is relevant here can be found in a work of the Leipsic zoologist, William Marshall, which was first known to me in November, 1899: "Neu eröffnetes, wundersames Arznei-Kästlein, darin allerei gründliche Nachrichten, wie es unsere Voreltern mit den Heilkräften der Thiere gehalten haben, zu finden sind." L., 1894 (127; 11 pages of bibliography at the end). I quote from it the following details, p. 84: "The Dresden taxation of apothecaries in 1652 contains 51 animal fats, amongst them human and monkey fat. Human fat was said to strengthen, disperse, alleviate pains, soften hardened scars, and dispel small-pox scars. Monkey fat works similarly, chiefly as dissolvent; lion fat strengthened and dispersed hardened glandular swellings, and for dry scabs they would rub in leopard fat with laurel oil." 89: "In the royal Prussian taxation of 1749 . . . occurs a spirit of human brains." 94: "Even human after-birth and the umbilical cord did not escape our ancestors' pharmacological art. The former was applied externally, and given internally for epilepsy and for the endurance of labour-pains. Secundinae occurred in German drug-stores right up to the middle of last century." 80: "Even the great Friedrich Hoffmann recommended in the previous century the following prescription for epilepsy: The whole ashes of a young crow still in the nest, and of a turtle dove, 2 lot (a lot is ½oz.) of burnt human skull, 2 lot lime-tree buds, 1 lot lion's excrement; all these substances were separately digested with brandy, after which the fluids were poured together." Cf. also ibid. 74 sq.

II HUMAN SACRIFICE

"BLOOD RITUAL"

A. The high significance which human sacrifices have possessed in many heathen religions, or still possess, is so well known that it need only be named, not proved (Assyrians, Phœnicians, Aztecs, etc.).—It is equally well known that such sacrifices were from the beginning most strictly forbidden to the Israelites, the possessors of the revealed religion of the Old Testament: Leviticus 18, 21; 20, 2 sq.; Deuteronomy 12, 31; 18, 10. As, however, even nowadays there are highly educated persons who believe such sacrifices were quite alien to the Greeks and Romans, as well as to the ancient Germans, I give here a list, at any rate, of the more important books.

Human sacrifices among the Greeks: *F. G. Welcker*, "Kleine Schriften," III. (Bonn, 1850), 160-4, and "Griechische Götterlehre" (Göttingen, 1858, sq.), II., 769, sq.; *K. F. Hermann*, "Die gottesdienstl. Alterthümer[2] (der Griechen)," Heidelberg, 1857, §27; *G. F. Schömann*, "Griechische Alterthümer,"[3] II. (Be., 1873), 250 sq.; *J. Beckers*, "De hostiis humanis apud Graecos," Münster, 1867 (69); *P. Stengel*, "Die griechischen Kultusaltertümer,"[2] Munich, 1898, 114-8. History, legends and first elements—"Rudimente"—(vicarious sacrifices) afford proof that before sea-voyages, at the beginning of a war, before battles, and altogether, when the lives of many people were in peril, human beings were sacrificed by the Greeks.

The Emperor Tiberius's severe ordinances certainly almost put a stop to such sacrifices; notwithstanding, human sacrifices in honour of Zeus Lykaios occurred in Arcadia even in the second century A.D.—Among the Greeks and Romans: *E. v. Lasaulx*, "Sühnopfer der Griechen und Römer" (in "Studien des klassischen Alterthums," Regensburg, 1854, 233 sq.); *O. Keller*, "Lateinische Volksetymologie und Verwandtes," L., 1891, 331-349 ("Einiges über römische und griechische Menschenopfer"), especially 340 sq.—Among the Romans: *M. Landau*, "Menschenopfer bei den Römern," in *Ur-Quell*, 1892, 283-6; *H. Diels*, "Sibyllinische Blätter," Be., 1890, 86 sq.*—Further, Cf. *V. Hehn*, "Kulturpflanzen und Hausthiere," 5th edition, Berlin, 1887, 438-44; *U. Jahn*, "Die deutschen Opfergebräuche bei Ackerbau und Viehzucht," Breslau, 1884, 61-9; *J. Lippert*, "Kulturgeschichte," II. (L., 1885), 34. About human sacrifices (especially pure virgins) in German fairy-tale and stories, v. *L. Freytag*, *Ur-Quell*, 1890, 197-9.

B. The so-called "Bauopfer," building sacrifices (the immuring of a human being, later also of an animal or other "rudiments"), in order to assure the foundation of a house, a dam, etc., are really only a special kind of human sacrifice. Bibliography: *F. Liebrecht*, "Zur Volkskunde," Heilbronn, 1879, 284-96 ("Die vergrabenen Menschen"); *O. Keller*, 331-4; *K. Müllenhoff*, "Sagen, Märchen und Lieder der Herzogthümer Schleswig, Holstein u. Lauenburg," Kiel, 1845, 242, 299, 601, 602; *G. Fr. Daumer*, "Geheimnisse," I., 137-147; *Grimm*, "Deutsche Mythologie," 1095, sq.; *Ad. Kuhn*, "Sagen aus Westfalen," I. (L.,

* The Roman Emperor Heliogabalus (218—222 A.D.) still offered up human sacrifices, v. Lampridius "Heliog."8. His contemporary, the renowned jurist, Julius Paulus, prescribes in the "Sententiae receptae" V. 23, 16: "Qui hominem immolaverint exve ejus sanguine litaverint, fanum templumve polluerint, bestiis obiciuntur vel, si honestiores sint, capite puniuntur."

1859), 115; *Wuttke*, §440; *Strackerjan*, I., 107-9; *P. Cassel*, 154-6; *F. S. Krauss*, "Das Bauopfer bei den Südslaven," Vienna, 1886; *Ur-Quell*, II., 25, 189 sq., 110 ("rudiments," ibid. III., 164 sq.); *P. Sartori*, "Ueber das Bauopfer," *Zeitschrift für Ethnologie*, 1898, 1-54.—The use of blood instead of chalk occurs already in the legendary cycle of the Round Table, v. "La Tavola ritonda, l'istoria di Tristano, per cura di *F. L. Polidori*," Bologna, 1864, 126.—*Pater Hieronymus Saucken* relates that in 1685 the inhabitants of Brunsbüttel, when a dam burst, wanted to bury a child alive, as he heard from its mother herself; it was, however, rescued. At Delve, in Dithmarschen, as is reported in the chronicles of the *Pastor Neocorus*, after a dam burst in 1597, as the elders declared, "animam quaeri" ("a soul was required"), a dog was drowned in the breach of the dam, v. *Urds-Brunnen V*. (1887-8), 165 sq.* In the Poschechon district of the Government of Jaroslaw runs the saying that in former times the millers in order to protect the mill-dam against the rushing spring flood, used to drown any belated pedestrian in the mill pond in propitiation of the water-sprite (*Löwenstimm* 16).—Immuring of a hen in order to make a quarry secure, Salzburg, middle of the nineteenth century, *Ur-Quell*, 1898, 230. In the foundation of old houses in Schleswig-Holstein may at times be found horse skulls, horse bones, or even the leg of a wild fowl. *Ur-Quell*, 1894, 157 sq.—In order to lend stability to a building, a corpse-bone or an animal skull is buried in the ground (Transylvania, v. *Ur-Quell*, 1898, 98).

Among the Szeklers in Transylvania the ballad of the wife of the builder Kelemen is widely known. (Contents: The master builders are alarmed to observe that their buildings are continually falling to ruins.

* Cf. the legends according to which the soul, which first enters an edifice, falls a victim to the devil, v. *UrQuell*, 1893, 206-8.

So they have taken an oath to sacrifice the wife of the builder among them who should be the first to see his wife, and they act accordingly.—In the " Märkisches Museum " in Berlin are remains of building structures, in which the bones of human beings or animals and birds' eggs are to be seen immured.

C. G. F. Daumer, in a book, which though extravagant in its conclusions, displays wide reading and keen perception, " Geheimnisse des christlichen Alterthums," Hamburg, 1847, 2 volumes, tried to prove that the characteristics of the *Christian religion* from its inception to the end of the middle ages consisted in human sacrifices and cannibalism and the use of human blood. I give here some of Daumer's examples in attempted proof of his position. One may gather from them what persons with vividly excited imaginations thought they saw, and how strongly realistic impressions were held admissible as facts, especially in more remote times.

I., 83. Amphilochius in the " Life of Basilius " (Herib. Rosweidi Vitae patrum [Antwerp, 1615], I., 156; " Leben der Väter," Augsburg, 1704, 739): When the holy office was celebrated, a Jew mingled among the crowd, as if he were a Christian, because he wanted to learn about the order of the Officium and the gift of the Communion. He there beholds how a little child is cut to pieces, limb by limb, in the hands of Basilius. He approached with the other communicants, and flesh was actually given him. Then he was also present at the handing of the cup, which was full of blood, and took part in drinking from it. Keeping some remains of both, he goes home and shows them to his wife.—I., 85 (Life of the Martyr S. George, " Acta Sanctorum," 23 April). A Saracen saw a priest kill and cut up a child, place the pieces in the paten, pour the blood into the cup, and eat one of the pieces and drink from the cup.—I., 118 sq., tells of the dissensions between the Dominicans and Franciscans in Bern 1507, after the Bernese Chronicle of Calonius Grönneirus, 1585, 615 sq., and Hottinger, "Helvetische Kirchengeschichte," Zurich, 1708 sq., Vol. II., 553 sq., 556 sq.: The Dominicans were alleged to have offered a consecrated wafer coloured with Christ's blood to Jezer, a tailor who had been received into their Order, whom they wanted to make their Saint. They are also said to "have handed him a drink composed of ointment, Easter baptismal-water, Easter-taper wax, consecrated salt . . . . and the hair and blood of a child."—In the confession cited by Grönneirus 622 it is asserted the Dominicans had made use of Jew blood, and the eyebrows of a Jewish child.—There is more in Daumer I., 36 sq., 73, 85 sq.

In the middle ages, appearances of Christ at Holy Communion in the form of a child or a lamb are not infrequently mentioned, vide e.g., Paschasius Radbertus, "De corpore et sanguine Christi," 14; Germanus in Edm. Martene, "Thesaurus novus Anecdotorum," V. (Paris, 1717), 96, 95. In fact, the fantasy required a small body, which should find a place at the table or altar. Berthold von Regensburg, the great popular preacher of the 13th century, says in reply to the question, Why Christ, as he is present at Holy Communion, does not let Himself be seen in it: "Wer möchte einem kindelîn sîn houbetlîn oder sînin hendelîn oder sînin füezelin abegebîzen?" ("Who would like a little child to have his little head, or his little hands, or his little feet bitten off?") ("Predigten," published by F. Pfeiffer, II., Vienna, 1880, 270.)

D. *Within the Church there has never been a blood-rite, but there has been among several of the Gnostics.*

Even Clemens Alexandrinus (d.c. 220 A.D.) found in the Epistle of Judas a prediction concerning the Karpocratians and related sects ("Stromata," III., 2). He relates, among other things, that among the Karpocratians, men and women, after the common meal, after the lights are extinguished, have sexual commerce with each other. Irenaeus (d. 202 A.D.) expressly testifies that the heathens were excited by such actions to repugnance against Christianity (I., 25, 3 = Epiphanius, "Haer.," xxvii., 3). Epiphanius, ch. 5, describes the conduct of these people as that of dogs and pigs. That the Karpocratians utilised blood in their rites has indeed not been expressly handed down, but is very probable on comparison with the related Gnostics.—Of the Cainites (they called themselves after Cain) Irenaeus says, I., 31, 2, that their doctrine was: The perfect knowledge was to proceed without repugnance to actions which it is not decent even to name.—Epiphanius xxvi., 5, describes as follows the conduct of the so-called Gnostics: After the common meal they turn to free concubitus. Next, men and women take semen virile in their hands and speak to the All-Father: "We bring Thee this gift as the body of Christ." They eat thereof, and say, "This is the body of Christ and the Passover meal." Likewise they take sanguinem menstruum: "This is the blood of Christ." If a woman has become pregnant they triturate the embryo, mix the mass with honey, pepper and herbs, and taste the dish at their gathering with the finger, which dish is esteemed the perfect Passover meal.

The contents of these documents are so revolting that one would be glad to agree with *H. Usener*, "Das Weihnachtsfest," Bonn, 1889, 110, and others, who contest their credibility. Epiphanius, the chief witness, they say, lived too long after the occurrences (he died, at the age of about 100, in 403 A.D.). But he appeals, xxvi. 17, 18, to the oral information of credible men, to original writings of the Gnostics, and to personal intercourse which, as a quite young man, he had with these "Gnostics."

Nevertheless, I hold with *R. Seeberg* it is very probable that the account of the use of the embryo, which is found only in Epiphanius, should be considered unhistorical. After all, Epiphanius was credulous enough to say about even the Montanists, that they employed in their sacrifices the blood of a child, whose body they had pierced with needles, xlviii. 14. The first part, however, of Epiphanius's last description is not merely confirmed by the remarks of Clement of Alexandria and Irenaeus, but also by two Gnostic writings which have only recently become known. Firstly, the Gnostic writing which was written in Egypt in Greek at the end of the third century A.D., but preserved only in Coptic, "Pistis Sophia . . . Latine vertit M. G. Schwartze, edidit J. H. Petermann" (Be., 1851, 53). The author, in the course of it, makes Jesus show the infernal regions to His disciples, and depict the punishments of wilful sinners. On this occasion Thomas puts the question, p. 386 sq.: "We have heard that there are men who put semen virile and sanguinem menstruum in a dish of lentils, and declare, 'We believe in Esau* and Jacob.' Is that proper or not?" Jesus answers that this sin is greater than all sins and misdeeds, and that such men shall be plunged into the outermost darkness. The query is only intelligible if the author, who was himself a Gnostic, knew other Gnostics, and wanted those to be condemned who acted in the manner indicated by Thomas's question. Secondly,

* The words "and Jacob" are beyond doubt an interpolation. The mention of Esau calls to mind the Cainites who, from hostility to the Jewish Deity, ascribed a higher power of light to Cain, Esau, Korah, the Sodomites, Judas Iscariot, in fine, all the bad men who occur in the Bible, and reverenced them as servants of the good God.

the second book of Jeû, also a Gnostic work, which, however is much older than the "Pistis Sophia," v. *C. Schmidt*, "Gnostische Schriften in koptischer Sprache, aus dem Codex Brucianus herausgegeben, übersetzt u. bearbeitet," L. 1892, 194. We read in it that Jesus is supposed to have told his disciples: "Keep these mysteries which I shall give you; reveal them to no man, unless he be worthy of them . . . . . Reveal them not to any man who believes in these 72 Archons or serves them; reveal them not to those who serve the eighth Dynamis of the great Archon, that is to say, those who consume sanguinem menstruum and semen virile, whilst saying: 'We possess the true knowledge and pray to the true God.' But their God is bad."

The partaking of semen virile and sanguis menstruus is ascribed also to the religious party of the *Manichaeans*, which was allied to the Gnostics, v. Cyrillus of Jerusalem's 6th Catechet. Discourse (348 A.D.), § 33, and Augustine, "De Moribus Manichaeorum," 18, 66, and "De haeresibus," 46.

The explanation of this action of many Gnostics is probably only partially to be sought in their dualistic conception of the world. The sparks of the higher power of light, which exist in the bodies of human beings, are gathered together by means of semen virile and sanguis menstruus, and brought to the Treasury of Light. In this way men earn reward from the highest good God (from whom the Creator-God has fallen away, with His angels and archons). First steps of the libertine conduct, without which rites like those described could hardly have arisen, are already adverted to in the New Testament: Rev. ii., 6, 15. (the Nikolaites), and the Epistle of Judas, especially vv. 7, 8, 10, 12.

E. Remarkable parallels are reported in Russian sects. Sectarianism in Russia, the *Raskol*, falls into two big groups: the Popowzy and the Bespopowzy ("the priestless"). The latter think the end of the world is near, and the dominion of Antichrist has already begun. Many of them made it their duty to dispatch the innocent souls of the newly born to heaven; others believed they were doing their friends and relations a service of love, if they kept them from dying a natural death. It not infrequently happened that whole families, even villages, united to offer themselves to God as a living sacrifice. The peasant Chodkin (under Alexander II.) persuaded some twenty persons to die with him of hunger in the forests of Perm. Others, especially in the 18th century, chose the baptism of fire by burning themselves. "Even in the 19th century such horrible scenes were not unusual . . . . . . in 1883 a peasant called Jukow burnt himself to death, while singing psalms. Baptism with blood. . . . . is perhaps even less rare; in most cases there are parents who wish thereby to preserve their children from the allurements of the Prince of Darkness. For instance, in 1847 a moujik from the government of Perm had intended to unlock the gates of heaven to his whole family with one blow; but as the axe failed him before he had finished his fearful work, he gave himself up to the law. Another peasant, from the government of Wladimir, who was called to account for the murder of his two sons, affirmed he wished in that way to preserve them from sin, and, in order to follow his victims, when in prison refused all nourishment. . . . . . In 1870 a moujik tried to imitate the sacrifice of Isaac. He bound his seven-year-old son to a bench, and ripped his belly open, after which he began to pray before the pictures of saints. 'Do you forgive me?' he asked the dying child. 'I forgive you, and God likewise,' answered the victim, whose part in the scene had been rehearsed." In a single year, 1879, the Odessa justices had to decide finally in one or more cases of self-sacrifice, crucifixion, self-cremation, and mutilation "from motives of piety." *A. Leroy-Beaulieu*, "Das Reich der Zaren und die Russen," German edition, III. (Sondershausen, 1890), 351-4. There are further instances of fire-baptism in *A. v. Haxthausen*, "Studien über die inneren Zustände . . . Russlands," I. (Hanover, 1847), 339.—Cf. inf., ch. 13.

The mystic sects of the Chlysty ("scourgers") and the Skopzy ("castrates"), which stand in close relations to one another, do not belong to the real Raskol. The gatherings of the Chlysty, or, as they are called, Ljudi Boshii ("God-men"), are outwardly comparable to those of the well-known "dancing dervishes" in Cairo and Stamboul. Whilst most Chlysty use only water and black bread for the celebration of the Holy Communion, some of them, according to more than one witness (*Leroy-Beaulieu*, 450, cites Philaret's "History of the Russian Church," Liwanow's "Raskolniki i Ostroshniki," Renzki's "Ljudi Boshii i Skopzy,") used the flesh and blood of a new-born child, and particularly of the first boy, who might be expected from a "holy virgin" chosen to be the "mother of God," after the ecstatic and obscene ceremonies following upon her selection. If a girl was born, she in turn became a holy virgin; but if a boy "Christosik" ("little Christ") he was sacrificed on the eighth day after his birth. The communion bread was renewed by a mixture of his heart and blood with flour and honey. That was called communicating with the blood of the lamb. Others, as is conjectured, communicated with the yet warm blood of the little Jesus.

Von Haxthausen, I., 349, mentions another way by which the Skopzys and Chlystys produced the materials for the solemnizing of their Communion: A virgin of fifteen, who has been persuaded by great promises, has her left breast severed, whilst she sits in a tub with warm water. The breast is cut into small pieces on a dish, which are consumed by all the members of the congregation present. Then the girl in the tub is lifted on to an altar standing near, and the whole congregation dances wildly around it and sings at the same time. . . . . My above-mentioned clerk made the acquaintance of several such girls, who were then always worshipped like saints, and says that at nineteen to twenty they looked as if they were fifty to sixty; they also usually died before thirty. One, however, was married, and had two children.

The Christian religion is not responsible for such abominations.

F. The following events are to be considered as *relapses into heathendom or as survivals from heathen times.* About two hundred versts (kms.) from Kasan is the village of Stary-Multan, whose inhabitants belong to the Russian Orthodox Church, with a church and a priest. Owing to bad harvests, famine and typhus visited them in 1892, and there was a fear of cholera. They began to doubt whether their way of worshipping God was the right. They thought they must appease the supernatural powers by sacrifice. Animal sacrifices helped nothing. Whereupon a sage of the village received the revelation that a "two-legged" sacrifice (kurban) was required, that is, a human sacrifice. There lived in the village a man from another district, so that he was without relations and friends in the place itself. This unfortunate man, on 4th (16th) May, 1892, was dragged into the Town Hall, stripped there, and hung up by his feet to the ceiling, and then fifteen persons with knives began to stab at his naked body. The blood streaming from the wounds was carefully caught in vessels, cooked and drunk by the sacrificers. The lungs and heart were also consumed. The village magistrate, the peasant-born policeman, and the chief elder of the church took part in the ceremony. The people were so convinced of the righteousness of their action that they did not take the least pains to conceal the murder. So it soon came to the knowledge of the authorities. After two and a half years the trial came to an end, and the perpetrators of the ritual murder were condemned to many years' hard labour. (*Urquell*, 1897, 118 sq., after the *Freies Blatt*, Vienna, 13 Jan., 1895, No. 145).

Government of Minsk, district of Nowogrud. In 1831 the country people, during a cholera epidemic, wanted to bury a priest alive; he only saved himself by begging his parishioners for a respite, in order to prepare for death. In August, 1855, the inhabitants of the village of Okopowitschi, in a similar epidemic, on the advice of an army surgeon Kosakowitsch, pushed an old woman, Lucia Manjkow, alive, as a sacrifice, into a pit, in which there were already corpses, and then quickly heaped earth upon it. In August, 1871, the inhabitants of the village of Torkatschi wanted to inflict the same fate on an invalid peasant woman; her husband and son-in-law came only just in time to the rescue; it is said that another woman who was ill, and by herself, was then sacrificed alive. The whole of the village authorities shared the conviction that they could save themselves from the cholera by the burying of a living person. In the Turuchan district, government Jenissei, a peasant P., by descent a Russian, buried alive, in 1861, a girl akin to him in order to save himself and his family from a prevalent epidemic disease by the sacrifice (*Löwenstimm*, 12-14).

A Samoyede, Jefrem Pyrerka, strangled in Nova Zembla, during the famine of the winter of 1881, a girl, Ssavanei, in order, as he openly stated, to bring an offering to the devil, because God, in whom he believed, did not help him in the time of the famine. Later he fashioned a wooden idol and wanted to sacrifice to it his tent comrade, Andrei Tabarei; he threw a noose round his neck, and only the entrance of P.'s wife saved Andrei from death (*Löwenstimm*, 10).

First element: Burying of living animals. District Nowogrud, in cholera time. District Grjasowez, government Wologda, after the peasant women, perhaps on account of a cattle murrain, had ploughed up a village (Löw. 12, 22 sq.). Human sacrifices, too, are said to have been offered on the occasion of the ploughing-up (Löw. 25).

G. The persons who took part in the following episode were also certainly quite untouched by Christian influence. " A woman, living in the Madras Presidency, was said to be possessed of the devil, and therefore barren. Her father accordingly asked advice of an exorciser, who declared a human sacrifice needful. So one evening the father, the exorcist, and five or six other men met together, and after a religious ceremony sent for the victim determined on. Without suspecting any evil, he came and was forthwith given so much spirituous drink, that he became unconscious. They then cut off his head and offered his blood mingled with rice to the Deity as a sacrifice; the corpse they cut in pieces and threw in a reservoir. The murderers, who were soon discovered, made a frank confession." (*L. Fuld*, *Neue Freie Presse*, Vienna, 4 May, 1888, No. 8510, reproduced from an English medical journal).

As to human sacrifices after a case of death (widow, bride, slaves), cf. *J. Kohler*, *Ztschr. f. das Privat- u. öffentl. Recht*, Vienna, 1892, 586 sq. (India, Central America, Ashanti, Fiji Islands, etc.)

III. HUMAN BLOOD SERVES TO RATIFY THE GIVEN WORD*

The drinking of human blood, or of wine mixed with such blood when friendship was sworn, and alliances were concluded, was the custom of many nations, in antiquity and in the middle ages.

Herodotus, IV., 70, narrates of the Scythians: "They conclude agreements in the following manner: They pour wine into a large earthen vessel, and, after the contracting parties have scratched themselves with an awl or a knife, mix the wine with their blood, and then dip sword and arrows and battle-axe and javelin into the vessel. Whereupon both the contracting parties themselves and the most distinguished of their following drink from it.†

F. Rühs, "Handbuch der Geschichte des Mittelalters," Berlin, 1816, 323 (following J. G. Stritter, "Memoriae populorum," Petersburg, 1771 sq.), observes of the Komani: "To increase the sanctity of

* *H. C. Trumbull*, "The Blood Covenant[2]" Philadelphia 1893 (390). *J. Goldziher*, "Die Fiktion der Blutsverwandschaft bei oriental. Völkern," in "Globus," 1893, p. 50 sq.—In general cf. *J. Kohler*, "Studien über die künstliche Verwandschaft" in *Zeitschrift für vergleichende Rechtswissenschaft*. V. (Stuttgart 1884), 415—40, especially 434 sq.—*P. Wilutzky*, "Vorgeschichte des Rechts," Be. 1903, in vol. 2 in the chapter, "Künstliche Verwandschaft und Blutsbrüderschaft."

† The same testimony is afforded by Pomponius Mela, the geographer, who probably lived in the time of the Emperor Claudius, "De situ orbis," I, 2 (cf. *Tzschukke*, on the passage). Cf. also Lucianus Samosatensis (200 A.D.; "Toxaris," ch. 37, and Athenæus (beginning of the third century A.D.), "Deipnosophisatæ," II., 45 E.

covenants, they let blood run from their veins into a goblet and drank it up on both sides, so as to be of one blood; also a dog was hacked to bits between the two covenanting parties."—When the Hungarian magnates in the ninth century had chosen Almus, the son of Ugek, for their ruler, they fortified the oath of allegiance by letting some of their blood run into a single vessel.*—As regards the Mongols, cf. *K. Neumann*, "Die Hellenen im Skythenlande," I. (Be. 1855), 268.

"The Medes and the Lydians," says Herodotus I., 74, "scratch the skin of the arm and then lick off one another's blood."—The Iberians (Radamistus) and Armenians (Mithridates) acted in precisely the same way. Tacitus, "Annals" xii., 47: "Kings, when they conclude a treaty, are wont to give each other the right hand, and to knot their hands together. They next produce blood by a slight prick and lick it up on either side. Such a bond is held to be something mysterious, as well as consecrated by the blood shed on both sides" (cf. *Lipsius* on the passage).

Even the Greeks and Romans are found to be doing similar things. The Greek and Carian mercenaries of Psammenitus butchered the children of Phanes, drank their blood mixed with wine and water, and thus bound themselves to fight bravely, Herodotus iii., 11.—Diodorus Siculus, contemporary with Augustus, relates how Apollodorus (in the first third of the third century B.C.) won lordship over the town of Cassandrea on the Macedonian promontory of Pallene: "When Apollodorus was struggling for the mastery, and wished to make sure of the conspiracy, he called in a youthful friend under the pretext of a sacrifice, killed him in honour of the gods, gave his entrails to the conspirators to eat, and made them

* *J. G. Schwandtner*, "Scriptores rerum Hungaricarum" I. (Vienna 1746), 6: *Mone*, "Geschichte des Heidenthums" I. 108.

drink the blood mixed with wine."*—In the conspiracy, which the banished Tarquinius Superbus arranged with sons of Brutus and others, a great and terrible oath was sworn, in the course of which they offered up the blood of a slaughtered man and touched the entrails.† . . . . . . Catiline and his fellow conspirators are supposed to have drunk human blood mixed with wine.‡—Cf. again the words of Festus, the grammarian, "The ancients called *assiratum* a composite drink of wine and blood, because the ancient Latins called blood *assir*."

"When the Ireni conclude treaties, the one drinks the blood of the other, which is shed voluntarily for this purpose" (*Gyraldus*, "Topographia Hiberno.," Cap. 22, p. 743).

When the French Prince Henry (from 1574, Henry III., King of France) was selected King of Poland in 1573, there came to meet him, on his journey to his new kingdom, 30,000 horsemen "dont un Seigneur s'étant détaché lui fit un compliment, qui le surprit par l'action dont il l'accompagna. Elle ressentoit un peu le génie des anciens Sarmates; mais d'ailleurs elle dut lui plaire. En s'approchant du Roi, il tira son sabre, s'en piqua le bras, et recevant son sang dans sa main il lui dit: 'Seigneur, malheur à celui de nous, qui n'est pas prêt à verser tout ce qu'il a dans les veines pour votre service; c'est pour cela que je ne veux rien perdre du mien,' et en même tems il le but," v. *G. Daniel*, "Histoire de France." (Amsterdam and L., 1755) xii., 316.

Among the South Slavs, when reconciliation of a blood feud takes place, elective brotherhood is even

* "Bibliotheca Historica xxii, Excerpta de virtutibus et vitiis," ed. *P. Wesseling* (Amsterdam 1746), II, 562 sq. Cf. Polyaenus, "Strategematica" vi, 7, 2.

† Plutarch, "Publicola," Ch. 4.

‡ Sallust, "Catiline," Ch. 18. Similarly Dio Cassius xxxvii.

now concluded with actual blood-drinking. "The representatives of the hostile clans cut open with a needle the artery of the right hand, suck one another's blood, exchange kisses and swear to each other unchangeable loyalty till the grave." (*Ur-Quell*, 1890, 196).—About blood-brotherhood, Cf. further G. Popović, "Recht und Gericht in Montenegro," Agram, 1877 (91), pp. 39, 45; S. Gopčevič, "Oberalbanien und seine Liga," L. 1881, 303.

Africa. Blood-brotherhood with drinking of blood by both parties. Madagascar: *Vinson*, "Voyage à M." 1865, 281 seq., 539; *J. Sibree*, "Madagascar," L. 1881, 249 seq.; *Ur-Quell*, 1897, 32 sq. (after the experiences of a merchant, T. Scluszanski).—East Africa: *Die Katholischen Missionen*, illustr. monthly, Freiburg, i. B. 1883, 32 sq.—Zanzibar: v. "Mélusine" iii., 402 sq. —Cameroons: "Mitteilungen aus den deutschen Schutzgebieten" V. (Be., 1892), 178 sq.; *E. Zintgraff*, "Nord-Kamerun," Be. 1895, 175, 202.

The Berlin paper DIE POST, 11th July, 1891, No. 187, gives information about the "Infame Legge," a band of brigands which was discovered in South Italy in 1891, after an existence of three years. It was noticeable that, in the ritual of the band, which was allied to that of the "Mala Vita" of Bari, "the neophytes drank blood-brotherhood with the leader of the band by sucking out and drinking the blood from a scratch wound, which the leader himself made in the region of his own heart."

ROCHHOLZ I., 52: "At Helmstädt and Leipsic the "Hasen" (so-called "Krassfüchse") used formerly to drink brotherhood by letting some blood drip into a bowl from cuts in their arms, and swallowing it kneeling."

C. The drinking of blood was foreign to the ancient Germans,* J. Grimm, "Deutsche Rechtsal-

* And not merely for the object here in question, but altogether. The fighting heroes at the end of the Nibelungenlied, 2051sq., decide upon an unusual drink, the blood of dead foes, only to save themselves in glowing heat from slow death.— The following examples are purely mythical. (1) The younger brother of Gunnar and Högni is supposed to be provoked to murder Sigurd by eating animal flesh,

terthümer "[2] (Gött. 1854), 193: "No German tradition makes mention of symbolical blood-drinking, the mixing of blood into wine, or else, what is related in 'Gesta Roman.,' cap. 67, of a treaty of friendship would have to be referred to German custom. 'Nunquid tibi placet unam conventionem mecum ponere et erit nobis utile; sanguinem quilibet de brachio dextro emittat, ego tuum sanguinem bibam et tu meum, quod nullus alium dimittet nec in prosperitate nec in adversitate et quidquid unus lucratus fuerit alter dimidietatem habeat.' "—*J. Grimm*, "Geschichte der deutschen Sprache," 136 sq. "The ancient Northern custom is attractive. When two persons concluded brotherhood between themselves, they cut a strip of turf so that it remained hanging with both ends on the ground, and a spear was placed under it in the middle, which lifted up the turf. They next stepped under the strip of turf* and each of them stabbed or cut himself in the sole of the foot or the palm of the hand, their flowing blood running together blended with the earth." This is the explanation of the passage in the Waltharius-Lied (v. Simrock, "Kleines Heldenbuch"):

v. "Brot af Brynhildarqvidhu" 4; "Some roasted a wolf, some cut up a snake, others laid before Gothorm a dish of the ravenous one" (i.e., the wolf, or some other beast of prey). Similarly in the prose Völsunga-Saga, ch. 30.—(2). In "Die ältere und die jüngere Edda nach den mythischen Erzählungen der Skalda," translated by *K. Simrock*, Stuttgart 1871, 200, it is told of Sigurd: "But when Fafnir's heart's-blood came upon his tongue he understood the birds' voice."—Cf. again "Altdänische Heldenlieder, Balladen and Märchen," translated by *W Grimm*, Heidelberg 1811, 152, 122.

*The original significance of this ceremony probably was that the persons thus concluding brotherhood wished to declare themselves sons of the same mother, the Earth, cf. *K. Maurer*. "Bekehrung des norwegischen Stammes zum Christenthum" II (Munich 1856) 170, and in *Germania, Vierteljahrsschrift für deutsche Alterthumskunde* 1874, 146 sq. and esply. *M. Pappenheim*, "Die altdänischen Schutzgilden," Breslau 1885, pp. 21-37.

"*Wir wurden Bundesbrüder and mischten unser Blut,*
"*Da galt uns diese Freundschaft wohl für das höchste Gut.*"*

Herodotus III., 8, speaking about the Arabians: "When two persons wish to seal faith with one another, a third party who has stepped between them, makes a cut with a pointed stone in the palms of the hands of both, then takes out of either of their cloaks one thread, and smears with the blood seven stones lying in the centre, calling upon Dionysus and Urania." In the period historically known to us, as early as the 6th and 7th centuries A.D., human blood is scarcely still mentioned, but the Arabians dipped their hands into a bowl filled with camel's blood and next into a bowl full of fragrant perfumes. *J. Wellhausen*, "Skizzen and Vorarbeiten," III. ("Reste Arabischen Heidentumes," Be. 1887), 119 sq.; cf. also *W. Rob. Smith*, "Kinship and marriage in early Arabia," Cambridge, 1886, 48 sq., 149 sq., 261, 284, and "Lectures on the Religion of the Semites, First Series,"[2] Edinburgh, 314-8.

The Dyaks celebrate blood-union in adoption by taking blood from both the parties, which is poured on some chewing betel and then eaten by them (*J. Kohler* in *Zeitschr. f. das Privat- u. öffentl. Recht der Gegenwart*, Vienna, 1892, 569, in an article well worth reading on "Recht, Glaube u. Sitte," 561-612.)

Mexican tribes form brotherhoods by smearing themselves with the blood of one and the same person. Similarly in the Dutch Indies. In the Society Islands it occurs that the mothers of the bridal couple let their blood flow together on a cloth (ibid. 565, 567).

D. In this connection might also be mentioned

* Roughly translatable:
"So we became bond-brothers, mingling together blood,
In sooth we deemed this friendship to be the highest good."

the use of personal blood in the signatures of agreements, cf. *Götz*, "De subscriptionibus sanguine humano firmatis," Lübeck, 1724; *Scheible*, "Die Sage vom Faust," Stuttgart, 1847.—Rochholz, I. 52, relates, as an absolute custom of German University freshmen ("Burschen"), that the parties wrote "mutually with their own blood leaves in each other's albums." "The leaf is still said to be in existence on which, with his own blood, Maximilian, the great Bavarian Elector, dedicated himself to the Holy Virgin."

E. This is also the place for the "Bahrrecht," i.e. ordeal of the bier, the belief that the wounds of a murdered person begin to bleed again in the presence of the murderer, cf. *Wuttke* §329; *Mannhardt* 24; *Ur-Quell* 1893, 275 sq.; 1894, 284; 1895, 175 sq. 212-4; *Chr. V. Christensen*, "Baareproven, dens Historie og Stilling i Fortidens Rets- og Naturopfattelse," Copenhagen, 1900 (289).

IV. THE BLOOD OF OTHER PERSONS USED FOR HEALING PURPOSES*

A. I start with two quotations from Pliny's "Natural History," XXVIII., 1, 2. "Thus epileptics even drink the blood of gladiators, and indeed out of living goblets. . . . They consider it the most effective method of cure to swallow down the blood, when it is still warm, still bubbling, out of the man himself, and thus simultaneously to swallow the very breath of life from the mouth of the wound."† 4, 10: "Human blood, from whatever part it has come, is said to be very efficacious according to Orpheus's and Archelaus's assertion, in inflammations of the throat, and should be smeared on the mouth of the patients who have become subject to epilepsy; for these are said thereupon to stand up immediately."—Scribonius Largus, the author of "Medicamentorum Compositiones," in the 1st century A.D. recommends in several passages the use of human blood for epilepsy. Physicians of the Byzantine epoch (3rd to 6th centuries), such as Aëtius and Alexander of Tralles, give similar advice.

B. "Die Chronik des Abtes Regino von Prüm"

* About the utilisation of blood in the actual medical art of to-day, cf. *L. Landois*, "Die Transfusion des Blutes," L. 1875 (358), "Beiträge zur Tr. des Bl." 1878 (58); *O. Hasse*, "Lammbluttransfusion beim Menschen," St. Petersburg 1874 (78); F. Gesellius, Die Transfusion des Blutes," St. Petersburg 1873 (187).

† Cf. also Celsus, "De Medicina," III. 23, towards the end; Coelius Aurelianus, "Tardarum s. chronicarum passionum," I, 4; Tertullian, "Apolog.," 9.—Cf. also inf. ch. 7.

(translated by E. Dümmler,[2] L. 1890, 93) writes about the Hungarians in 889 A.D.: "They eat, as report goes ('ut fama est') raw meat, drink blood, swallow as a remedy the hearts of their captives cut into pieces." Bishop Liudprand, of Cremona, "Antapodosis," II., 2 ("Opera Omnia," recogn. E. Dümmler,[2] Hanover, 1877, 28) gives like information, after having told of the death of Arnulf of Carinthia: "ut magis magisque timeantur, interfectorum sese sanguine potant."

When in 1649 the Huron Mission Station at St. Louis was captured by the Iroquois and the Jesuit, Jean de Brébeuf was most horribly done to death, and did not show a tremor when they scalped him; the savages came in crowds to drink the blood of so brave a foe. A chieftain then tore his heart out and devoured it. (*Parkman*, "Jesuits in North America in the 17th century," 389 sq.)

C. The medical folk-belief, or (relatively) the superstition, respecting menstrual blood remained and remains in rank fulness.* For the middle ages the best evidences are the numerous penance books which for the most part arose in the period between 600 and 1000 A.D. Cf. *H. J. Schmitz*, "Die Bussbücher und die Bussdisciplin der Kirche," Mainz, 1883. The so-called penance book of Theodore of Canterbury, 7, 3 (Schmitz, p. 530), "Qui semen aut sanguinem biberit III annos poeniteat." 14, 15 (536): "Sic et illa, quae semen viri sui in cibo miscens, ut inde plus amoris accipiat, poeniteat (tres annos)." 14, 16 (536): "Uxor quae sanguinem viri sui pro remedio gustaverit, XL. dies vel LX. minusve jejunet."—"Poenitentiale Cummeani" I., 17. 35. 36. (617 sq.)=Theod. vii. 3; xiv. 16, 15. The three passages are repeated xxiii. 2 (668)"—"Poe-

* Cf. also *H. Ploss*, "Das Weib in der Natur- und Völkerkunde," anthropological studies, 8th. ed. publd. by M. Bartels, 2 vols. L. 1904, 1905, in the chapters on "Menstrualblut als Arznei- und Zaubermittel," and "Liebeszauber."—For §§ *C.* and *D.* cf. v. Wlislocki, "Zigeuner," 75 sq.

nitentiale Parisiense " 18 (683): "Qui sanguinem suum aut semen causa amoris vel alterius rei bibere aliquem vel aliquam facerit, tribus poeniteat annis," 91 (691) =Theod. xiv., 16.—"Ordo Poenitentiae, Codex Barberini" (748): "Bibisti sanguinem vel manducasti ullius pecudis vel hominis, tres annos poeniteas."—Another repetition in the Prague synodal decrees, v. *C. Höfler*, "Concilia Pragensia," Prague, 1862, XI., XII.—That the blood of female persons generally meant sanguis menstruus, is apparent from Bishop Burchard of Worms's (1000-1025) "Kanonensammlung," 19th Book ("Corrector et Medicus"), §39. "Fecisti quod quaedam mulieres facere solent? Tollunt menstruum suum sanguinem et immiscent cibo vel potui et dant viris suis ad manducandum, ut plus diligantur ab eis. Si fecisti, quinque annos per legitimas ferias poeniteas"; also from Abbot Regino of Prüm's (ob. 915), "De synodalibus causis," II., 359. 378 sq. (Edition of Wasserschleben, L. 1840, 354. 359); from Hrabanus Maurus's (ob. 856) "Liber Poenitentium" ("Opera," Cologne, 1627, Vol. VI.); from the "Regesta rerum Boicarum," for 1421 A.D., etc.

Hildegarde,* Abbess of the convent on the Rupertsberg, near Bingen, d. 1179, in her "Libri subtilitatum diversarum natur. creatur" (Ed. Migne, Paris, 1855), the oldest work of monastic medicine composed in Germany, which also gives experiences of popular therapeutics, praises baths of menstrual blood for leprosy. Warm uterine blood of a virgin, applied to gouty limbs, would alleviate the violent pain.† A shirt stained with this blood would ensure

* P. Kaiser, "Die naturwissenschaftlichen Schriften der Hildegard von Bingen," Be. 1901 (24); "Hildegardis causae et curae," ed. P. Kaiser, L. 1903 (254).

† "Hauss-Apothec" 50: "The pains of podagra are alleviated by the menstrual blood of a virgin, when it is smeared warm upon the place."—*Fossel*, "Steiermark" 166: "Linen rags steeped in menstrual blood are poultices against gout well known from of old."

against blow and stab,* and would quench outbreaks of fire, when thrown into the flames.

In the "Cosmography" of the Arabian, Zakarija ben Muhammed al-Qazwīni (ob. 1283 A.D.), Edtn. of F. Wüstenfeld, Göttingen 1848 sq., it is observed I. 366: "The blood of menstruation, if the bite of the mad dog is smeared with it, cures it, and likewise tubercular (knotig) leprosy and black scab (Räude). (In regard to these names of diseases, Cf. *J. M. Honigberger*, "Früchte aus dem Morgenlande," Vienna, 1853, 542 sq.); 367: "The blood of the menstruation of a virgin helps against the white spots on the pupil, if it is applied as an eye-salve."†

"Birthmarks, red moles, and freckles vanish if they are smeared with warm menstrual blood, the placenta, or with blood from the umbilical cord. . . . of a woman bearing her first child. (Unter- und Oberfranken)," *Lammert*, 184 sq. (ibid. original documents). "Moles . . . are cured by smearing with the blood of a fresh umbilical cord, by rubbing with a fresh afterbirth. . . . The red mole is covered with a linen clout which is moistened with fresh menstrual blood (Ennsthal)," *Fossel* 134. 56. "The freckles, especially of women, are sought to be dispelled by smearing. . . with warm menstrual blood (Oberland and neighbourhood of Graz)," *Fossel* 135.—"The smearing of warts with fresh menstrual blood. . . . is universally practised," *Fossel* 140. Slightly different is the practice in Oldenburg: "To dispel warts, they are smeared with the blood of another person's warts; the blood of one's own warts generates more of them." *Strackerjan* I.

* "Hauss-Apothec" 45: "How a man may always conquer in tilting or the lists. Take a piece of a virgin's shift, who has for the first time had the menses. Wrap it in a new trousers belt, which a pure virgin has made, and bind it on the naked skin beneath the right arm, so wilt thou feel the effect. Staricius in the 'Heldenschatz,' page 97."

† Cf. also *W R. Smith*, "Religion of the Semites," 2nd ed., I. 133.

83.—" For itch, wear a shirt, in which a woman has menstruated, during three days on the belly (Hieflau)," *Fossel* 135.—" Hauss-Apothec," 45: "Above all, the first virgin menses, preserved on the shift or a piece of linen, is held in high esteem, and when steeped in vinegar or rose-water, and, according to the greatness of the disease, laid and repeatedly laid on diseased glands, small-pox, apostemes, is prized as an excellent remedy."

In the Franche-Comté a good table-spoon of a woman's menstrual blood, or better still a young virgin's, in a glass of hot wine with sugar, is recommended for corrupt blood (sang gâté). (" Mélusine " I., C. 402).

Love-potion*. " In the Oberpfalz . . . sweat, a few drops of menstrual blood . . . are mixed in the drink of the person, whose liking it is desired to win," *Lammert*, 151 sq.

In 1885 in the assize circuit of Colmar, Dr. L. Fuld of Mainz, a barrister, had to work up a divorce case, in which, among other things it came out that the wife, in order to keep the affection of her husband, a farmer, had put a few drops of sanguis menstruus in his coffee.—An unmarried woman, B. (I intentionally indicate the name only with a letter) in Schleswig in 1888 gave her sweetheart some drops of her sanguis menstruus in his coffee. " He shall not run away from me," she cried triumphantly; in spite of which he was unfaithful to her. (Information from *H. Carstens*, Dahrenwurth, near Lunden, July, 1892).—The same thing was done by Lella d'Errico, in order to chain to herself her lover, the Prince of Venosa. About the proceedings taken against her in 1603, v. *Luigi Amabile*, " Il santo officio della Inquisizione in Napoli," Città di Castello 1892, Cf. *Ur-quell*, 1895, 12.

* Cf. sup. p. 9, line 13, and *Herklots*, "Canoon e-Islam or the customs of the Moosulmans of India," London 1832, p. 341 sq.

—The same is found in the Magyar folk-belief, v. Ur-Quell, 1892, 269. Likewise among the Gypsies. *H. v. Wlislocki* 77, 83-5. Cf. also *J. W. Wolf*, "Beiträge zur deutschen Mythologie" I. (Göttingen, 1852) 210.—In Oldenburg it is believed that a man too can win the affection of his beloved by the help of his blood. "The commonest remedy is, that one should give the other person . . . . . something of his own body, e.g. three drops of blood in a glass of wine or in coffee." *Strackerjan* I., 96.—In the province of Prussia, *Frischbier* 159: "If one wishes a beloved person to return one's love, one must put secretly a drop of one's own blood in that person's food or drink."—"The wife buries the hairs of a dead person and her own menses at the place where the husband is used to draw water in order to assure his marital fidelity." (Transylvania, v. *Ur-Quell*, 1893, 98).

First Elements: "He who is unable to conceive any love for the beautiful sex, should on Friday evening put on silently in moonshine a girl's shift, and take it off again Sunday morning. Love is awakened (Konow, District of Kammin)," U. JAHN, No. 547.—Tatjana Timoschtschenkow, in 1880, made her judges, in order to bewitch their goodwill for herself, drink the water in which she had washed herself, LÖWENSTIMM, 77.—The girl spits secretly in her sweetheart's beer-glass. (Neighbourhood of Cottbus).

(Cessation of the menses). "One should drink some of the water in which the blood of a first menstruation has been dissolved or the girl's bloody shift has been washed, or one should put on a shift moistened with fresh menstrual blood (Franken)." *Lammert* 148.

D. Some examples of the employment of other persons' blood.

Taken from mediæval medicine. The surgeon Henri de Mondeville (about 1304 in Montpellier; about 1306 and following years in Paris), says in his "Chirurgie," published by J. L. Pagel, Be. 1892, 555,

"Similiter dicit Thedericus, episcopus Lerviensis [also a famous mediaeval surgeon] in libello secretorum suorum, quod nervi contracti, si fricando humectentur cum aqua sanguinis humani septies distillati curabuntur," etc. He is followed by *Guy de Chauliac*, the most eminent surgeon of the middle ages (who practised in Montpellier, Bologna, Paris, ending as Papal Physician-in-Ordinary in Rome) in his great "Chirurgie," written about 1363, or at any rate then published, "Tract." VI. 1, 1 (Paris, 1891, 401) in respect of the treatment of indurations both after fractures and in articular and nervous disorders, "et aqua sanguinis humani septies distillati est ad hoc per alchimistas et per Henricum laudata."

(Against hydrophobia.) *J. Wellhausen*, "Reste arabischen Heidentumes," Be. 1887, 142: "Hydrophobia is cured by King's-blood ("Kitâb al-Aghâni," ed. Bulaq XIII., 36, 22 sq. XIV., 74, 28. "Arabb. Provv." I. 488. "Hamasa," 372, 9. 725, v. 5. Versio lat. II. 583 sq.). It can be seen from the quantity of instances, how widely-spread this belief was among the Arabs. It can hardly be explained otherwise than by assuming King's blood to be divine blood. The nobility is the centre of the stem, represents the straight branch of genealogy, and is nearest connected with the divine ancestor. King's blood, that is, does not signify the reigning King's blood, but the blood of the family from which the Kings or Princes are taken, e.g., that of the Quraishites, to whom the Khalifs belong. The poets flatter a Quraishite, by saying: "Thy blood is a help against rabies."—Cf. also *Caussin de Perceval*, "Essai sur l'histoire de l'Arabie."*

(Against children's convulsions). "The father pricks himself in the finger, and puts into the child's

* "Son sang (du roi Djodhayma) reçu dans les vases, fut conservé précieusement, car on croyait alors généralement que le sang des rois était un spécifique contre la folie ou possession, Khabal."

mouth three drops of blood from the wound," *Lammert*, "Bayern," 125, Cf. sup. Ch. 4A.

"Against distemper in little children: The father should give the child three drops of blood out of the first joint of his ring finger (Rackow, district of Neustettin)," U. Jahn, No. 519.

"Hauss-Apothec," 40 sq. "The wondrous virtue of human blood is this. If one distills into an alembic the blood of a young, healthy person about thirty odd years old, it makes all poor complexions again blooming, is good for all weakness of the brain, memory and spirits, banishes all poison from the heart, cures all manner of lung complaints, purifies the blood beyond all other medicaments, and is good for diarrhœa and lumbago, and increases the blood and semen," etc.

E. Human flesh. *Fr. L. Walther*, "Von Menschenfressenden Völkern and Menschenopfern," 1785.—*R. Andree*, "Die Anthropophagie," L., 1887 (105).—*H. Gaidoz*, "L'anthrophagie," in "Mélusine," III., column 337-46, 361-3, 385-9, 409-11, 433-5, 457-60, 481-7, 505 sq. (385 sq. contain instances of the fact that there is a belief in China and in Tonquin that he who has eaten of the flesh, especially of the heart or the liver, of a man has his courage communicated to him.—*P. Bergemann*, "Die Verbreitung der Anthropophagie über die Erde und Ermittelung einiger Wesenszüge dieses Brauches," Bunzlau, 1893 (53).—*R. S. Steinmetz*, "Endokannibalismus," Vienna, 1896; *H. Kern*, "Menschenfleisch als Arznei," in *Ethnographische Beiträge*, Festgabe zur Feier des 70. Geburtstages von Prof. Ad. Bastian (Leiden, 1896), 37-40. Corroborations of these four works from South Slav sources are given by *F. S. Krauss*, "Menschenfleischessen," in *Ur-Quell*, 1897, 1-5, 117-9. If a brigand kills anybody in the Masur district, he tastes a little of his blood in the belief that the blood of the murdered man will in that case not overtake him. When the Montenegrins cut a Turk's or Arnaut's head off they licked the blood off the yataghan, with the notion that the blood would not then descend into their feet—*i.e.*, they would not lose their presence of mind. If two persons in the Mazur district want to seal brotherhood they let blood on each other's fingers and suck it out mutually (p. 117). 347-350 (about the unrest in Croatia, 1897).

F. Incidentally may be mentioned here the longing for human blood or flesh in lunatics and pregnant women; v. regarding the former, *C. Lombroso*, "Der Verbrecher," translated into German by Fränkel, II. (Hamburg, 1890), 89 (Verzeni), 111; regarding both, v. *R. Leubuscher*, "Uber Wehrwölfe und Thierverwandlungen im Mittelalter," Berl., 1850, 57-63 (Bichel, the murderer of girls, Bertrand, the mutilator and outrager of corpses, etc.). Cf. also *Daumer*, I., 148-155 ("Kannibalismus des christl. Alt."), and inf. Ch. 13.

G. Blood of the Saints. *Daumer*, I., 191. When St. Blasius (under Diocletian) was murdered, seven Christian women smeared themselves with his blood, v. Wicelius, "Chorus sanctorum omnium," Cologne, 1554, 39.

H. The Communion wine and the consecrated wafers are referable here in so far as the partaking of them was also believed to affect a person's corporality. In respect of Christ's blood shed in the Holy Communion cf. (as early as about 348 A.D.), the 23rd "Catechesis" of Cyrillus of Jerusalem: "If a drop remains on your lips, smear your eyes and forehead with it, and sanctify them." About the legends regarding the blood of the Crucified Saviour, v. especially *J. N. Sepp*, "Das Leben Jesu Christi," V. (Regensburg, 1861). For Iceland, v. *Feilberg*, *Ur-Quell*, 1892, 87 sq.; for Poland, v. *Schiffer*, ibid. 147 sq. A good many criminals think they can perjure themselves with impunity if they have with them a piece of consecrated wafer from Holy Communion.

The doctrine of transubstantiation, which was brought forward as early as the middle of the 9th century A.D. by Paschasius Radbertus, and ecclesiastically established in 1215 at the fourth Lateran Synod, afforded the possibility that coarse-minded, and therefore also superstitious, ideas might be connected with the consecrated wafers. Cf. supr., p. 34, Jezer at Berne. From the end of the 13th century the appearance of the "bleeding holy wafers"* gave frequently rise to the charge that the Jews had pierced or cut through the wafers, and thus outraged them, and the accusation led to numerous persecutions of the Jews.†

It is the merit of the Berlin naturalist *Ehrenberg* to have shown the possibility of an explanation for a portion of these cases, v. "Verhandlungen," of the Academy of Sciences at Berlin, of 26th October, 1848, 349: "Herr Ehrenberg exhibited in fresh condition the old-time famous prodigy of blood in bread and food as a phenomenon now appearing in Berlin, and explained the same as conditioned by a hitherto unknown nomadic animalcula." Ibid. 349-62, E.

* Several points about "bleeding wafers and altar-cloths" in Daumer II., 111-20.

† Besides what has been dealt with by Ehrenberg, cf. *McCaul*, "Reasons for believing, etc." 12 sq.; *Cäsarius von Heisterbach* (first half of the 13th century) in 9th Book of the "Dialogus Miraculorum" (edition of J. Strauge, Cologne, 1851); *Johann von Winterthur's* "Chronik," trltd. by B. Freuler, Winterthur, 1866, 179 sq.; *O. Stobbe*, "Die Juden in Deutschland während des Mittelalters, Brunswick 1866, 187 sq., 283: *E. Breest*, "Das Wunderblut von Wilsnack" (1383—1522). Authoritative statement about the "Wunderblut" historical facts (in "Märkische Forschungen" (1881) 131-302); *F. Holtze*, "Das Strafverfahren gegen die märkischen Juden im Jahre 1510" ("Schriften des Vereins für die Geschichte Berlins," part 21).Be., 1884, 22. 28, 173; *G. Sello*, in R. Koser's "Forschungen zur Brandenburg. u. Preussichen Geschichte," IV., L. 1891 (about the same proceedings); the names of the 36 Jews burnt are given, according to the day-book of Minden, by *D. Kaufmann*, in *Magazin für die Wissenschaft des Judenthums*, Be. 1891.

gives an abundant list of cases in which the visual appearance of blood on the wafers and other objects —blood which was apparent and therefore held to be real—was to be explained by the appearance of a species of bacteria which was quite unknown till 1819 (Dr. Sette at Padua), and was only more intimately investigated in 1848 by Ehrenberg himself. The immediate conclusion is that the Jews were unjustly reproached with desecration of the wafers on the ground of that phenomenon. 362: ' I have been able very easily to propagate the phenomena on consecrated wafers. It makes its most flourishing appearance on boiled rice. It develops with striking facility in warm air in covered vessels and plates.—What a capacity for production! What a power!" Ehrenberg gave publicity, on 15th March, 1849, to further "Mitteilungen über Monas prodigiosa oder die Purpurmonade," 101-116.* Again Cf. *C. Binz* in *Verhandlungen des naturhistorischen Vereines der preussischen Rheinlande u. Westphalens*, Bonn, XXIX. [1872]; *Sitzungsberichte*, 166-9, 210†; *J. Schroeter*, "Ueber einige durch Bakterien gebildete Pigmente" in "Beiträge zur Biologie der Pflanzen." Published by Ferd. Cohn. 2nd part, 2nd impression, Breslau, 1881, 109-19; *F. Cohn*, "Untersuchungen über Bacterien" (in *Beiträge*, etc., 153); *Leunis*, "Synopsis der Pflanzenkunde,"[3] III., 634.

* Schroeter: "Bacteridium prodigiosum." Cohn: "Micrococcus prodigiosus."

† Here B adds, after Rainald, "Annales ecclesiastici," VI. 125 (Lucca 1750): "He (Benedict XII. in 1338) who was well instructed about the fabrication of miracles that blossomed in his time, answered the Duke of Austria's question about the 'bleeding holy wafers' at Passau, to the effect that the matter should first be carefully examined into, as in that regard there had already been deceptions proved. He also wrote to the Bishop, to carry on the investigation, taking particular heed of the falsifications that had already occurred, and canonically to visit severe punishment on those who were guilty of them."

How is it to be explained that the charge of descecrating the consecrated wafers was so often brought against the Jews? Precisely the high esteem in which the wafers were held by many Christians conduced for more reasons than one to exciting in Jews the desire to get possession of such valuable objects—*e.g.*, as security for loans.

Another proof of the belief in the efficaciousness of the blood (only apparently contradictory) is the widespread repugnance against the consumption of blood (*Frazer*, "The Golden Bough," 2nd edition, I., 353), nay, even against the beholding of women's blood (ibid. p. 360, sq.).

V. HUMAN BLOOD CURES LEPROSY

The opinion was extraordinarily widespread, pre-eminently in mediæval times, that leprosy could be healed only by human blood. The brothers *Grimm* say ("Der Arme Heinrich von Hartmann von der Aue." Published and elucidated, Berl., 1815, 172 sq.): "Health, which has been shaken to its centre and spoilt, can only be restored by the approach and invigoration of the *pure;* ordinary aid by means of herbs, juices, stones, which only operate for particular things, is futile; a complete annihilation of the evil and a new *rejuvenated* life are requisite. Leprosy and blindness were regarded as such generally incurable diseases which could only be removed by a miracle. . . . The *pure blood* of a virgin or of a child was, above all, thought to be the source of life which would abolish those diseases and engender a new flourishing life. . . . The patient had to bathe in it or be sprinkled with it; whereupon he was pure and fresh, like a maid or a child."

Doubtless the oldest evidence for the existence of this belief occurs in Pliny's "Nat. Hist.," XXVI., 1, 5. He says of elephantiasis: "This disease was chiefly at home in Egypt, and when kings were attacked by it, it was bad for the people; for then the seats in the baths were warmed with human blood for the sake of the cure." Herewith the old Jewish exegesis (called the "Midrash Shemôth [Exodus] Rabba"), of Exodus II., 23, is in striking agreement: "'The king of Egypt died,'—*i.e.*, he had become leprous, and a leprous person (Numbers XII. 12) was considered dead. 'And the children of Israel sighed.' Why? Because the hieroglyphic experts of Egypt had said to the king: There is no cure for you, unless every evening 150 little *Israelite children are slaughtered*, and every morning 150, and thou bathest twice daily in their blood. When the Israelites learnt of this grievous doom they began to sigh and complain." Cf. also the Paraphrase usually termed "Pseudo-Jonathan": "The king of Egypt was eaten away. So he bade kill the first-born of the children of Israel, in order to bathe himself in their blood."

Constantine the Great, according to the legend, when he was still a heathen, was, owing to his persecution of the Christians, punished with leprosy. Neither native doctors nor Persian savants could prevail against the fearful malady. The priests of Jupiter Capitolinus thereupon declared he must bathe in children's blood. Children were procured; but the lamenting of the mothers moved the Emperor to such an extent that he declared he would rather suffer alone than make many suffer. Referred in a dream to Pope Sylvester, he is converted, and is restored to health after baptism. Cf. Simon Metaphrastes in the Life of Sylvester, Michael Glykas, Nicephorus Callisti and "Reali di Francia," cap. 1. So early a writer as the Armenian Moses of Chorene (ob. A.D. 487) relates that the advice was given by heathen priests. Georgius Cedrenus's story that Jewish doctors had counselled the bath in children's blood rests upon prejudiced distortion of the older form of the legend.

"Pentamerone III., 9. The Great Turk (i.e., the witchmaster, Giant, great Enemy) has the leprosy, and cannot be cured unless he bathes in the blood of a great prince." He gets one caught, but the captive runs away (GRIMM, 178 sq.). — "Histoire de sainct greaal (Paris, 1523, Fol. 225). When Galaad, Perceval, and Boort travel together, and Perceval's sister is with them they reach a castle. . . and hear that the Lady of it has been sick of leprosy for two years, and no physician has known a cure for it. At length a wise man had said a basin, full of a virgin's blood, was needed. . salved with it, the sick woman would at once become clean" (GRIMM 180).—"Histoire de Giglan de Galles et Geoffrey de Mayence, cap. 19. A giant is leprous, and wants to bathe in children's blood in order to cure himself. His servant has already kidnapped eight children, slaughtered them, and gathered their blood in a bowl, and is just on the point of kidnapping the ninth" (GRIMM, 181).

We may also allude here to the touching story of Amicus and Amelius (Ludwig and Alexander,* Engelhard and Engeltrut, Oliver and Artus, the pilgrims of St. James de Compostella, v. GRIMM, 187-97. Cassel, 182-6), which has been disseminted in several variations (just named) which, however, are secondary to our purpose. One of the friends becomes leprous. When the other learns that cure is only possible by children's blood, he kills his own children, and brings their blood to his friend. The friend is cured, but God rewards the other's loyalty by raising the children to life again. Cf. also the fairy tale "Der treue Johannes" (in the collection of the brothers Grimm, No. 6).

"Der arme Heinrich," by the Swabian poet, Hartmann von Aue, may here be assumed to be known.

The story of HIRLANDA belongs to the same period. King Richard of England (1189-99) suffering from leprosy, sent for a Jew renowned for his skill, as no other doctor could help him. This doctor did his best, but the illness grew quickly worse. At last he spoke: I know of "a powerful remedy, if your Majesty had heart enough to employ it. Know that you will recover your health completely, if you can make up your mind to bathe in the blood of a new-born child, since I can swear to your Majesty by my Law, that nothing in the world works so vigorously against the corruption that has settled on your body, as the fresh blood of a new-born child. But because this remedy is only external, it must be helped out by an additional recipe, which extirpates even the inward root of the malady. Namely, the child's heart must be added, which your Majesty must eat and consume quite warm and raw, just as it

* In "Die sieben weisen Meister," which story, e.g., *K. Simrock* has printed in "Die deutschen Volksbücher," vol. XII. Frankfort (a.M. 1865) cf. esply. p. 237: "Then he (Emperor Ludwig) betook himself into the chamber wherein the (his) five children lay, and killed them all five together, and took a vessel and filled it with the children's blood. Whereupon he went to King Alexander and washed him all over with it. Now when King Alexander had been washed with the blood, he suddenly became fresh and quite whole."

has been taken from the body." (SIMROCK, "Volksbücher," XII., 31 sq.)*

The story of the foundation of the Schongau Bad at the Lindenberg relates how a libertine, having become leprous, wanted to bathe in the blood of twelve virgins, so as to be healed, but, after he had already killed eleven, he was despatched by the brother of the twelfth, whom he had already chained up. E. L. Rochholz, "Schweizersagen aus dem Aargau," I. (Argau, 1856), 22 sq.

Valerius Anshelm (from 1520 onward, municipal physician at Berne) narrates of Louis XI., King of France (1461-83), in his "Berner Chronik," I. (Berne, 1825), 320: "Now, when he was very ill, he seeks for and tries everything, especially much children's blood because of his illness." *G. Daniel*, "Histoire de France," IX. (1755), 413: "Il avoit recours à tous les remedes naturels et surnaturels; et pour le guérir, dit un Historien contemporain, furent faites de terribles et merveilleuses médecines. Un autre dit plus en particulier, qu'on luy fit boire du sang, qu'on avoit tiré à plusieurs enfans, dans l'esperance que cette potion pourroit corriger l'acreté du sien, et rétablir son ancienne vigueur." (In the margin as authority: "Gaguin," who wrote about 1498.)

Two evidences for the attitude of medical science. The celebrated physician, *Theophrastus Paracelsus von Hohenheim* (1493-1541), mentions as remedies for leprosy: "Dosis sanguinis humani, semel in mense in secunda die post oppositionem." Even the Zürich professor and municipal physician, *Joh. v. Muralt*, prescribes in the "Hippocrates Helveticus," Basel, 1692, 645, human blood for hereditary scab.

* The narrative is not based upon actual happenings. Richard did not suffer from leprosy; he died as the result of a wound he received. Accordingly the Jewish physician, together with his advice, also belongs to fiction. Cf. besides, the report given in Ch. 15 on the death of Pope Innocent VIII.

VI. UTILISATION OF ONE'S OWN BLOOD

Very common, too, is the use of personal blood—*i.e.*, the blood of the person upon whom an effect is to be produced. The blood is customarily either (A) taken inwardly, or (B) disposed of in a special manner, more rarely (C) applied externally.

A. (Hæmorrhages.) In violent uterine hæmorrhages "the woman in labour is given one or more spoonfuls of her own blood mixed with water," *Lammert*, "Bayern," 167.—"In May or between the two Lady-days catch two green frogs, dry and pound them, and give some of it in red wine with some pomegranate pods and human blood, and you will stop all bleeding with this (Suabia)," (*Lammert*, 194).—*Höfler*, too, "Oberbayern," 210, alludes to "the drinking of one's own blood in blood-letting" as an ordinary remedy.

B. (Dropsy.) "A dropsical person should bleed himself on the right arm, pour the blood into any empty egg-shell, and bury this in the dung till it grows rotten." Buck, "Schwaben," 44.—(Ischiagra): "In Nuremberg, where they scratch the spot till it bleeds, and plug some wool, soaked in blood, into the tree." *Lammert*, 270.—(Epilepsy): He who is attacked by epilepsy should have his blood let. This blood should be poured into a hole, which is made in a tree. Thereupon one must close the hole with the bored-out wood. *Lammert*, 272.—(Fever): "If owing to great febrile heat the patient is bled, wet a clean rag somewhat with this blood, and lay it, without letting it get otherwise wet, in a cool place, in the cellar, or in the side of a well; then will the heat directly disappear (Unterfranken)." *Lammert*, 198.—The invalid goes before sunrise to a small tree, scratches his left little finger, smears the blood on the tree, and speaks: Go away, fever; go away into the tree, etc., *v. Wlislocki*, "Zigeuner," 82.

(Freckles.) "Go Friday morning before sunrise into the wood, bore a hole in a tree, put some blood from the nettlerash into the shavings that have been bored out, put them back into the hole, and shut it tightly (Unterfranken)." *Lammert*, 179.—(Malignant skin-eruption): The Transylvanian tent-gipsy lets some drops of blood fall before sunrise from his left ring-finger into running water; if a water-sprite swallows this blood the evil is turned aside, *v. Wlislocki*, 82.

(Toothache.) In Northern Lithuania the following remedy is applied to toothache: You cut a chip from a living tree, and bore a hole in the tree; you then clean the teeth and the gums with the chip (usually another person does it) till blood comes; stick the chip in the hole and set light to it. The sufferer turns his back to the tree and goes off; but he must never look at the tree again.—According to Pisanski (*Wöchentliche Königsbergische Frag-und Anzeigungs-Nachrichten*, 1756, No. 22) it must be an elder-tree.* With the splinter cut out of it, you worry the gums till they bleed; then "you must plug it again into its former place, and let it grow together again." *Frischbier*, 102.—"If anyone has toothache, let him take a nail when the moon is waning, bore with it into the tooth so that blood comes, then let him knock it silently into the north side of an oak, so that the sun does not shine on it, and as long as the tree remains standing he will never again have toothache." (*Ad. Kuhn*,

* About this tree, Cf. *Urds-Brunnen* I. (1881-2) part 9, p. 16.

"Märkische Sagen und Märchen," Be., 1843, supplement p. 384.)—In Bischofsheim, District of Molsheim, you take a new nail, and after it has become blood-stained you knock it "into a place which neither sun nor moon reaches." *Jahrbuch für Geschichte, Sprache u. Litteratur Elsass-Lothringens.* VIII. (Strasburg, 1892), 13.

(Hæmorrhages). "Burning of a linen rag, on which three drops of blood of the bleeding person have fallen," *Höfler* 210.

(Against gout and rheumatism). The South Hungarian gipsy cuts himself in the left arm and lets the painful place be rubbed in, first with the blood, then with the grains of hip and haw berries. *v. Wlislocki*, 82.

"How to make a young married pair sterile. Cut a strip out of the bride's shift which is stained with the blood of her menses. When the young couple are declared one in church, stick the rag into a padlock and close it as soon as the Pastor says Amen. Afterwards cast it in a well or else in a place where nobody can find it. As long as the padlock lies unopened in its place, the pair will remain childless (Hinterpommern)." *Jahn*, "Pommern," No. 546.

Quite similar is the method described in No. 521 from Liepe auf Usedom.*

C. (Hæmorrhages). Qazwini I., 366: "If anyone has nose-bleeding, he writes his name with his blood on a rag and lays it before his eyes; the blood is then stopped."

* Magic for the same object, but *without* blood. *Kuhn*, "Märk. Sagen," supplement, p. 358: "Sometimes there are, among those present, envious opponents of the bridegroom, who, during the time the blessing is pronounced, open and shut three times an heirloom lock, in order that the married couple may remain barren." In the palaest. Talmud "Sanhedrin" VII., fol. 25d, the sea is obliged, at the command of R. Josua, to vomit forth again the magic knot which has been cast into it.

(Against decline). A communication was sent from Kreuzborg in Upper Silesia to the *Köln. Zeitung* (15th July, 1892, No. 567): "Widow Skroka, of Gusenau, had acquired the reputation of a 'wise' woman through the cures to which she subjected children suffering from decline. As she announced before the Court, she had inherited a razor from her father, with which she made cut-wounds behind both ears of the sick children, so that blood flowed properly. She next dipped the middle finger of the left hand in the blood, made three crosses in the sick child's pit of the heart, and spoke at the same time some words, which she did not dare disclose. However, according to the statement of witnesses before the sheriff's court at Landsberg in Upper Silesia, three children—one of them as early as the second day—died after this 'treatment,' probably from blood poisoning. The 'wise' woman Skroka escaped with 14 days' imprisonment."

VII. BLOOD OF EXECUTED PERSONS: HANGMAN'S ROPE

A. The blood of people who have died a violent death, especially executed persons, is held to be even more efficacious than menstrual blood. In fact everything belonging to such individuals is considered effective. Pliny, "Nat. Hist." XXVIII., 1, 2: "Treatises by Democritus are still in existence, according to which, in one case, the head bones of a criminal are more serviceable, in another, those of a friend and guest. . . . Antaeus made out of a hanged man's skull pills for mad dog bites."

"The blood of executed criminals, drunk warm, is good for epilepsy," *Buck*, "Schwaben," 44. The same evidence in *Lammert*, "Bayern," 271.—*G. F. Most*, "Die sympathetischen Mittel und Kurmethoden," Rostock, 1842, 150, tells how somebody, to get rid of this complaint, drank the still warm blood of an executed person, but fell down dead after he had run a hundred paces.—*Strackerjan* I., 83 sq. "Blood of an executed person, when drunk, helps against epilepsy and (Ovelgönne) fever. One must if possible drink it fresh, and then run as long as one can (Wildeshausen)".—For Denmark and Sweden Cf. *Feilberg*, *Ur-Quell* III., 4. The celebrated fairy story-teller *Andersen* describes in his autobiography an execution which he witnessed at Skelskör in 1823: "I saw a poor sick man, whom his superstitious parents made drink a cup of the blood of the executed person, that he might be healed of epilepsy; after which they ran with him in wild career till he sank to the ground."

Also according to the popular belief of the Transylvanians the blood of a hanged person is helpful in epilepsy, v. *Ur-Quell* 1893, 99.

"On 6th June, 1755, K. G. Zeibig, who when drunk had murdered a man, was beheaded on the Rabenstein at Dresden. . . . Before the execution two foremen of the tailor fraternity at Dresden begged the Prime Minister, Count Heinr. v. Brühl, on behalf of their brother member, Joh. Ge. Wiedemann, who suffered severely from epilepsy, that the same be allowed to drink the blood of the murderer for his restoration to health. An entry in the register announces that Brühl assented to the request, and also that Wiedemann, after drinking the blood of the individual beheaded, 'ran off.'" *Th. Distel*, "Neues Archiv für Sächsische Geschichte u. Alterthumskunde," IX. [Dresden, 1888] 160, rightly adds: "It is remarkable in this connection that even the highest official should have granted the request for the drinking of such human blood, and thus simply promoted crass superstition." For more about this superstition readers are directed to "Breslauer Sammlungen 1721 June; 'Winterquartal' 1721, pp. 654-7, class IV., art 17: Cf. also Oct. 1720, class IV. art. 9." He also refers to the article "Epilepsie," in *Zedler's* "Universallexikon."

Carl Lehmann, "Chronik der freien Bergstadt Schneeberg" III. (Schneeberg, 1840), 299 describes the execution at Zwickau of the murderer Karl Heinr. Friedrich on 15th Dec., 1823 (Cf. inf. ch. 12). He says at the end: "And with our own eyes we saw how a pot full of the blood of the executed man was drunk dry by various persons, and how these persons, mostly children, were driven with blows from whips to run at utmost speed over the field."

When the murderer Carsten Hinrich Hinz had

been executed near Tönning on 16th April, 1844, the epileptic son of a farmer, P. Ketels, of Gunsbüttel, drank, by permission of the executioner, who came from Oldenburg, some of the criminal's blood (communication from *H. Carstens*, of Dahrenwurth).*—"I was a pupil of the famous Prof. Herrmann at Göttingen. At his suggestion, at the beginning of January, 1859, I attended the public execution of a female poisoner at Göttingen. It was done with a sword. When the head was severed from the body, and the fountain of blood sprang up about 1½ feet high, the populace broke through the square formed by the Hanover Schützen, rushed upon the scaffold, and possessed itself of the blood of the dead woman, collecting it and dipping white cloths in it. It was positively a gruesome impression. To my horrified question I got answer that the blood was applied for the cure of epilepsy." (Communication of the Attorney-General ("Oberstaatsanwalt") *Woytasch*, of Marienwerder, August, 1892).—"A woman in an Outer-Rhodes (Appenzell) almshouse suffered from epilepsy, and received from the properly qualified directorate of the institution permission to go on the day after execution [of a butcher] to Trogen [in Appenzell] and try the gruesome remedy. Three draughts must be swallowed whilst the names of the three Highest are invoked. She was already standing at the scaffold, when a fresh access of her illness occurred, and hindered the carrying out of the plan. *Aargauer Nachrichten*, of 26 July, 1862." (*Rochholz* I., 40).

"Pommern,"† *U. Jahn*, No. 522: "The value of the

* Such blood is also mentioned by *H. Volksmann*, *Ur-Quell* 1893, 279, as a remedy against convulsions, believed in in Schleswig-Holstein.

† About the significance of the blood of an executed person, *O. Knoop* has collected further authentic documents from Pomerania in "Blätter für Pommersche Volkskunde," I. (Stettin 1893), 62-4.

blood of an executed person: When a criminal is executed, some of his blood must be obtained in a piece of linen. Bakers and brewers must dip such a rag into their dough and their beer, merchants and inkeepers into the broached brandy barrels, then they get a large number of customers; horse-owners must rub in their horses with it, that they may become sleek and shiny. The power of the blood, however, only extends to the third member (general)." —The story of "Der Sündenfinger," well known in Stolp, in its essential point (v. *Urds-Brunnen* VI. [1888-9], 76 sq.) amounts to this: A merchant in Stolp had concealed in the spirit cask a finger of an executed person. In consequence of which customers flocked to him in crowds, and the business flourished. The ostler denounced his master, who was severely punished, and the finger taken away from him. After fulfilling his term of prison the merchant had no luck any more; the customers remained away.

"Preussen," *Frischbier* 24: "Skinners' families preserve the blood of executed people as a magic remedy." 106: "The finger or blood of an executed person brings luck into house and into business (Dönhoffstädt). If such a finger be put in the stables, the horses thrive well (Ermland).—As is evident from the Report on the Conitz witch-trial in 1623 ("Preussiche Provinzial-Blätter" II., 133 sq.), in former times not only were the fingers and other limbs of corpses hanging on the gallows lucky, but also gallows-chains and gallows-nails; they helped to good beer-brewing and sale of beer, quickened manual work, made horses indefatigable, etc." Cf. also *Tettau and Temme.* 265.—*Mannhardt* 49: "A good many [executioners and skinners] keep the blood of the executed as a magic specific."

"Masuren," *Töppen* 107: "The blood of the

executed brings luck, and they often go several miles to get some of it (Neidenburg). Because, since a big crowd of people meet at the execution (at any rate they used to at the earlier public executions), buyers stream into their shops (Willenberg)."

After Andreas Hofer had been executed in 1810, some soldiers, among them Müller, the subsequent Director of Prisons in Vienna during the fifties, banded together to get hold of a limb of his body, because they regarded such as an amulet. They were, however, caught and punished (communicated by *Prof. G. Wolf*, of Vienna).

"Shanghai, 15 July. (East-As. Lloyd). In Foochow at the beginning of the month, occurred the execution of a pirate. After the criminal had been made a head shorter, the executioner opened the corpse with his sword, tore out the liver and distributed it in pieces among his assistants. The fact is that the liver of persons who have been hurried into the beyond by the executioner's sword is deemed a radical cure for various illnesses, especially consumption." (*Voss. Zeitung*, 26 Aug., 1892, No. 397).

B. Particular value is attached to the rope used by a hangman and a suicide. Pliny "N. H." xxviii. 4, 12, alludes to the belief that the rope by which a person has been hanged, wound round the temples, alleviates headaches.—*Lemke*, "Ostpreussen" I., 57: "It is considered a 'Glückszwang' (compeller of luck) to appropriate secretly some of the property of the fresh corpse. A suicide's rope and the blood of an executed person have a quite special value." I., 115: "'When W. hung himself in Gerswald, the man, who, people said, brought the rope home with him, came into good luck. But those in whose house he had hanged himself, and who had been deprived of the rope, came to grief.'"

"Poland," *Schiffer*, *Ur-Quell*, 1892, 200: "He who

wishes to have well-fed cattle, and that they should consume all the fodder in the crib, let him rub the crib with a rag which comes from a hanged person. Certain articles of the dress of a hanged person are needful to the efficacy of certain magic formulae."—P. 201: "Udziela tells about a peasant, who buried the rope of a hanged person in his garden, so that the passing river might not overflow its banks and press further into the field. He who carries with him a piece of the rope, with which anybody has hanged himself, has always luck. If a publican desires a brisk demand for brandy, let him put into the brandy barrel a thread from the dress of a hanged person. Lukaszewicz relates that in 1559 in Posen a certain Anna Maciejowa Sieczczyna was whipped and hounded out of the town on account of dealings in magic, amongst other things because she escorted a female innkeeper to the gallows, in order to get the rope with which a criminal had recently been hanged. The peasants explain the powers of attraction wielded over them by the brandy barrel by the circumstance that the host has put in it the rope of a hanged person."

"The dying can be kept very long alive, if part of a hangman's rope is laid in their beds. My grandfather told me this. . . . . about a widow, who was kept alive in that way more than a year. . . . . When the rope was taken out of the bed, in order 'to lighten the woman's anguish,' she died even in the course of the same day." "Transylvania," *H. v. Wlislocki, Ur-Quell* 1893, 100.

The well-known soubrette Josefine Gallmeyer (not of Jewish extraction) took with her on her pilgrimage to Maria-Zell, a "Mesusa"* and a piece of

* The "Mesusa" is a small metal box, attached to the doorposts of Jewish dwellings, with a small parchment scroll on which are written the Biblical words in Deuteronomy VI., 4-9, and XI., 13-21.

hangman's rope. (Communicated by *Prof. G. Wolf*, of Vienna, according to the narration of several persons friendly with J. G.)

C. In place of the rope, a nail from a cross, gallows, or bier, is also occasionally mentioned. Pliny, "N. H." xxviii., 4, 11: "Some, in cases of quartan fever, bind round their necks a piece of a nail from a cross wrapped in wool, or also a rope taken from a cross, and, as soon as the invalid is free from fever, they hide it in a hole where the sun cannot penetrate." Cf. p. 73, and inf. Ch. 15 B 4.

VIII. CORPSES AND PARTS OF CORPSES

A. *Strackerjan* justly remarks I, 70: "In the use of 'sympathy' for the cure of diseases, it is generally a question of firstly establishing the necessary connection between the malady and another object, and secondly in some way to set the object aside or completely to destroy it." I. 78: "Nothing can be more certainly destined to destruction, to corruption than a human corpse; wherefore there is scarcely a means more powerful for destroying hostile influences than when those influences are brought into connection with a corpse. Tumours, eruptions, outgrowths, warts, gout, etc., are dispelled, if one strokes the sick part with the hand (with the left hand) of a corpse.—If one puts in a coffin any part of an injured limb, say the scar of a wound, rags soaked in pus or blood, clothes covered with sweat, or a piece of wood which has been in contact with the suffering part, the illness passes away."—Hereditary lice can be got rid of, if a few in a pen-tray be put with a corpse in the coffin, Dithmarschen, v. *Ur-Quell* 1895, 217.—Let him who has a wound clean it with a cloth, lay this under the corpse's head and speak at the same time: Take this with you into the beyond! Portugal, *Ur-Quell* 1898, 208.

B. But the idea of the majesty of death has also had influence in another direction, namely to the effect that in many cases the quality of directly curing and protecting has been attributed, and is still, to corpses and their parts.—*Rochholz* I, 232: "The Swedes believed that on the possession of Frey's corpse depended the fertility and peace of the land; he was therefore not, according to custom, cremated, but buried in the hill untouched; in like manner King Hâlfdan Svarti was buried in four places in order to give the country fourfold fertility, and his different graves were pointed out (Grimm, "Kleine Schriften" II. 266."—"When the Northern Viking Ivar, son of Ragnar Lodbrok, died in England, he commanded on his death-bed that he wished to be buried there, where the kingdom was most exposed to hostile attacks." Likewise the Irish Prince Eoghan Bell was "buried with his red javelin in his hand, his face turned in the direction whence the foe were bound to make inroads into the land," v. *Feilberg*, *Ur-Quell* III, 118.—Cf. also *F. Liebrecht* "Zur Volkskunde" (Heilbronn 1879) 289 sq., who quotes *Jul. Braun*, "Naturgeschichte der Sage" (Munich 1864) I, 225. II, 407.—*J. Grimm*, "Geschichte der Deutschen Sprache" 149: "Those bones of Orestes or Theseus had a tutelary force for the whole land. Out of Pelops's bones Abaris is said to have constructed the Palladium and given it the Trojans (Julius Firmicus "Astronom." p. 435; Clemens Alexandr. "Ad gentes" p. 30). His shoulder blade was exhibited, and regarded as powerful to cure: "quorundam partes medicae sunt, sicuti diximus de Pyrrhi regis pollice, et Elide solebat ostendi Pelopis costa, quam eburneam affirmabant," Pliny xxviii, 4, 4. But there was not evolved from it so general, all-comprehensive a worship as among the Christians." "They scarcely liked to build a church in which mouldering bones and old rags of clothes were not deposited; these saints, whose altars rose up next that of the Deity, whose festivals filled the whole year, were also lords of justice and of diseases; for all oaths were sworn on their relics, all incurables besought cure on their knees before their graves and relics."—*Rochholz* I, 230: "The head of S. Makarius in the Marienkapelle at Würzburg is laid every year [2 January] on believers; it is a security against headache. ("Bavaria" iv. [Munich 1866], 220)."

C. Drinking out of skulls. J. Grimm, "Geschichte der Deutschen Sprache" 144: "The monks at Treves had S. Theodulf's skull set in silver and gave fever-patients to drink out of it ("Acta Sanctorum" May I, 99a). Leo von Rozmital came to Neuss in 1465: There we saw in the church a costly coffin; therein lay the dear holy Saint Quirinus, and we saw his skull, therefrom they gave us to drink."—The author of a pilgrimage undertaken about 570-80 A.D. ("Antonini Placentini Itinerarium" cap. 22, Be. 1889, published by Gildemeister) writes after describing the Church of Sion at Jerusalem: "There is a nunnery there. I saw there enclosed in a gold casket adorned with jewels a human skull, of which they say, it is that of the martyr Theodota. Many drank water out of it for a blessing ('pro benedictione,') and I also drank."—*Rochholz* I, 230: "The Benedictine monastery 'zum S. Gumpertus' in Ansbach received its name originally in 750 A.D., and is endowed with charters by Charlemagne in 787 A.D.; it suffered the neighbouring Wend heathens to drink cures out of the wonder-working skull of Gumpertus, grew in consequence to a place of pilgrimage, and so gave the first occasion for the foundation of the future city. When S. Anna of Klingnau's corpse was dug up, a sick nun drank out of her skull (*Murer*, "Helvetia Sacra" 334 b). 'As long as S. Sebastian's skull set in silver is kept at Ebersperg in Upper Bavaria, and the consecrated wine is given those pilgrimaging thither to drink out of the skull, the plague has never more dared to take its seat in these parts.' ("Vierte Festpredigt zum hundert-jährigen Jubiläum der Sebastiansbruderschaft zu Aichach." Augsburg 1757, 101.) Likewise in S. Nantwein near Nandesbuch, S. Vitalis in Au am Inn, S. Marinus in Rott am Inn, S. Alto in Altomünster, the skull as a drinking vessel has been assimilated into the Christian religion, v. *M. Höfler*, "Wald- und Baumkult in Beziehung zur Volksmedizin Oberbayerns," Munich 1894, 13. 46. 79. 87; Cf. also "Archiv für Anthropologie, Correspondenzblatt," xiii (1882), p. 46. The skull or other relics of S. Valentine (7 January) are said to cure epileptics.—About skull-worship Cf. further *W. Powell*, "Unter den Kannibalen von Neu-Britannien" (translated by *F. M. Schröter*, L. 1884, 144 b); *G. A. Wilken*, "Het Animisme bij de Volken van den Indischen Archipel," Leyden 1885, Ch. 4, and in: "Bijdragen tot de taal-, land- en volkenkunde van Nederlandsch Indie" 1889, 89-130.

The superstition that pigeons which are made to drink out of a dead person's skull always return to their dovecot, is not infrequently testified to, v. *Rochholz* "Schweizersagen" II, 160.—In order to compel a thief to restore what he has stolen, it is customary in Banzenheim, district of Mülhausen, to lay a criminal's skull and a stone on a juniper bush, or to take three nails from a bier smeared with some melted fat of an executed person—adding in both cases a fixed formula of incantation, v. *Jahrbuch für Geschichte, Sprache u. Litteratur Elsass-Lothringens* VIII. (1892) 22.

D. The *corpse-hand.* Pliny, "N. H." xxviii. 4, 11; "Stroking with the hand of a person who has died early is supposed to cure goître, glandular swellings near the ear, and throat complaints; nevertheless, a good many think this can be effected by any corpse's hand, provided only the dead person be of the same sex, and the thing is done with the left hand upturned."—*Grimm*, "Der arme Heinrich," 177: "Carpentier (v. miselli) quotes from an authentic document of 1408 a passage in which a leper is stroked with the hand of a still-born (therefore sinless) child, in which was put some salve, and is healed. There is even now a popular belief in parts of Austria, that malignant tumour is cured by the laying-on of a dead hand."—Hauss-Apothec 48: "Other credible people have affirmed that if the hand of a corpse is rubbed against a goître or other swellings, the same are said, as the corpse rots away, to decrease and gradually vanish, although quicker in summer, slower in winter. If one rubs the swelling on a hand with a dead hand, the swelling goes down."—"Oldenburg," *Strackerjan* I, 71: They stroke "the painful part with a dead hand. . . . . what afterwards. . . . . happens to the dead hand, happens also to the disease."—In Pomerania the memory of this superstition has been preserved, especially in numerous incantations or benedictions, in which the "cold corpse-hand" is mentioned: as protection against fire, *U. Jahn*, no. 118-20. 140-3; against water and fire, no. 132; against inflammatory swelling (Einschuss, lacteal metastasis in the breast and udder), no. 228; against "Rückblut" (an internal illness of cows, in which the urine is coloured red) no. 336; against warts, no. 387. —"Preussen," *Frischbier* 103: "The custom is universal, in toothache, to press with a corpse's finger the gums or aching tooth. The right hand index finger is the most efficacious. The same is also applied for herpes, red moles, etc."—*Lemke*, "Ostpreussen" I, 47: "It is recommended to lay a corpse's hand on the red mole; one must not, however, omit to utter at the same time: 'In the name of God the Father, the Son, and the Holy Ghost'!" 55: "The sufferer from toothache is moreover advised to stroke the gums with a corpse's finger. 'It cured my daughter in Gerswald immediately, when she went to her little dead godchild and rubbed her gums with one of his fingers.' "—*Ur-Quell*, 1890, 137: "The most infallible remedy for toothache is to press the tooth three times with a corpse's finger, saying: 'To thee, dead one, I bewail my distress. Take away my toothache, and take it with thee into the grave. In the name of the Father, etc. Amen.' (Neighbourhood of Insterburg)."—"Masuren," *Töppen* 54 sq.: "Apophyses on the human body, which are called 'Knöchel' (little bones) are cured in the following fashion: (1) One goes into a house in which is a corpse, takes the hand of the corpse without uttering a word, and thrice presses the apophysis with the corpse's finger."—107: "Toothache is cured by pressing the corpse's index finger on the aching tooth (*Königsberger Hartung'sche Zeitung*, 1866, No. 9)."—Birthmarks, freckles, and apophyses disappear, as soon as they are touched with a dead hand (Natangen), *Ur-Quell*, 1892, 247.—"Steiermark," *Fossel* 134: "Birthmarks are cured. . . . . by contact with a dead hand, especially the hand of a child's corpse." 140: For the banishing of warts "contact with a dead hand is. . . . generally practised."—In Dithmarschen, burns and carbuncles too are stroked with a dead hand, v. *Urds-Brunnen* V. 127. "The herpes is stroked with a dead hand," Sehestadt in Schleswig-Holstein, *Ur-Quell* 1893, 278. Also among the Transylvanians (Henndorf): "A tumour or warts are cured by stroking them oneself with a dead hand." *Ur-Quell* 1893, 70.—To get rid of a goître let it be stroked thrice with a dead hand, with the words: Even as this hand is decayed so too may the goître subside. (Bosnia), *Urquell* 1892, 303.—After Russian popular belief a dead hand protects from bullets, *Löwenstimm* 113.

E. Fossel, "Steiermark" 172: "The belief in the use of a corpse as a drug, which is a mania prevailing over the whole country, reaches strange expression, as follows: The Brothers of Mercy at Graz are supposed to enjoy the privilege of being allowed every year to exploit one human life for curative purposes. With that object a young man, who goes into the hospital of the Order for toothache or other slight complaint, is seized, hung up by the feet, and tickled to death! The honourable brethren thereupon boil the corpse to a paste and utilise the latter as well as the fat and the burnt bones in their drug store. About Easter, the people say, a youth annually disappears in the hospital in this way."

F. This mania serves to explain the disturbances that have so frequently broken out during three centuries in China against Europeans, especially the Roman Catholic Missionary Establishments (houses for sick persons, foundling-hospitals, educational institutions, etc.) The riots, as I know directly from persons who have lived long in China, almost always begin by the "litterati" issuing appeals to the people, in which it is said: "Down with the foreigners! Kill the missionaries! They steal or buy our children and slaughter them, in order to prepare magic remedies and medicines out of their eyes, hearts, and other portions of their bodies." Baron Hübner narrates, following the best authorities, in his "Promenade autour du monde" II. (Paris, 1873), 385-455, the story of the massacre at Tientsin on 21 June, 1870. From his description which, in more than one respect, is rich in lessons, a few sentences at least may be cited here.

392: "Vers la mi-mai . . . . des bruits alarmants furent mis en circulation: des enfants avaient disparus. Ils avaient été volés par des gens à la solde des missionaires. Les sœurs les avaient tués. Elles leur avaient arraché les yeux et le cœur pour préparer des charmes et des remèdes. Ce n'était pas la première fois que se disaient de pareilles absurdités. 393: Les accusations se multiplièrent. On cita des faits et on y crut . . . . Le hasard semblait conspirer avec les auteurs de ces bruits sinistres. Une épidémie se déclara à l'orphelinat des sœurs. Plusieurs enfants moururent . . . . 397 (June):

Deux chinois étrangers . . . . . portaient un sac sur les épaules et conduisaient par la main deux petits enfants . . On les arrêta. Dans leurs sacs furent trouvés des dollars mexicains . . et quelques paquets de drogues. Mis à la torture, ils déclarèrent avoir effectivement ensorcelé les enfants au moyen de ces drogues. Les dollars leur avaient été donnés par les sœurs en paiement du crime. Les deux hommes, convaincus sur leur propre aveu d'un crime commis à l'instigation des sœurs, furent condamnés à mort et exécutés. C'était implicitement condamner les sœurs et rendre un arrêt de mort contre les Européens. 399: Plusieurs cadavres furent exhumés et examinés. A quelques-uns les yeux manquaient: cet effet naturel de la décomposition fut interprété comme une preuve convaincante de la culpabilité des sœurs et des missionaires. 400-3: The lying statements of Wu-lan-tchên about the magic means by which the missionaries attract people (retracted after the massacre, v. 437). On 21 June occurred the butchery. 426 sq.: Une femme fut jetée dans la rivière et retirée après qu'elle eût promis de deposer contre les sœurs (déjà massacrées!) et de déclarer avoir été ensorcelée par elles.

Everybody knows that in 1891, and in later years persecutions, due to the same cause, of Europeans living in China, especially of missionaries, have taken place.

Towards the end of 1891 a charge was brought in Madagascar against the foreigners, particularly the French, that they devoured human hearts, and for this purpose bought and killed children. Hence a decree of the Malagasy Government, which states amongst other things: "(1) Aucun étranger, ni Anglais, ni Français, ni d'aucune autre nation, ne cherche à acheter des cœurs humains. Si des gens mal intentionnés repandent ce bruit et disent que les étrangers achètent des cœurs humains, saisissez-les, attachez-les et faites les monter à Tananarive pour y être jugés. (2) Si on répand des bruits quels qu'ils soient, il est de votre devoir, gouverneurs, de réunir le peuple, de l'avertir et de lui prouver le fausseté de ces bruits, qui sont formellement interdits dans le royaume; c'est un crime de les propager," v. the Paris paper LE TEMPS, 1 Feb., and 25 March, 1892.

IX. ANIMAL BLOOD

A. The blood of sacrificed victims has a special position to itself. Attention may in the first place be drawn to the well-known necromantic episode in Odyssey, Bk. XI. According to ancient and wide-spread belief, inspiration is produced by sucking the fresh blood of a sacrificed victim, v. *Frazer*, "The Golden Bough," 2nd Ed., I., 133-5. As regards Egypt v. sup. p. 5.

B. In the middle ages, I refer to the collection of the learned Dominican, *Vincentius de Beauvais* (born 1194), "Speculum naturale," xxiii. 66.—*Ibn Baitar's* great medical and naturalist work prescribes, in the article "blood" (Ed. Bulak I., 96; French by Leclerc in "Notices et Extraits," xxv. [1881], 93) different kinds of animal blood as materia medica; human blood, however, is not mentioned.—*Qazwini*, "Kosmographie," I., 293: "If you desire that the vine be not fallen upon by worms, cut off its shoot with a pruning knife, which is smeared with bear's or frog's blood." (Instead of *dubb*—"bear"—read, with Dr. *G. Jacob*, *dabb*—"lizard.")

C. *Daumer* II., 194: "Even in the last quarter of last century it was customary in some parts of Germany on St. James's Day (25th July) to throw from a church tower or even from the Guildhall, amid strains of music, a he-goat adorned with gilded horns and ribbons, and to draw off its blood as it lay below, which when dried was esteemed a powerful remedy in many illnesses.* Something similar used to happen in Ypres, where cats were thrown from the tower on the Wednesday of the second week of fasting; so that that day is even now called in Ypres 'cat-Wednesday,' or the 'cat-day.' "†

D. In the most recent times. The following summary by *Buck* (used by Lammert 264, 221, 226), applies to Suabia, 44 sq.:" Cat's blood is useful against fever. A hole must be cut in the ear of a black cat, three drops of blood must be let fall on bread and the bread eaten (*Birlinger,* " Volksthümliches aus Schwaben " [Freiburg i. B. 1861] I. 488). Ox-blood is a violent poison. An ache or pain which is not outwardly manifested is cured by letting warm water flow over the place. Whoever bathes in warm blood becomes very beautiful. Hare-sweat helps against erysipelas. But the hare must be shot on Good Friday before sunrise; it must be at once gutted, and its sweat collected in an unbleached cloth (two ells), so that it becomes quite wet, and this must be wrapped round the inflamed limb. The cloth may afterwards be used pretty frequently.—Blood from a jenny-ass, and in particular three drops from the ear, if mixed in a strawberry drink and a 'vögle' (the eighth part of a Würtemberg beer measure) drunk two days running, restores speech which has been lost through an apoplectic stroke. Ass's blood extracted from behind the ear, soaked up with a cloth and steeped in well-water, if this be afterwards drunk, gives courage and banishes fear of ghosts.—If the eyes are smeared with bat's blood, a person can see as well by night as by day. . . . . Dry pigeon blood, mixed with snuff is

* *Kosche,* " Charakter, Sitten und Religion aller bekannten Völker " IV. (L. 1791), 481: and later, *Sommer,* "Sagen, Märchen u. Gebräuche aus Sachsen und Thüringen " (Halle 1846) I., 179.

† *Coremans,* " L'année de l'ancienne Belgique " 53; Sommer I., 180. —Cf. besides, Schröder's " Arzneischatz," v. sup. p. 8.

helpful for nose-bleeding."—(Bavaria). I extract from *Lammert* the following further details. In the Pfalz, in cases of pimples on the eye, fresh he-goat's—or sparrow's—blood is trickled in (228), in jaundice or other diseases she-goat's blood is drunk in wine (249). "In Suabia it is believed that weasel-blood is useful to strumous patients. . . . For the same purpose a band dipped in the warm blood of a shrewmouse is wound round the neck" (239).

(Pomerania). "If a man has lost his manhood: If thou art bewitched by a woman, so that thou dost not wish to have to do with any other, take he-goat's blood, and smear the testicles therewith, then wilt thou be right again." *Jahn*, No. 604 (after "Albertus Magnus . . . . Geheimnisse," cf. sup. p. 3, a book very widely disseminated in Pomerania).—"That people may love one: Carry bat's blood about you (Swinemünde)," *Jahn*, No. 612 (after A. Kuhn and W. Schwartz, "Norddeutsche Sagen, Märchen u. Gebräuche," L., 1848, No. 448).

(Prussia). *Frischbier*, 22: "In Lithuania such [ill-behaved] children are given three drops of blood, which has been taken from the left ear of a black sheep or lamb." 73: "In Samland a remedy for convulsions consists of drinking three drops of blood from a young sow which has littered for the first time, and a portion is given in the name of God the Father, etc." 94: "If warts are thrice pressed with a bleeding pike's head which has just been cut off, and the head is then buried beneath the eaves, the warts vanish as soon as the pike's head rots (Dönhoffstädt)."—*Lemke*, "Ostpreussen," II., 278: "For all manner of convulsions, but not for epileptic. . . . a potion is recommended, composed of Hungarian wine and (raw) hare's blood. (The hare's blood is collected and kept for a long time with this object in view.")

X. WASTE AND EVACUATIONS OF HUMAN AND ANIMAL BODIES

The waste and evacuations of the human and animal body are variously used. If from one's own body, they are often laid apart for curing purposes, even like one's own blood; if belonging to another person's body, they usually serve some object of magic (conjuring away of thieves, etc.). There are numerous examples in the works mentioned, pp. 2-5. Here it may be merely observed that the "Areolae" of *Johannes de Sancto Amando*, Bishop of Tournay, at the beginning of the 13th century (published by *J. L. Pagel*, Be., 1893), was in the middle ages a much esteemed compendium of the science of drugs: in the present book the different stercora are often specified.

XI. THE BLOOD SUPERSTITION AS A CAUSE OF CRIME

The blood superstition has often led to crime, in proof of which I have collected a large number of authentic documents. They are intended to show legal officials, ecclesiastics, and teachers that this superstition has not remained merely theoretical, and alien to our common life. And that it cannot be described as a peculiarity characteristic only of bygone times, but that it is a frequent cause of crimes perpetrated for therapeutic or magical purposes.

A. Murders. *Michael Wagener*, "Beiträge zur philosophischen Anthropologie, Psychologie," etc., II. (Vienna, 1796), 268, asserts that desire for beauty has been a source of inhuman cruelty, and goes on to relate: "A story of a Hungarian lady, which is very noteworthy in this respect, can be found in some Hungarian historiographers, e.g., in Ladislaus Thurotz, Istwanfy, etc. I detail the circumstances which are relevant here, both according to the aforesaid historiographers and (mainly) according to the existing legal documents. Elizabeth (Bathori)* was

* The name, which W. omits, I have filled in from Meyer's "Konversations-Lexikon[3]" II., 668: "E. B. (d. 1614), wife of the Hungarian Count Nadasdy, is notorious for the unparalleled cruelty with which, after enticing young girls into her castle, she had their blood extracted from them, which presumably was used for the beautifying of her skin, and in which she bathed herself . The Count Palatine Georg Thurzo surprised the Countess red-handed in 1610. The result of the examination showed that 650 girls had been the victims of this thirst for blood. A man-servant, who was an accomplice, was beheaded; two female servants were burnt alive. The Countess was condemned to life-long confinement."

excessively fond of making herself up to please her husband, and spent as much as the half of a day at her toilette. It happened, as Thurotz relates, that one day one of her chamber-maids once made some mistake in her coiffure, and received for it such a violent box on the ears, that the blood spurted on her mistress's face. When the latter washed the drops of blood off her face, the skin on the place appeared to her to be much more beautiful, whiter and more delicate. She at once came to the inhuman decision to bathe her face, nay her whole body, in human blood, so as thereby to increase her beauty and attractions. With this horrible intention, she took counsel of two old women, who accorded her their entire sympathy, and promised to assist her in the ghastly project. A certain Fitzko, a pupil of Elizabeth, was also made a member of this bloodthirsty society. This madman usually killed the unfortunate victims, and the old women collected the blood, in which that monster of a woman was wont to bathe in a trough about four o'clock in the morning. She appeared to herself always more beautiful after the bath. She therefore continued her operations even after her husband's death in 1604, in order to win new worshippers and lovers. The wretched girls who were allured into Elizabeth's house by the old women under the pretence of going into service, were taken into the cellar on various pretexts. Here they were seized and beaten until their bodies swelled. Not infrequently Elizabeth tortured them herself, and very often she changed her blood-dripping clothes and then began her cruelties anew. The swollen bodies of the poor girls were then cut open with a razor. It was not uncommon for this monster to have the girls burnt and then flayed; most of them were beaten to death. She herself beat her accomplices when they did not wish to help her in her torturings; whilst, on the other hand, she abundantly rewarded the women who brought the girls to her and let themselves be used as tools for the execution of her cruelties. She was also given to supposed magic, and had a peculiar magic mirror in the shape of a cracknel, before which she used to pray for hours at a time. Finally her cruelty reached such a pitch that she pinched her servants and stuck pins into them, especially the girls who drove with her in her carriage. She had one of her serving-maids stripped naked and smeared with honey, in order that she might be eaten up by flies. When she became ill and could not practise her usual cruelties, she had a person come to her sick bed, and bit her like a wild cat. About 650 girls lost their lives through her in the way described, partly in Cseita (in the County of Neutrau, in Hungary), where she had a cellar specially arranged for the purpose, partly in other places; for murder and bloodshed had become a necessity to her. When so many girls from the neighbourhood, who were brought into the castle on the pretext of entering service or of receiving further education, disappeared, and the parents never received satisfactory, but generally ambiguous, answers to their enquiries, the matter became suspicious. . . . At last, by bribing the servants, it was discovered that the missing girls went hale and hearty into the cellar, and never made their appearance any more. A denunciation followed both at Court and to the then Count Palatine Thurzo. The Count had the castle of Cseita surprised, commenced the strictest investigations, and discovered the horrible murders. The monster was condemned to life long incarceration for the terrible crimes, but her accomplices were executed."*

* [A Viennese pamphlet, communicated by *Grimm*, "Armer Heinrich," 181 sq. probably refers to the same episode, although the number of girls tortured to death is given as only 29, and the

From DAUMER, "Geheimnisse," II., 266, I extract the following: "There may also be mentioned here a well-known story by E. T. A. Hoffmann (ob. 1822) which, as far as I know, is based upon a criminal case authenticated by documents. There lives in Naples an old doctor; he has, by several women, children, whom he inhumanly slaughters amid special preparations and solemnities; he cuts open their breasts, takes out their hearts, and prepares from the heart's blood precious drops that afford resistance to any disease." Hoffmann's "Nachtstücke," 1817 (Be.) "Ignaz Denner," I., 47 sq.

Nurgalei Achmetow, of the village of Stary Ssalman, Govt. Kasan, had an apoplectic stroke, and suffered in consequence from paralysis of the right arm, and constant trembling of the head. When he heard he would recover if he ate a human heart, he murdered a six year old girl with his father's help, cut her heart out of her body, and devoured it. *Löwenstimm*, 145.

Rochholz, I., 39: "The murderer Bellenot, a native of the Bernese Jura, who was executed in 1861, confessed, at his trial, he had killed the woman, who was nicknamed the *Doktorfraueli* (doctor-woman) because she used to sell medicinal herbs which she gathered herself, in order to drink her blood, and so get rid of the epilepsy to which he was said to have been subject (*Aargauer Zeitung*, 19th May, 1861)."

B. Desecrations of graves. "Next appeared [on 15th February, 1890, before the Court at Hagen, in Westphalia] a servant, 70 years of age, named A. S(ander), of Wengern, on the serious charge of robbery of dead bodies, and desecration of graves. The accused . . . . . has already been punished with ten years' imprisonment for a similar crime in 1873; according to the new legislation the maximum punishment is two years' imprisonment. The accused confesses that on the night of 6th December last year

" beautiful and distinguished lady in Hungary " is alleged to have been " burnt alive in the public market-place " with the old woman who shared her guilt.]

he went to the cemetery of the parish of Wengern, looked at the fresh graves, and dug up with a spade lying on the spot a child's grave, from which he then raised the little coffin, took it under his arm, and wandered off to his dwelling. He then hid the coffin under the hay on the house floor, and next day, after opening the coffin with a screw-driver, cut out of the thigh of the corpse a piece of flesh, which he laid on a wound he had had many years on his body. The deed of the accused is therefore, like the former one for which he was condemned, the result of a fearful superstition. S. says he got the recipe many years ago from an old doctor as a remedy for his wound. He even imagines, at least he said so in to-day's hearing of the case, that the remedy has done good. The little coffin was accidentally noticed by the employer of the accused on the ground beneath the hay, and thus the affair came to light. . . . . The accused was condemned to two years' imprisonment." (*Hagener Zeitung*, 18 Feb., 1890, No. 41).

In 1865, a peasant in the neighbourhood of Mariensee (West Prussia) injured himself whilst carrying to the cemetery the coffin of an old woman he knew. A "wise-woman" declared the man could only be saved, if he burnt a piece of the dead person's coffin and of her shift, and swallowed the ashes. His wife, together with a friend of the watchman's, were arrested, when she tried one night to extract from the grave the articles mentioned to her. *Mannhardt*, 18.

In April, 1871, the churchwarden, Peter Woroshenzow, of the village of Bobinskoje, District of Wjatka, Russia, took out of a fresh grave a little child's liver and coagulated blood, in order to cure himself with them from an illness. He drank the blood, after mixing it with wine. *Löwenstimm*, 109 sq.

In 1862 four shepherds of the borough of Janow,

Govt. Radom, opened two graves, cut portions from the corpses, boiled the portions, and sprinkled sheep with the brew. This treatment was supposed to protect the animals from infection. *Löwenstimm*, 110.

In 1890 the "magician" Wawrzek Marut was condemned to five months' close arrest by the judicial court at Rzeszow (Galicia), because he had taken two children's corpses from the Jewish cemetery at Rozwadow, in order to fumigate typhus from a peasant's hut. The accused asserted there were two kinds of typhus; one, the "Catholic," which could be banished by the Lord's Prayer, and the other the "Jewish," which could only be banished by Jews' bones. Marut had already been condemned for similar proceedings in 1881. (*Ur-Quell*, 1891, 179 sq.)—Cf. *Ur-Quell*, 1892, 126 sq., for a similar crime committed in January, 1892, at Raźniów.

"In Kjelce (Russia) two Christian peasants were recently condemned to six months' imprisonment each, who stole the bodies of two Israelites from their graves, and cut them in pieces, in order to use the latter for the 'cure of diseases'." (*Oesterreich. Wochenschrift*, 1886, 452.)

W. Mannhardt, "Preussen," 19 sq.: "The notion is widespread that if parts of a corpse are put in connection with a living person, the latter will pine away and decline in the same period and degree as the corpse putrefies. Now this may happen in two ways, either by suspending one of the limbs of the dead person in the chimney of the dwelling of the person who is to be injured, or by putting with the corpse in the coffin some article of clothing or any other property of the intended victim [Cf. sup. Ch. 8A]. 'Double does not tear,' thought the gardener's widow, Albertine Majewska . . . when she resolved in May, 1875, to revenge herself on her former lover, the father of an illegitimate child who had been buried three months before. Soon after the gendarmes received information that the corpse of Majewska's child was damaged. By order of the Public Prosecutor the little body was dug up, and found in a mutilated condition. The sexual organs and all the fingers of the left hand had been torn off, and the stump of the hand and the face strewed with gunpowder. . . . It transpired that she [Majewska] had removed the above-mentioned parts of the body in order to hang them in the chimney of her erstwhile lover, so that his hand, with which he had perjured himself, and, at the same time, the source of his manhood might dry up and wither away; and also that the gunpowder strewed in the coffin was taken from the man's belongings to ensure that he should gradually pine away and disappear together with the powder and the corpse."

A village shepherd, Casimir K., in the Rajew district of the Government of Warsaw, in May, 1865, cut, with the help of two comrades, the liver out of a woman's corpse, in order to bury it in a spot over which the herd must pass, in the expectation that all the sheep belonging to the peasants would then rot away. He had wanted a corpse's tooth, in order to pulverise it and sprinkle it in his brother-in-law's snuff; but the person to be poisoned was a man, and in the opened coffin lay a woman. *Löwenstimm*, 111.

C. Outrages on virgins. The unhappily not uncommon cases of rape of innubile girls are not ordinary crimes against morality, but find their explanation in the maniacal idea that contact with a virgin (a rudimentary element in the sacrifice! v.p. 1, 28 sq., 37 sq.) is requisite for the cure of sexual disease in men. Cf. *Wuttke*, §532; *A. Vogel*, "Lehrbuch der Kinderkrankheiten,"[7] Stuttgart, 1876, 426; "A wretched superstition prevails among the populace that gonorrhœa of the male organ vanishes if the organ is brought in contact with a hymen, and many an enticement to immorality is yielded to because of this belief." *Henoch*, "Vorlesungen über Kinderkrankheiten," Be., 1881, 548: "I can refer to a whole series of cases of children between 4 and 10 years old who fell victims to savagery, demoralisation, or a certain superstition." *Casper-Liman*, "Handbuch der gerichtlichen Medizin[8]," Be., 1889, 122 sq.: "But it is well known that among the common people, and not alone in our country, the absurd and dreadful prepossession rules that a venereal evil can be most surely and quickly cured by coitus with a pure maiden, and most certainly with a child."—Hirt relates an instance in J. L. Friedrich's "Blätter für gerichtliche Anthropologie," V. (1854), 4. The punishment of a youth, who in 1862 outraged a girl of eight in Berlin, is related by *Mannhardt*, 10.—On 27th July, 1881, a child of eleven, Christine Hämmelmann, was murdered and outraged at Rellinghausen, in the Essen district. The murderer was, unfortunately, not discovered. The state of the district, however, had made it likely that the poor child "fell a victim to this morbid, mad idea," v. *Das Tribunal, Zeitschrift für prakt. Strafrechtspflege*, I. [Hamburg, 1885], 621-3.—Persian soldiers, according to Polak, have commerce with horses for the same purpose (*Wiener Medizinische Wochenschrift*, 1861, p. 629, in *Löwenstimm*, 147).

D. Vampires (a widespread superstition, especially in the province of Prussia).* *Mannhardt*, 13: "Those who have fallen ill through a vampire's bite are healed by having mixed with their drink some of the blood (*i.e.*, the thickish product of decomposition so described by the populace) of its head when cut

* About the vampire, cf. especially *W. Hertz*, "Der Wehrwolf, Beitrag zur Sagengeschichte," Stuttgart, 1862, 122-8. Also *C. Gander*, *Ur-Quell* 1892, 288-90 (after Joh. Pilichius, "Drey predigten zum eingang des newen Jahrs," Wittenberg, 1585).

off." 17 sq.: "Only a few months ago (March, 1877), at Heidenmühl, in the Schlochau district, the body of a recently-deceased child . . . was mutilated in its grave, and a small bit of the corpse-flesh was given internally to a sick child as a cure [for a vampire's bite]."—Cf. *Tettau and Temme*, 275-7 (especially about a case that happened about the middle of the 18th century in the family of Wollschläger, at Jacobsdorf, in West Prussia).

Graves are not seldom desecrated in Russia, because the people believe the dead person is going about sucking their blood, or causing epidemics, or producing drought by milking the clouds. *Löwenstimm*, 95-103.—In the Greek island of Andros (Cyclades) a countryman suffered from a swelling in the face. He attributed it to a dead enemy, opened his grave, stabbed the heart of the corpse, and also mutilated the bones. An old man knew about it and told everybody; he also intended to denounce it to the authorities, but stopped on learning that his own son had done a similar thing. For he had desecrated his mother's body in the same way, had even dismembered it and scattered the portions, in order to dispel his wife's puerperal fever. *Freisinnige Zeitung* (Berlin), 1893, No. 86 (after the *Kölnische Zeitung*).

E. Witches. Mannhardt, "Preussen," 59 seq.: "The test of witchcraft [swimming ordeal*, fumigation with "devil's dung"] is generally not carried out; but when there is an urgent conjecture of witchcraft, the person suspected is seized and beaten till her blood flows, in order to give it the sick man to swallow or to wash him with it, or until she promises to withdraw the spell. . . . That takes place in our Kas-

* "Schwemme": the person suspected is thrown into the water and is made to swim (must try to swim), and if she cannot, she is drowned.

subian villages as it were daily, and only a few cases come to the knowledge of the courts and to publicity. Nevertheless, the number of them is not inconsiderable. . . . In 1874 we again see a country-schoolmaster in the Strasburg district an accomplice in a deed of the kind. He and his wife, on the advice of a somnambulist woman, beat their own aunt with a pair of tongs till blood flowed, with which they sprinkled their child, whom they supposed bewitched by their victim.—57: "A peasant in Jaschhütte had . . . his leg broken. He did not seek any professional help . . . and was taken ill, in addition, with typhus. Neighbours who visited him persuaded him he was bewitched by a woman in the village, who had sent to plague him her twenty-fifth devil, called Peter. The witch, a young relative of 26, living opposite, is made to enter the house of the possessed man, and asked by those present to give him some of her blood to drink, because only then would the devil Peter quit him. . . [She is] forced by blows of the fist from two of those present to let the salving blood be drawn from her nose. The attempt is a failure. . . . One of the two men goes to the courtyard, dirties his hands with manure, whilst at the same time he makes three crosses with it on them. Flesh blows of the fist on the nose with the blessed hands had the desired effect. The witch was now obliged to lay herself on the bed of the possessed man, and to let the blood trickle into his opened mouth. The devil then, indeed, seemed to give way, for soon after the patient was able to utter the words: 'Nu wart mi beeter' [I'm better now!] The still-flowing blood was then collected in a cup for possible relapses. . . . The two exorcists were condemned to three months' imprisonment by the District Court at Berent on 16th October, 1868."

"The wife of a farmer G., in Niederhutte (Kassubei) was suddenly taken ill. The neighbours arrived . . . at last at the conclusion that it was not entirely owing to natural causes, but there was also witchcraft in the business. Very soon, too, a scape-goat was found in farmer K., a relative of the invalid. He unsuspectingly approached the sick-bed, when he was suddenly surrounded by all his male and female cousins, who violently demanded blood from him, red, warm blood; for the Kassubians, in their therapeutical anxiety, had recognised the wizard's blood to be the only effectual remedy. In order to avoid violent attacks on the part of the fanatical crowd, K. wounded himself in the little finger. But . . . an 'expert' affirmed the blood must come from the middle finger, and the wretched victim of this superstition had also to cut himself in the middle finger." (*Ur-Quell*, III., 46.)

According to *Joh. Scherr*, "Deutsche Kultur-und Sittengeschichte[7]," 1879, 585 sq., the following happened in Steiermark in 1867: "The son of a peasant was suffering from a leg injury. Instead of calling in a doctor, the father went to a 'wise-woman' for advice. She declared the boy was bewitched, and would not recover till the witch, whose name and abode were given, had named the necessary remedies. The peasant went to the 'witch,' and by brutal intimidation forced from the poor woman the recipe of a potion, the use of which, however, did not cure the boy's sick leg. The peasant thereupon went again to the 'wise-woman,' who gave him the advice to use force, and in the following way. He must bind the witch fast hand and foot, then tear out a tuft of the hair of her head; dip this in the blood coming from a deep transverse wound in the sole of the right foot, and mix it with her excrement, and use the result as a fumigation cure for the leg. No sooner said than punctually and earnestly done and executed; only in regard to the excrement the torturer had to content himself with remains that were in a pot, because the poor wretch could not immediately satisfy his desire. By a coincidence the healing of the leg-injury began after the fumigation had taken place. At the trial of the case of the woman, who had been crippled by the cut-wound, the accused, who was convicted, stood all the more upon the justice of his act because the cure of the leg had begun."

A village elder's wife fell ill in the Ranenburg district, and declared her old aunt had bewitched her. The peasants dragged the old woman to the invalid, knocked her down with a thrust with a hedge-pole, made cuts in her fingers, and collected the flowing blood in a vessel. *Löwenstimm*, 58, after the Russian periodical *Ssewerny Wjestnik*, 1892, No. 9.

In Tübingen, at the beginning of October, 1896, George Speidel was condemned for perjury. It came out in the case that he had once, at the request of a peasant, performed a piece of magic, so as to kill a witch. The peasant had to pull the coffin-boards out of a fresh grave; on these Speidel stuck a figure of clay, and then told the peasant he need not now fear the witch any more. (*Löwenstimm*, 73 sq., after *Vossiche Zeitung*, 10th October, 1896, No. 478.)

F. Hidden treasures. About a crime perpetrated in Hamburg in 1783, I have had placed at my disposal two printed documents from the Commerz-Bibliothek: (1) "Richtige Auszüge aus den Akten der Inquisition Namens Borchers, gewesenen Bürgers in Hamburg, Anna Catharina Neumanns, seiner Stief-Tochter, und Anna Lüders, Borchers Dienstin, wegen Ermordung eines Juden-Burschen in Hamburg. Frankfurt, 1785" (45), and (2) an extract, marked with the page numbers 187-192, from a journal printed outside Hamburg in 1785, in small quarto, whose name I unfortunately cannot ascertain.—According to them, the facts were these. A band of swindlers, consisting of an Altona Jew, Meyer Südheim, a certain Freudentheil, a one-eyed fellow who went by the name of Pater Flügge, and a certain Montfort or Musupert, whose tool was Lüders, a woman of 65 who was fooled by them, persuaded the uneducated simpleton Neumann, a woman of 36, to disburse considerable amounts of money on the pretext that money was needed in order to dig up the treasure of a Count von Schaumburg, which was buried in Ottensen. Neumann had several times given money directly; she then found notes in her house, mysteriously thrown in, in which she was asked to place ready in the parlour, at punctually fixed times, certain definitely named sums of money, and frequently meals also. What she handed over vanished in a most extraordinary way. When, impelled by curiosity, she once played the spy, she suddenly received so severe a box on the ears that she was deafened. It was repeatedly demanded in the notes "that a girl should be produced and killed as a sacrifice to the treasure, and particularly a Jewish girl, or, what would be better, a Catholic girl; for if this were not done, fifteen persons would lose their lives in this affair, and old Lüders and the Master [Borchers] would be smashed to pieces." An attempt to kill a Catholic girl, Maria Johanna Sardach ("Auszüge," p. 32), failed. Then came a note saying "that the treasure could not be dug up otherwise than with blood; because it was sealed with blood. A Jewish youth must also be killed, who was possessed of as much as 83 marks in value, and these 83 marks would also have to be brought to the sacrifice." ("Auszüge," 37, 41). In consequence of which Johann Jürgen Borchers, who had already for some time been told about the buried treasure, his stepdaughter, and Lüders murdered, on 13th October, 1783, a young

Jewish pedlar called Renner, with whom Lüders had made an appointment at the house of Borchers. Of 110 marks received for pawning the things, 83 were, in accordance with the instructions contained in the note, placed in the ante-room, and vanished like the amounts previously demanded. A few days after the murder there was a demand in a new note, firstly for the Jew's clothes, secondly that "the breast-cloth [probably the so-called small prayer-cloak or Tallith], which the Jew wore on his naked body, should be burnt as a sacrifice" ("Auszüge" 34). These commands were likewise executed. Borchers wounded himself mortally by cutting his throat immediately after his arrest; the two women, of whom Lüders was indubitably the most guilty, were broken on the wheel from top to toe, their heads stuck on posts.—The thieves were only concerned with money and money-values. They would hardly have brought their sacrifice to the point of robbery and murder, solely for such a purpose. They therefore played upon Neumann's proved superstitiousness. Neumann was a Protestant; so she might consider a Jew's blood to have a special virtue, and still more the blood of a Catholic; for there was at that time in Hamburg only quite a small number of Catholics. Cf. Ch. 20.

On the morning of 14 April, 1892, the body of a corporal in the artillery, Ilija Konstantinowitsch, was found on the banks of the Danube not far from the rampart of Fort Semendria. It lay stretched out on a bed-covering perfectly nude, the larynx had been cut out, the heart torn from the pectoral cavity. The murderer soon came forward of his own accord; he was a friend of the murdered man, an artillerist called Vasilje Radulowitsch. He said Ilija had come to him in the night and told him he had already dreamt five nights running there was a big treasure to be dug up at a fixed spot outside the walls of the fort, but he would have to sacrifice his life for a short period of time. Ilija begged him to accompany him, and took his bed-covering also with him, and when they reached the place, he asked his friend to kill him by stabbing with a knife, to cut out his larynx, to take his heart out of his breast, and then to besprinkle a certain spot with the blood of those parts of the body; Vasilje was then to dig quickly, whereupon he would find a small iron rod and a bottle of brandy—he was to stroke the whole body twice with the small rod, replace the heart and larynx, and pour the brandy on the raw places. Thereupon he (Ilija) would again come to life, and have the power to dig up the treasure which would make them among the richest people in the world. After Ilija had given these instructions, he stripped and lay down on the bed-clothes. After some hesitation, Vasilje killed Ilija by a stab in the neck; Ilija made no resistance, and only gnashed his teeth through pain. Vasilje next cut out Ilija's throat and heart with difficulty; he then dug till day-dawn, but found neither the bottle nor the rod. When he despaired of success, he returned the throat and heart into the murdered man's body, and betook himself secretly back to the barracks without anybody having seen him. The investigations showed Vasilje had spoken the truth. Ilija had spoken to several comrades about his dream, and his intention to get the treasure by sacrificing himself, and there was not the least trace of resistance on the corpse. (*Vossische Zeitung*, 24 April, 1892, No. 191).

Ilija's sacrifice was intended as a propitiatory sacrifice to the Earth Spirit, the guardian of the treasure. Cf. Milan Vesnič's work, "Praznoverice i zločini s naročitim pogledom na praznovericu o zakopanom blagu" ["bigoted faith and crime, with special reference to beliefs concerning buried treasure"], Belgrade, 1894 (62). *Ur-Quell*, 1895,

137-40, contains an account according to V. of two other crimes perpetrated in Servia which arose from the same superstition.

XII. BLOOD-SUPERSTITION AMONG CRIMINALS AND ITS CONSEQUENCES

A. "Pommern," *Jahn*, No. 524: "To prepare thieves'-tapers: Take the entrails of an unborn child and mould tapers out of them. The same can only be extinguished with milk, and as long as they burn, nobody in the house is able to wake up." (Meesow, Regenwalde District). 526: "If a thief gets the fat of a pregnant woman, makes a candle of it, and lights it, he can steal where he likes, without anxiety. No one will see him, no sleeper can awaken (Konow, Kammin district.)" 576: "If a thief dries an unborn child, lays it in a wooden casket, and then carries it about with him, he is invisible to everybody, so he can steal to the top of his bent(Konow, Kammin district.)"—Cf. *E. M. Arndt*, "Märchen und Jugenderinnerungen," II. (Be., 1843), 348 sq. ("Der Rabenstein," ad init.)

"Oldenburg," *Strackerjan*, I., 100: "The finger of an unborn child is useful to thieves by keeping the dwellers asleep in a house into which they have penetrated; it is simply laid on the table (Vechta).—The saying goes in Wardenburg that robbers and murderers cut open the bellies of pregnant women, and make candles of the fingers of the unborn children. When these candles are lit, they allow no sleeper to wake up as long as they burn. The candles can only be extinguished by dipping them in sweet milk."

"Bayern," *Lammert*, 84: "According to a wild

delusion circulating in the Pfalz, the finger of a child that has died unbaptized renders invisible, so that even 40 or 50 years ago, the churchyard at Speyer had to be watched ("Bavaria, Landes-und Volkskunde des Königreichs Bayern," IV., 2 [Rheinpfalz], Munich, 1867, 347). A similar superstition dangerous to public safety prevailed in Mittelfranken among thieves, namely, that the blood, which is collected with three wooden sticks from the genitals of an innocent boy, and carried about on the person, renders invisible in thieving."

According to a popular belief obtaining in Iceland and Jutland, inextinguishable lamps can be made of human fat, as well as of the finger of an executed person, v. *Feilberg*, *Ur-Quell*, III., 60 sq. Feilberg relates, 89 sq., that there is still in existence "in Denmark and Norway the notion of the magical power of an unborn child's heart." Also in Sweden, the last-named article of magic was well-known, v. *Harsdörffer*, "Der grosse Schauplatz jämmerlicher Mordsgeschichten,"[7] Frankfort, 1693, No. 182.

"Preussen," *Lemke* (East Prussia), I., 114: "'Human fat' yields a light which is useful to thieves. 'Many a one murders a man simply for the purpose of making a candle out of his fat'—at least so everybody says—whether it's true, it is impossible for me to tell. Such a candle is supposed to be the best thing a thief can have. But when they've lit it, they must hold it under the soles and under the noses of the sleepers; then the sleepers don't wake till the thieves are away. Such light can be put out neither in water nor in brandy, nor by kicks; such light can only go out in milk."—*Töppen*, 57: "A candle of human tallow puts all in the deepest sleep with its light. Such an article has therefore quite a special value for a thief (Gilgenburg.)"

Poland, especially Ukraine. *Schiffer*, *Ur-Quell*,

III., 148: "The first vein met with in a corpse, when dried and set light to, renders a thief invisible. A taper of corpse-fat has the effect that sleepers do not wake up, and the thief can steal quietly. The sleeper, on whom the shine of such a taper falls, abides in a heavy, invincible sleep. The hand of a five-year-old child's corpse opens all locks."

People in Little Russia believe (Papirnia, near Trembowla) corpse-fat candles have the faculty of sending everyone, except the persons holding them, into a swoon. With these candles in their hands, thieves need not fear to be caught. *Ur-Quell*, 1894, 163.

In Russia thieves attribute a narcotic effect also to the hand of a corpse. *Löwenstimm*, 116, says: "The proverb, 'The people slept, as if a dead hand had travelled about them,' has not sprung up without cause." From a Russian folk-song, which in truth sounds like a survival of cannibalism, Löwenstimm, 120 sq., quotes the following passage: "I bake pastry out of the hands, out of the feet, I forge a drinking-cup out of the mad head, I pour drinking-glasses out of his eyes, out of his blood I brew intoxicating beer, and out of his fat I mould candles."

H. v. Wlislocki, "Zigeuner," 94 sq.: A cloth, on which are some drops of blood of a hanged person, preserves a thief from discovery. Parts of the limbs and shreds of the clothes of a hanged person have the same result. He who drinks of the blood of a hanged person can go in the darkest night as well as in the brightest daylight. When the robber-murderer Marlin was hanged at Hermannstadt in 1885, a gipsy, Roska Lajos, got some of the blood and drank it, after mixing it with a strong decoction of hempseed flowers. He who consumes the little finger of the left hand of a still-born child, can by his breath bring it to pass that people who are already asleep will not be awakened by he loudest noise. The nomadic gipsies of Servia and Turkey therefore stick a needle through the above-mentioned finger of such children so that no one may consume the finger after digging up the corpse. Thieves who possess a taper made of a white dog's fat, and the blood [95] of still-born twins can be seen by no one. He who eats some of a paste composed of that material, can see hidden treasures on S. John's Eve and New Year's Eve. The South Hungarian gipsies rub such salve into their soles, in order to make their footsteps inaudible whilst stealing. A nomad gipsy, in November, 1890, paid a peasant woman, Lina Varga, of Vörösmart, four kreutzers for every drop of blood yielded by her still-born twins.

Further authentic documents proving the wide currency of the belief in the magical properties of the fingers of children who were unborn or died unbaptised. *Grimm*, "Deutsche Mythologie," p. 1027, quotes: Schamberg, "De jure digitorum," p. 61 sq.; Praetorius, "Vom Diebsdaumen," 1677; "the 'coutume de Bordeaux,'" § 46. *R. Köhler*, in the treatise immediately to be named, cites: Philo (Bartholomäus Anhorn), "Magiologia, Augustae Raurac." 1675, 768 sq.; H. L. Fischer, "Buch vom Aberglauben," I. (L., 1791), 155; F. Wolf, "Proben portugiesischer und catalonischer Volksromanzen," Vienna, 1856, 146; Rochholz, "Alemannisches Kinderlied und Kinderspiel aus der Schweiz," L., 1857, 344.—Here may also be added, "Das Lied von der verkauften Müllerin," v. *R. Köhler's* careful homonymous essay in the *Zeitschrift für deutsche Mythologie und Sittenkunde*, IV. (Göttingen, 1859), 180-5. There are also supplements by *L. Parisius*, "Deutsche Volkslieder . . . . in der Altmark und im Magdeburgischen," Part I. (Magdeburg, 1879), 45-9. In Lower Saxony the song is shown to be in existence by *H. Sohnrey*, v. *Urds-Brunnen*, I., Part I., 16 sq.,; a variation from Dithmarschen, Part III., 16.

—*L. Strackerjan* has found in a prosaic form this story, which indeed testifies to the existence of a popular superstition, in the Oldenburg region, II. (1867), 127: "A good fifty years ago a hired-man in Schwege, parish of Dinklage, sold his pregnant wife to a Jew at Vechta for 400 rx., who wanted to use the foetus for purposes of magic. The children listened and told their mother, who repeated it to her three brothers. The latter gave the Jew a thorough hiding on the night when the woman was to have been taken away, but the man went to prison." Direktor K. Strackerjan, of Oldenburg, wrote me on May 1st, 1889, in answer to my question as to the source of the information which appeared to me to lack historical value: "In the papers my brother left behind there is nothing that could serve as an elucidation. . . . . I judge the story in this way. The fifty years mentioned are an arbitrary artifice, which goes back far enough to thrust aside at once the hearer's critical faculty, but not so far that it exceeds his circle of experience through traditions of living persons (grandparents, etc.), and so weakens the interest. Formerly there were no Jews anywhere in the Oldenburg Münsterland except in Vechta . . . so that if the story were to be brought closer home to the hearer, the buyer had to be a Jew of Vechta. Poetic justice required the imprisonment of the Jew. The district prison is at Vechta: I do not doubt that the story also assumed the man 'came to Vechta,' as readily occurs in popular tales in such cases. If the basis of the story were in the main historical I am old enough myself, as well as the lawyers among my acquaintances . . . . to recollect the circumstances not exactly directly, but in any case indirectly. . . . . I consider the story altogether to have come from outside. . . . . An examination into the public documents of the courts of justice would be futile; for the departmental conditions in our

Münsterland have so altered during the last 60 or 70 years, that no documents can be now in existence, even supposing any ever existed at all."

B. Montanus, "Die deutschen Volksfeste, Volksbräuche und deutscher Volksglaube," Iserlohn, 1858, 130 sq.: "This peculiar superstition of illumination with a child's limbs seems to hang together with folk-beliefs about will-o'-the-wisps. Thieves are said to have also wrought very powerful magic results, pertinent to their night work, with the hearts of new-born or innocent children as well as with their blood, and even with children cut out of their mothers' wombs, which superstition has then demonstrably had as a consequence several murders of innocent children and of wives about to become mothers.—The following incident* put together from the documents of investigation may serve for the explanation and significance of a superstition even now prevailing among the masses. . . . . After the Thirty Years' War had very much decivilised human beings, crowds of thieves roamed about the lower Rhine. On 7 October, 1645, Heinr. Erkelenz, a poor rural worker, who was hardly a year married, went from his lonely dwelling towards Angermund, to buy oil and other trifles there, when he was knocked down by two robbers in the forest. 'I am poor,' he says, 'and my wife is near her confinement; I have to buy what is necessary for her.' Whereupon the robbers. . . . . 'Your gold you shall have back and 100 gulden in gold in addition; but you must bring your wife here to us in return' . . . . . After some deliberation, the barbarous man, seduced by filthy lucre, agrees to the bargain." He tells his wife he has sold their little house for 100 gulden in gold, and when she talks against it, entices

* [The author, v. Zuccalmaglio (Montanus is a pseudonym), has been dead for some time. For that reason I could not ascertain the sources of information he used.]

her into the forest on the pretext he intends to cancel the transaction there. The wife becomes afraid, but starts on the road, after secretly praying her brother to follow her. "Erkelenz approaches her with one of the robbers, while the other leans on a tree. The robber holds up a heavy money-bag; her husband seizes it and runs aside with it, and the poor victim is dragged away by the robber's strong arm. She screams, she struggles, but all resistance is useless. She is gagged and bound to a tree, she is stripped naked, and the elder robber pulls out a big sharp knife, in order to slit up her belly—then comes the crash of a bullet, and one of the robbers, hit in the heart, lies in his own blood." The other robber is knocked down by the woman's brother, gagged, and dragged to Angermund. "The robber was, according to the judicial sentence, on 12th October, before the Ratinger Thor, at Düsseldorf, first pinched with red hot tongs, and then broken alive on the wheel from toe to top. Erkelenz was hanged. The reason why the robber was visited with the severer penalty was the confession that he and his accomplice, among many other outrages committed by them, had cut two unborn children from their mothers' wombs, and extracted their little hearts. Had they got the third heart as well, they would have become masters of magic powers which no one could have withstood; they would thereby have been able to make themselves invisible, and to perform a number of devil's tricks."

Lammert, 84: "A horrible example of superstition about the magic power of unborn children is afforded in more recent times by Hundssattler, who was executed in the middle of last century at Bayreuth. He was under the delusion that a man could fly if he ate nine hearts of new-born children. With this object he had already butchered, cut up, and eaten the still-throbbing, warm hearts of eight pregnant women (Meissner, "Skizz." xiii., 107). The Nuremberg reports* of 1577 and 1601 are lamentable for a similar reason."

Tettau and Temme, 266: "The hearts of unborn children were held by robbers and thieves to be a means of protection; in a raw state, even as they are torn from the mother's womb, and from the child's body, they were cut into as many pieces as there were partakers, and a piece was eaten by each of them. He who had thus partaken of nine hearts could not be caught, whatever thievery or other crime he might commit, and, even if he accidentally fell into his opponents' power he could make himself invisible, and so again escape his bonds. The children, however, had to be of the male sex; female were no good for the purpose. The band of the robber captain, King Daniel as he was called by his men, "Kix Teufel aus der Hölle" ("King Devil from Hell") as he was called by the populace, which terrorised Ermeland in the middle of the 17th century, admitted after their capture, that they had already killed 14 pregnant wives with that object, but had only found male children in very few of them." 267: "Moreover, there were not only means of insurance against earthly punishment, but there were also means for quieting the conscience. For he who had killed a man had only to cut a piece out of the man's body, to roast and eat it, and he never thought again about his evil deed."

* The Nuremberg executioner, Meister Frank, broke on the wheel in 1577, at Bamberg, a murderer who had cut open three pregnant women; in 1601 he executed a monster at Nuremberg, who had slain 20 persons, among them also several pregnant women, "whom he afterwards cut open, cut the children's hands off, and made little candles of them for burglary." Cf. "Meister Franken, Nachrichters allhier in Nürnberg all sein Richten am Leben, sowohl seine Leibsstraffen, so er verricht, alles hierin ordentlich beschrieben, aus seinem selbst eigenen Buch abgeschrieben worden. Genau nach dem Manuscript abgedruckt und herausgegeben von *J. M. F. v. Endter*," Nuremberg, 1801.

In the defile behind Wiemes-Hof, near Süchteln, stands, amid the underwood of ferns and briars, an old cross with the inscription: "Anno 1791 den 14. Merz ist Anno Margaretho Terporten alt 9 biss 10 Johr durch eines Mörders Hand grausamlich umgebrocht worden" (On 14 March, 1791, Anna Margareta Terporten, aged 9 to 10, was cruelly killed by a murderer's hand). *R. Freudenberg*, in his book, "Söitelsch Plott," Viersen, 1888, attaches the following note to the poem, "Et Krüz an den Hoalwäg": "The cross is in memory of a little Süchteln girl who was murdered towards the end of the last century. . . The murderer committed the crime because he had been told that anybody possessing the heart of an innocent child, might steal without being discovered. Shortly after the finding of the body he was convicted, beheaded in Jülich, and his corpse broken on the wheel on the so-called Galgenhaide ("gallows-common") outside Dülken." I also take the following details, which rest upon the statements of the oldest inhabitants, from the *Crefelder Zeitung*, 1892, No. 197: "It was alleged the child had been seen to go into the forest with a strange Jew. For that cause, and because the heart was extracted, people gave credence to a 'ritual murder' . . . . The Jews in the neighbourhood were persecuted for three months, till the real criminal was found. A child of the murderer wore a hairpin and a little ring belonging to the murdered girl. So the murderer was found in a mason and day labourer of Anrath, who had also frequently worked here in Süchteln. . . . . He confessed he had committed the murder of his own accord, in the belief that he could steal without being caught, if he possessed the heart of an innocent child."

A. F. Thiele, "Die Jüdischen Gauner in Deutschland[2]," Be., 1848, 7: "The handsome Karl made the wives and concubines belonging to his band swear by the prince of darkness, and by everything evil, to deliver up unhesitatingly for that ghastly purpose [thieves' candles] the fruit of their wombs, if they were required so to do by himself or any other graduate of the band. The foetus was then, before it had reached maturity, expelled and roasted!"* Theodor Unger (that was 'handsome Karl's' real name), who was executed at Mageburg in 1810, was not a Jew, and there is no proof discoverable that the Jews concerned in the robbery disorders of that period had the superstition here under notice.

On 12th December, 1815, Claus Dau was executed on the Galgenberg, near Heide, district of North Dithmarschen, for killing three children, and devouring their hearts. He fancied he could make himself invisible by eating seven hearts.†

Lehmann, "Chronik der Stadt Schneeberg," III., 299, says under date 15th Dec., 1823: "We have still to mention a horrible custom, whose existence could scarcely be still thought possible in the 19th century. Friedrich's place of execution was close by the road from Zwickau to Werdau. Already early the next morning the two thumbs of the corpse were cut off, and a portion of the criminal's clothes stripped off.

* "The notorious concubine of Horst, *Luise Delitz*, has uttered remarkable revelations regarding these and similar facts."

† "Rede nach der Hinrichtung des Mörders Claus Dau am 12 Dez. 1815, vor der Richtstätte an das Volk gehalten, von *Karl Schetelig*, erstem Prediger zu Heide," Heide 1816. The well-known poet *Claus Groth*, a native of H., says about Dau in the "Quickborn" ("Hans Schander beim Rugenbarg"):

> He wehr sin Tid en argen Sünner,
> He drüssel dre unschülli Kinner,
> Mit säben Harten—as he swahn—
> Kunn he bi Dag unsichtbar gahn."

Roughly translatable:

> "He was in's time a sinner bad,
> Three harmless bairns he strangled had,
> With seven hearts—for he thought so—
> He could by daylight unseen go."

Within a week, however, the corpse lay on the wheel, deprived of all its toes and fingers as well as all its clothes, and caused an unparalleled scandal, so that the authorities saw themselves compelled to order its burial at once. And whence came the aforesaid despoiling and mutilation of the body? In order by means of the various single items to obtain safety whilst thieving, and so forth." (Then follows the passage quoted supr. p. 71).

Mannhardt, 21 sq.: "On New Year's Eve, 1864, a fearful murder with robbery was perpetrated at Ellerwald, near Elbing, on Elizabeth Zernickel, 23 years old. . . . . A piece of flesh, nine inches long, and the same in breadth, had been cut out of her belly. For a considerable time there was no trace of the criminal, till on the evening of 16th February, 1865, during the committal of a thief. . . . a working man, Gottfried Dallian, of Neukirch, in the Niederung, was caught, and there was found on him a strange candle, consisting of a tolerably firm mass of fat, poured round a wick, and contained in a leaden cylinder. . . . The murderer made a frank confession at the trial. He had intended merely thieving on 31st December, but Z.'s loud screams for help had caused him to strike her senseless by blows on the head with his knotty stick. . . . . After he had packed everything together . . . . he cut out of the body. . . . a piece of belly-flesh, which he roasted at home. He had made the thieves' candle out of the roasted human fat by the addition of beef tallow, but had eaten the residuum. At the Elbing Assizes he was condemned to death on 23rd June, 1865. The motive of the . . . deed was the delusion instilled into Dallian by hearsay, that a candle or small lamp prepared from the fat of a murdered person would not be extinguished by any draught, and the flame could only be put out with milk; the person who carried it would be invisible, whilst all living people round about would be held in a deep slumber. In that way the thief was ensured against any interference in his business. And if the murderer cut a piece out of his victim's belly, roasted and consumed it, he would have peace in his conscience, he would never again think of the crime."

U. Jahn reports on "the murder-trial of the working man Bliefernicht, of Sage, heard at the Assizes at Oldenburg," in the spring of 1888, in the "Proceedings of the Berlin Anthropological Society," 7th April, 1888, 135: "As the statements of two witnesses informs us, B. was of the opinion that he who ate the flesh of young innocent girls, could do anything in the world, without anybody being able to make him answerable. He killed two girls of six and seven years old respectively, and one of the two corpses not only had its throat cut from ear to ear, but had also its stomach ripped up, so that the entrails, lungs, and liver were exposed. A large piece of flesh had been artistically cut out of the rectal region, and could not be found in spite of search being made, for the reason that the monster had eaten it."

In March, 1895, a man-servant, called Sier, of Heumaden, dug up in the cemetery at Moosbach, in the Bayrischer Wald, the body of a child recently dead, knocked out one of its eyes, and likewise appropriated the little shroud. By getting its eye he imagined he could make himself invisible, so that he might then follow unseen his bent towards stealing. *Ur-Quell*, 1895, 200.

In the night of 27th February, 1873, three Russian soldiers in the village of Sheljesnjaki, District of Grodno, opened the grave of a comrade recently dead, and took the entrails out, because they had heard that they could steal without danger by the light of a candle composed of human fat.—In 1884, in the town of Perejaslawl, Govt. of Poltava, three youths were arrested as they were opening a fat man's coffin, in order to use his fat for the preparation of a thieves' candle. *Löwenstimm*, 114 sq.—In 1872 three horse thieves in the district of Kanew, Govt. of Kijeff, took out of a girl's grave one of her hands and her waxen cross. They thought it was enough to put the dead hand into the window, and set light to a taper made of the wax of the little cross, to cast the inhabitants of a house into deepest sleep. *Löwenstimm*, 115.

Russian criminals are not frightened even to commit murder in order to get thieves' candles. *Löwenstimm*, 117-20 quotes four cases. In April, 1869, Kyrill Dshuss murdered a boy and flayed the skin off his stomach in the Wuikowitsch forest, district of Wladimir-Wolynsk; but the rustling of the leaves disturbed him and drove him out of the forest.—In 1881 two youths of 18 or 19 killed a peasant with the same object in the Tschembarsch district, Govt. of Pensa.—In 1887, Jefim Semljanin, after he and his two accomplics had failed in three other attempts, strangled a girl in a wood in the Bjelgorod district, Govt. Kursk, and made a candle of her fat. The criminal was only discovered more than seven months later, when his house was searched on account of a theft, and a bundle with cooked flesh was found; the cloth in which the flesh was wrapped had belonged to the murdered girl. —In 1896, two men of the Korotojak district, Govt. Woronesh, throttled a boy of twelve in order to mould a candle from his fat.

A weakened form of this superstition occurs in the Govt. of Nishnij-Nowgorod: he who wants to become a magician must cut off the toe of a married woman's right foot. That was done at the beginning of the eighties by an inhabitant of the village of Fokin. *Löwenstimm*, 126.

XIII. SUPERSTITION AMONG DEMENTS CRIMES OWING TO RELIGIOUS MANIA

The dividing-line between superstition and dementia is often only recognisable with difficulty or not at all, particularly as both may occur combined in the same individual. Yet it may be said in general: Superstitious ideas arise in single instances chiefly through conditions of up-bringing, society, hearsay, reading, more rarely through influences from facts; madness, on the other hand, is mainly based either on hereditary derangement, or on a terrible shock either to the body or to the mind (to the body, e.g. a fall, wound, debauched life; to the mind, accumulation of misfortunes).—Lively religious feeling, when clean of every impure alloy, shows us man from the side of his similitude to God; otherwise it may, if—what we have solely here to consider—superstition or madness be superadded, lead to horrible deeds.

In referring to the "Bernstein case" (Ch. 15), I here collect a few facts, which may be characterised partly as "superstition among dements," partly as "crimes due to religious mania."

A. "A tradesman's assistant, 27 years old, suffered from persecution mania, was confined in the lunatic asylum at Cadillac, quieted down, and engaged in useful occupation. One day he met in a dark corridor an old, weak invalid, split his skull open with an iron stick, extracted his brain, ate a portion of it at once, and saved the rest in his cell. He confessed, when asked, what he had done, and also that he wanted still to eat the remainder. Five whole years afterwards he remained quiet, till he one day found himself with the doctors in the mortuary of the institute, and in an unguarded moment seized hold of a brain, and began greedily to devour it. He was put back again among the 'dangerous' patients, and he was more than once surprised eating the brains of birds he caught in the yard.—The persecution mania had altered in him. As he noticed he was ill in his mind, he fancied he could help himself and increase his understanding by swallowing the brains of others." (*C. Lombroso*, "Der Verbrecher," done into German by Fränkel, II. [Hamburg, 1890], 154).

B. Margarete Peter, daughter of a peasant, who was born in 1794, at Wildisbuch, was disposed from youth upwards to morbid religious enthusiasm; and, the remainder of her understanding having been ruined by the confused mystic, Jakob Ganz, she fought, together with her family, on 13th March, 1823, with such vigour against Satan with axes, wedges, and rakes, that the floor of the house partially gave way. On 15th March she declared: "If Christ is to conquer and Satan to be completely overthrown, blood must flow!" She then seized an iron wedge, pulled her brother Kaspar to her with the words: "Behold, Kaspar, the Evil Enemy wants your soul," and planted several blows on his head and breast, so that he began to bleed in both places. Kaspar is led away by his father; some others, too, go away. She now says to those who have remained behind: "Blood must be shed. I see my mother's spirit, which requires of me to quit my life for Christ. And you, will you also surrender your life for Christ?" "Yes," they all replied. Her sister Elizabeth cries out: "I shall gladly die for the salvation of my father's and my brother's souls. Kill me dead, kill me!" and she beats herself on the head with a wooden mallet. Margarete attacks her sister with an iron hammer, wounds her brother-in-law, Johannes Moser, and his intimate friend, Ursula Kündig, and then orders those present to kill Elizabeth downright. Without uttering a single cry of pain, the latter passes away with the words: "I quit my life for Christ!" Margarete: "Some more blood must be spilt. Christ in me has given his Father a pledge for many thousands of souls. I must die. You shall crucify me." And she strikes herself with the hammer on the left temple, so that it begins to bleed. Johannes and Ursula are obliged to deal her further blows, and make a circular cut round her neck with a razor, and a cross cut on her forehead. "Now I want to be nailed to the cross, and you, Ursula, must do it. You go, Zäsi [her sister Susanna], and bring up the nails, and you others meanwhile get ready the cross." The victim's hands and feet are nailed to the cross. The strength of the crucifying woman is again about to fail her. "Go on, go on! May God strengthen your arm! I shall awaken Elisabeth, and within three days shall myself arise again." Continuance of the hammer blows; a nail is driven through both of the victim's breasts, likewise through the left elbow-joint, then by Susanna also through the right one. "I feel no pain. Only be *you* strong, that Christ may conquer." In a firm voice she further commands a nail or a knife to be driven through her head into her heart. In raving desperation Ursula and Konrad Moser rush upon her and smash her head to pieces, the former by means of the hammer, the latter with a two-bevelled chisel.—On Sunday, 23rd March, there was a pilgrimage of Margaret's adherents to W. One of them scraped blood from the place where the bed was, broke a blood-stained piece of chalk out of the wall of the room, and carefully wrapped up these relics. (*J.*

Scherr, "Die Gekreuzigte, oder das Passionsspiel von Wildisbuch," S. Gallen, 1860 [219].—Precisely according to the public documents preserved at Zürich. Unfortunately the author has distorted his book by blasphemous attacks on the Bible, especially the Old Testament, and on the Christian religion).

SCHERR has the audacity, reminding one of Daumer and Rohling, to remark: "Even in our days we have lived to find a pietist, emulous of Abraham and Jephthah, slaughtering his five children as a sacrifice to the El-Schaddai: Georg Hiller at Oberjettingen, in Suabia, in March, 1844."—Prof. EB. NESTLE, now at Maulbronn, has at my request read through the newspaper reports: "No mention of religious motives, either in the first conjectures or in the professional opinion of the medical faculty, nor in the proceedings at Court.—SCHWAEBISCHER MERKUR, 1844, 10th March: 'Great poverty and drunkenness are supposed to have been the causes.'—11th March: 'probably in desperation owing to financial ruin and disaster.'—11th November: consigned to Tübingen for observation by the medical faculty.—1845 19th June, a short report, 23rd June, a detailed report (6 columns) about the judicial proceedings. Speech of the public prosecutor: death penalty because of wilful murder: speech of defending counsel: emotional manslaughter: lessened responsibility owing to passing emotional disturbances: verdict of 18 years' imprisonment for manslaughter. According to the reasons for this decision some of the judges were for murder, others for emotional manslaughter, some adopted full responsibility, others—the majority—diminished responsibility. (The man had no more money, sent for brandy and rolls of white bread for the evening meal, and as the children went to sleep through it, he used the occasion to free them by death from the misery of the world. He had not determination enough to kill himself. I found it nowhere mentioned in the MERKUR that the man was a pietist)."

"The 'heiligen Männer' (holy men) at Chemnitz, in Saxony, whose society had been founded by a religious enthusiast shoemaker called Voigt [carried on their life in 1865] with truly Molochistical piety, by persuading two mothers in the sect to slaughter their sick children, because the same were 'possessed of the devil.'" (*J. Scherr*, "Deutsche Kultur-und Sittengeschichte,"[7] L., 1879, 585).

"Two sisters from Briançon, the one 45, the other

47 years old, were rich, and had no other occupation but going to church. One morning the elder sister informed the younger, God had appeared to her in a dream, and had asked that she (the younger sister) should sacrifice herself as a sign of love for him. The other finds it all right, agrees to offer herself as a sacrifice to God, lets her hands and feet be cut off with a razor, and dies crying: 'Jesus and Maria!' whilst the sister collects her blood as a relic, then carefully adorns the corpse, goes to the notary, to whom she announces her dream and her sister's murder, and deposits a will, by which all her papers of money-value are to be burnt." (*Lombroso*, II., 146 sq.)

"A certain Kursin, a very pious man . . . killed his seven-year-old boy, convinced he was offering up a sacrifice pleasing to the Lord. . . . 'The thought that the whole of mankind must perish, had disturbed me so that I could not sleep. I got up, lit all the lamps before the eikon, and prayed God to save me and my family. . . . Then the idea came to me to save my finest and best son from eternal damnation.' . . . . . When brought to prison (after he had killed the child), Kursin refused all nutriment, and died of starvation." (*Lombroso*, II., 152 sq.)

The awful crimes committed in the last centuries of the middle ages, and yet later on even in the 17th century, and connected with alchemy, magic, Satanism ("black masses!") and sorcery of all kinds, cannot be gone into here. Only one example: Gilles de Rais, Marshal of France, a contemporary, and for a time, a companion of Jeanne d'Arc, murdered about 200 children between 1432 and 1440 for purposes of magic.

XIV. WHAT DOES THE JEWISH RELIGIOUS LAW SAY ABOUT THE PARTAKING OF BLOOD AND THE UTILISATION OF PORTIONS OF CORPSES?

A. The Jews have always, and also since their "dispersal among the people of the earth," been strongly influenced by their environment (e.g. in dress, food, language, etc.), likewise in the matter of superstition.* Superstitions, too, of Jewish origin are not wanting.† For both reasons it is not permissible to assert à priori, that such views and customs as

* *M. Lidzbarski*, "Jüdische Sagen aus Russland u. Polen," in *Urds-Brunnen* IV., 55-61, is also of the opinion that the Jews had taken over with the German language several of the German popular beliefs.

† Cf. *D. Joël*, "Der Aberglaube und die Stellung des Judentums zu demselben," 2 parts, Breslau 1881 (116). 1883 (65); *M. Güdemann*, "Geschichte des Erziehungswesens und der Cultur der abendländischen Juden während des Mittelalters und der neueren Zeit." Vienna I. (1880), especially 212 sq.; II. (1884), especially 219 sq., 333 sq., 255 sq.; III. (1888), especially 128 sq.; *G. Wolf*, "Die Juden" [part of the compilation, "Die Völker Oesterreich-Ungarns"], 113 sq.; *S. Rubin*, "Geschichte des Aberglaubens," L. 1888 (159. From the Hebrew). In the Tosephta (a very ancient Halakhish work running parallel to the Mishna) in the Treatise on the Sabbath, ch. 7, 8 (edition of Zuckermandel 117-9) several matters of superstition are collected, in many cases with the remark that it is heathen (belongs "to the ways of the Amorites"). *H. Levy* has translated both chapters and explained them in the *Zeitschrift des Vereins für Volkskunde*, 1893, 23-40, 130-43.—Cf. also: *G. Brecher*, "Das Transcendentale, Magie und magische Heilarten im Talmud." Vienna 1850 (233). *J. Bergel*, "Die Medizin der Talmudisten." L. 1885 (88). *L. Blau*, "Das altjüdische Zauberwesen," Budapesth 1898 (167). *J. Hamburger*, "Böser Blick" in the "Real-Encyclopädie für Bibel u. Talmud" II. (1883), 117 sq.

we have learnt about in the first main portion of this work never occur among Jews, because they are impossible among them. Assuredly, however, not only a Jew, but also an unbiassed Christian inquiring into the matter may point out, that several precepts of Judaism are bound to form a great obstacle at any rate to the wide dissemination of the thoughts and acts described or alluded to in the preceding chapters.

B. The most important of these precepts is the *prohibition of the consumption of blood and of meat with blood in it*, which several times occurs in the Pentateuch.

Genesis ix. 4: "But flesh, with the life thereof, which is the blood thereof, shall ye not eat." Leviticus xvii. 10: "And whatsoever man there be of the house of Israel, or of the strangers that sojourn among you, that eateth any manner of blood; I will even set my face against that soul that eateth of blood, and will cut him off from among his people. 11: For the life of the flesh is in the blood: and I have given it to you upon the altar to make an atonement for your souls: for it is the blood that maketh an atonement for the soul. 12: Therefore I said unto the children of Israel: No soul of you shall eat blood, neither shall any stranger that sojourneth among you eat blood. 13: And whatsoever man there be of the children of Israel, or of the strangers that sojourn among you, which hunteth and catcheth any beast or fowl that may be eaten; ye shall even pour out the blood thereof, and cover it with dust. 14: For it is the life of all flesh; the blood of it is for the life thereof: therefore I said unto the children of Israel, Ye shall eat the blood of no manner of flesh: for the life of all flesh is the blood thereof: whosoever eateth it shall be cut off."—Leviticus vii. 26: "Moreover, ye shall eat no manner of blood, whether it be of fowl or of beast, in any of your dwellings. 27: Whatsoever soul it be that eateth any manner of blood, even that soul shall be cut off from his people."—Cf. Lev. iii. 17, xix. 26; Deut. xii. 16, 23, xv. 23, besides I. Samuel xiv. 32-4; Ezekiel xxiii. 25; Acts xv. 29.

The first quotation gives at the same time an important *reason* why the Israelites must abstain from partaking of blood. *God has fixed upon blood as the means of atonement*; therefore it must serve no other aim.

C. The later Jewish legislation goes even further than the Old Testament. In the "Schulḥân 'Arûkh," written by Joseph Qaro (1488-1575), whose work in combination with its acknowledged commentaries is considered the chief authority in Jewish Law matters for those who are either not in a position or have not the time to refer back to the original authorities (Talmud, the oldest decrees of the Law, etc.), we read in "Jore De'a," LXV., 1: "There are veins, the consumption of which is forbidden because of the blood contained in them, e.g. the veins of the fore-arm, the shoulder and the lower jaw." LXVI., 1: "The blood of cattle, of beasts of the field, and of birds, no matter whether these animals be clean or not, must not be partaken of." LXVI., 3: "If a drop of blood is found in an egg, the blood should be removed and the rest eaten; but only if the blood was in the white. If it was, however, in the yolk, the whole egg is forbidden." The gloss of the Cracow Rabbi Moses Isserles (ob. 1572/3), which is held in equal esteem with the text, especially among the East European Jews, remarks on this passage: "In these countries it is customary to declare without distinction every egg forbidden, in which there is a drop of blood." LXVI., 9: "Fish blood, although [because not forbidden in the Pentateuch] allowed of itself, must nevertheless not be partaken of, if it has been collected in a vessel, because it might be thought to be a different kind of blood. It may, however, be consumed if it is easily recognisable as fish blood, e.g. if there are scales in it."

The watering and salting, that have to be carried out in the case of meat intended for eating, for the sake of thoroughly getting rid of the blood, are treated of by e.g. Eleazar of Worms (beginning of 13th century) in his work entitled "Roqēaḥ," Ascher ben Jeḥiēl (ob. 1327); Jakob ben Ascher (ob. c. 1340) in

"Arbaʿā Ṭurîm;" Joseph Qaro; Naphthali Benedict Sêpher Beríth Mélaḥ," Prague, 1816 sq.

D. The practice of the present time, corresponding to the traditional Law, is related by *Ludw. Stern,* "Die Vorschriften der Thora," Frankfort a. M., 1882, §118:

"*After all forbidden parts have been separated from the animal, the flesh, which is intended for cooking,* must, before the lapse of 72 hours after the butchering of the animal, be laid in a vessel specially used for the purpose for half-an-hour in water, so that it is quite covered with water ("soaking in water").—Next, the meat is thoroughly washed in this water and cleansed of blood sticking to it, then laid on a slanting board also used for the purpose, or on a perforated vessel, so that the water may run off properly ("watering off").—When that has been done, every piece is singly sprinkled with fine-grained salt so abundantly on all sides and in all crevices that it looks as if it were covered with hoar-frost ("salting").—The meat remains lying with the salt for an hour, as after the watering off on the slanting board or on the perforated vessel, so that the blood drawn out by the salt can trickle down; then every piece is so abundantly watered on all sides that all the salt is washed away ("moistening with water"). Only after this treatment may the flesh be cooked. . . . If the flesh was frozen before the treatment, or if it is frozen during it, the whole treatment must be again performed when the flesh has again been thawed.—4. . . [the liver which is rich in blood], after being cleansed by thorough washing from the blood attached to it, must, sprinkled with some salt, be roasted directly by the fire, but not lying on paper or on the leaves of plants; but on a spit, on a gridiron, or freely on the*

* [The salting-out of blood is not needed in meat which is roasted, v. "Jore Deʿa" LXXVI., 1, because the fire is held to suck up the blood; about blood, which remains in the limbs, v. LXVII., 1.]

coals. It must remain at the fire till the blood has been extracted and it is perfectly well-cooked for immediate eating. After being taken away from the fire it must be thrice watered abundantly on all sides. —5. . . . In the case of the heart, milt, lungs, head, feet with claws, as well as birds, there are yet especial prescriptions to be observed.—More detailed instructions about it in . . (the supplement to) 'Amirâh l·bêth Ja'aqôb,' by Rabbi S. B. BAMBERGER *[2nd edition, Fürth, 1864].*"

E. The prohibition of the consumption of blood, according to its phrasing, certainly holds good only of animal blood, or, more accurately, the blood of warm-blooded animals (quadrupeds and birds). The consumption of human blood is not expressly forbidden in the *O. T.*; it does not follow, however, that it was allowed. The lack of an express pronouncement may be explained very simply, if the following is taken into consideration. Firstly: It is altogether beyond the imagination of Israelites as such to conceive that anyone could have the idea of partaking of human blood. Secondly: The Pentateuchical Law forbids the partaking of animal blood particularly because it ordains animal sacrifices; whilst human sacrifices are strictly prohibited, v. Leviticus xviii., 21; xx., 2 sq.; Deuteronomy xii., 31.—In the whole of the literature concerned with the Jewish religious law there is no passage whence it could be concluded that the Jews are, or were, permitted to eat human blood. *Moses Maimonides* (1135-1204) writes in his great ritual code, "Laws about forbidden foods," Ch. 6 (Venice, 1524, No. 361 b): "§1. Whoever eats blood to the amount of an olive, if he does it intentionally, incurs the punishment of extirpation; if it happened unintentionally, he brings the usual sin-offering. But the guiltiness is only imputable in regard to the blood of cattle, game, and birds, no matter whether they are clean or unclean; v. Leviticus vii., 26; Deuteronomy xiv., 5. But there is no guiltiness because of the prohibition of blood* with the blood of fishes and locusts and creeping and swarming animals or with human blood. It is accordingly explicitly allowed to eat the blood of clean fish, and also to drink it after it has been collected in a vessel; but the partaking of the blood of unclean fish and beasts is, like the milk of unclean cattle, forbidden solely because it is a component part of their bodies; the blood of reptiles, as well as their flesh, is likewise forbidden [because those animals are unclean].—§2. Human blood is rabbinically prohibited, when it is separated from the body, and the transgression is punished with disciplinary scourging. Blood from the gums may be swallowed [because it is still in the mouth, not separated from the body]. But whoever has bitten into bread and then finds blood on it, scrapes the blood off and only eats the bread, because the blood was separated from the body."—Already in the first unrevised edition of the "Schulḥan Ărûkh," Venice, 1565, it is stated, "Jore Dea," lxvi, 1, without mention of human blood: "Blood of cattle, game and birds, be they clean or unclean, is forbidden, likewise the blood of a foetus; but the blood of fishes and locusts is allowed." Cf. again ibid. §10: "Human blood when separated from the body, is forbidden on account of its appearance [because it might be regarded as Biblically-forbidden animal blood]. Therefore, whoever eats bread must scrape off the blood which has perhaps come on the

* [Because the Bible, when forbidding the eating of blood, does not expressly mention these two kinds of blood. The Mishna, "Bikkurim" ii, 7, states on similar lines: The blood of human beings and the blood of creeping animals are in so far alike, that their consumption is not visited with the penalty of extirpation.]

bread from his gums; if, however, it is still between his teeth, he may swallow it."

"Talmud, Makkoth," 16 b: "Rab Bibi bar Abaje has said: Whoever drinks from the horn of an 'Aderlasser' (a kind of cupping-glass) transgresses the prohibition in Leviticus xx., 25."

It is true that in circumcision the Mohel sucks the blood from the wound (usually with the mouth; during some years in Germany also by means of a glass tube, in whose middle is sterilised wadding); but that is only ordained with the object that the wound may heal more easily, and because, according to the "Talmud," the wound, if not sucked out, would be dangerous to the child's life (Cf. "Sabbath," 133 b), and he immediately spits out the blood, Cf. M. BAUM, "Der theoretisch-praktische Mohel," Frankfort a. M., 1884, 35 sq.; JAKOB MÖLLN Ha-Levi, "Minhagim," Cremona, 1558, No. 89 b. — According to the "Zohar" to Leviticus xiv. and xix., the blood of the circumcision is preserved by God for the healing of the child (in case it should be necessary), and in order that it may not be injured by the female demon Lilith.—Concerning the covering of the blood of circumcision with earth Cf. Pirqe de Rabbi Eli'ezer 29 (in the notes to Josh. v., 2 sq., and Numb. xxiii. 10).

All partaking of human blood (because the swallowing of a few drops of one's own blood, when the gums are bleeding, cannot be taken into account) *is accordingly forbidden the Jews unconditionally by their religious law.*

F. Yet another precept of the Jewish religious law puts obstacles in the way of the superstitious utilisation of other men's blood and altogether of all parts of corpses, viz., the sentence: "*Utilisation of a dead person is prohibited,*" "mēth 'āssûr bah^a^na'ā^h^" (Talmud, "'Aboda zara," 29 b). Maimonides, "Laws about mourning," xiv. 21: "Utilisation of a dead person is prohibited, with the exception of his hair,* because this does not belong to his body." Schulḥan 'Arûkh, Jore De'a 349, 1: "Utilisation of a

* "*Jore De'a*" 349, 2, says more precisely: The utilisation is only allowed when it is false hair and when the deceased before death has expressly determined, that son or daughter should get it.

dead person, be he 'Goj' (non-Jew*) or Israelite, is prohibited." Cf., too, Talmud, "'Arakhin" 7ab, "Sanhedrin" 47 b. sq., "Ḥullin" 122a, "Nidda" 55a; Salomo ben Adreth (Rabbi at Barcelona, ob. 1310), "Legal Opinions," No. 375.† On this are based the following ordinances referring to burial (after *J. Rabbinowicz*, "Der Totenkultus bei den Juden," Frankfort a. M., 1889, §21-3): "No employment must be made either of the corpse itself or of its clothes. . . . The clothes must be intended for the deceased, and have already come in contact with him. . . . In this case the objects in question, if for any cause whatever they have failed in their purpose, must be buried or burnt. If, however, they had not yet come into any contact with the deceased, they may assuredly be used for something else, but . . . not just as they now are . . . but the coffin must be knocked to pieces and the clothes must be torn asunder. . . . Even if anyone had testified in his will that his hair shall be used after death and for a certain purpose, it is not permitted to derive benefit from it. But if he wore false hair, it may be utilised

* The famous *Jakob Emden*, in the collection of technical opinions, "She'ilath Ja'beç," I., No. 70b sq. (Altona 1739) forbids a Jewish doctor the dissecting of corpses, and declares all prohibitions of utilisation expressly as also holding good of the corpses of non-Jews (Cf. *D. Hoffmann*, "Der Schulchan-Aruch2," Be. 1894, 83 sq.). Even now orthodox Jews are averse from the dissection of corpses, and allow it only in consideration of the saving of human life possibilised thereby. — Respecting dissection of corpses in Talmudic times, v. "Bekhoroth" 45a, and *J. Hamburger*, "Real-Encyclopädie für Bibel und Talmud" II. (Strelitz 1883), 685-7.

† On the Talmud treatise "Ta'anith" ("fasting") 15b: "They scattered ashes on the holy ark," the commentary "Tosaphoth" (12th and 13th century) says: "These ashes were of human bones; because these ashes were to recall the 'Aqeda [binding of Isaac and the following sacrifice by Abraham, Genesis XXII.], in which instance also bones were burnt." According to this passage parts of corpses were even used ritually. But there were no ashes of human bones among the Jews, since corpses were not allowed to be burnt! The text is corrupt: the word "'adam" ("men") must be struck out.

after his death, if he permitted it during life-time. . . . A murdered person, and a woman who has died in child-bed, to whose clothes blood adheres, are in several places not washed before burial, also they are not undressed, but the burial costumes are drawn over their clothes. . . . All blood they have lost since passing away, as well as all articles of clothing, utensils, parts of the bed and suchlike, to which any of this blood sticks, are laid in the grave with the body. . . . Everything that has been cut from or has fallen from the dead is consigned with him to the grave."*—Much that is relevant here also occurs in *J. Ch. Korn*, "Der Talmud vor Gericht," Part I., Vienna, 1884 (46).

G. Finally, the fact may be also alluded to that the corpse and all parts of the corpse make unclean, according to Jewish religious law, Cf. Numbers xix.; Mishna treatise "Ohalôth"†; Maimonides, "Laws about defiling by a dead person (Ṭum'ath mēth)." The want of the means of purification, according to the Law (ashes of a red cow), has caused several alterations in the practice. But even now the numerous Kohanim, i.e., the men who, by tradition, belong to the priestly caste, *must* avoid all pollution through corpses, so that they may not even be in the same house together with corpses.

* Cf. *Landshuth*, "Sēder biqqûr ḥōlîm maʿabar Jabbōq wʿsepher ha-ḥajjîm" ("Prayer and devotion-book for the use of invalids, dying persons, and at burials" (Be. 1867 XXXVI. sq.; Schulḥan ʿArûkh, Jore Deʿa, 364, 3.4 with the commentaries.

† *S. Jerome*, Epistle 109 to Riparius: "Samaritanum et Judaeum, qui corpora mortuorum pro immundis habent et etiam vasa quae in eadem domo fuerint pollui suspicantur " (Opera ed. Vallarsi 1., 719).

XV. POPULAR THERAPEUTICS AND BLOOD-SUPERSTITION WITHIN THE JEWISH PEOPLE

A. In Judaism the opinion prevailed: "At the head of all diseases stand I, the blood [out of the blood come most diseases]*; at the head of all remedies stand I, the wine," "Talmud Baba bathra," 58 b. Thence it is declared in "Sabbath," 41 a: "It has been taught: If any one has eaten and not drunk, his eating is blood. 'ᵓakilathô dām' [ie., he is consuming his vital power, he is becoming emaciated], and that is the beginning of indigestion; if anyone has eaten and not walked four ells, his eating causes putrefaction, and that is the beginning of bad smell." —The Jew has naturally a disgust for partaking of blood, as is clearly stated in "Makkoth" 23 b: "Rabbi Simeon bar Rabbi said: It is written (Deuteronomy xii. 23), 'But take heed that thou eatest not blood, for the blood is the soul,' etc. If, then, man, whose soul loathes blood, receives reward because he abstains from blood, how much must it be counted to him for a merit if he abstains from robbery and forbidden carnal intercourse, on which, nevertheless, his lust is set!" Cf. also "Siphrê," No. 76, on Deutero-

* The British Museum Greek papyrus, 137, says of the pre-Aristotelian doctor, Thrasymachus of Sardes, that he regarded the blood as the cause of all illnesses. It is the teaching of Galen about the plethora, which doctrine was also the cause of the excessive use of blood-letting in the East, Cf. *J. Bauer*, "Geschichte der Aderlässe," Munich 1870 (230).

nomy xii. 23 (Friedmann's Edit., No. 90 b).—These views and the contents of Ch. 14 justify the assumption that *only rarely, at least considerably more rarely than heathens or Christians, have Jews used, or do they use, blood for therapeutical or for magical purposes.* The assumption is confirmed by the consistency of tradition.

B. Antiquity. Except what follows, it would be hard to find anything requiring elucidation in the whole Talmudic literature. Several points here brought forward are neither superstitious nor loathsome, but simply component parts of an all-comprehensive "popular medicine"; they should, however, be mentioned here, so that they may not appear to have passed unnoticed (e.g., the consumption of animal milt). Of what an altogether different species are the "Hauss-Apothec," the "Dreck-Apotheke," and what may be read in the Ebers papyrus, in Pliny, etc. (v. Ch. 1)!

1. Animal blood. For the eye-disease "Barqîth," the eye is smeared with woodcock's blood, for "Jarôd" with bat's blood (Cf. p. 57, l. 3). "Sabbath," 78 a.—"Against one-sided headache take a woodcock, butcher it with a silver 'Zuz' (a coin) above the side on which the head aches, so that the blood flows on that side; care, however, must be taken that the eye is not blinded (by blood flowing in). Next hang the woodcock at the door in such a way that the patient rubs against it on entering and on going out," "Giṭṭin," 68 b.—For the cure of jaundice it is recommended in "Sabbath," 110 b, etc., that the blood of a very young donkey should be let run over a place shaven clean on the centre of the patient's head, but so that the blood may not flow into the eye.— "Ḥullin," 28 a supr., 85 b fin.: Bird's blood as a means for dispersing moth ("janibā,") which have got into the flax. Palestinian Talmud Maʿaser sheni V., fol. 56 b. Rab,

whose flax had turned out a failure, asked Ḥijja the Great, whether a bird might be killed, and its blood mixed with the flax-seed (to better its growth). (The consideration was that then the command to cover up blood would not be fulfilled).

Whoever smears himself with salamander's blood, is, according to "Ḥagiga," 27 a, immune against fire. Ahas wanted to sacrifice to Moloch also his son Hiskia; but Hiskia's mother had smeared her son with salamander blood, v. "Sanhedrin," 63 b. Together with the name of "Salamandra," the Jews also took over from the Greeks their wondrous notions about the idiosyncrasies of that creature.

2. Parts and refuse of animals. For nyctalopia, eating roasted animal-milt is among, other things, thought a remedy, "Giṭṭin," 69 a. Mar Samuel is of opinion that after a blood-letting milt-food is strengthening, "Sabbath," 129 a. A Mishna teacher, who had been in Rome, advises for hydrophobia that one should eat a lobe of the mad dog's liver, "Joma," 84 a * —"Sabbath," 109 b sq.: "If anyone is bitten by a snake, let the fœtus of a white jenny-ass be taken and divided, and let the bitten person sit on it. An official in Pumbeditha was bitten by a snake. Now, there were ten white jenny-asses on the spot. They were slit open one after the other; but they were all found to be tʿrephāh (i.e., afflicted with an injury of the womb)."—"Kethubboth," 50 a.: Abaje heard from his mother that should a boy of six be stung by a scorpion, one should dip the gall of a white kite in beer (schikhrā), and make the boy drink it.—"Sabbath," 67a: For tertian fever, collect several [counted singly] objects in the number of seven of each, among them also seven threads from an old dog's beard, and bind all to the neck with ʿnîrā barqā (white thread? tuft of hair?). "Giṭṭin," 69b: For the disease of "Karsām," touch a white dog's excrement with balsam. But, if possible (i.e., if one has another remedy, or if the malady is endurable), the excrement should not be eaten.—"Sabbath," 67a: Whoever has a bone stuck in his throat should take a bone

* *M. Sachs*, "Beiträge zur Sprach-und Alterthumsforschung," I. (L. 1852), 49, compares here Aelian, "De Natura Animalium" XIV. 20, and [Pseudo-] Dioskorides "Περὶ εὐπορίστων φαρμάκων" II., c. 113 —Cf. also Galen, "Περὶ τῶν ἁπλῶν φαρμάκων" κ.τ.λ. xi., 10 (ed. Kühn xii., p. 335). The same remedy also found among the aborigines of the present day, e.g., the Haussas, v. *Zeitschr. für Ethnologie 1896, Verhandlungen*, p. 31.

of the same kind, lay it on the crown of his head, and say: "One, one, go down, be swallowed, be swallowed, go down, one, one."

3. Parts of corpses. Among a series of popular remedies for diseases of the spleen* (e.g., take the spleen of a she-goat which has not yet had young, stick it to an oven, stand opposite, and say: Even as this spleen shrivels up, so let the spleen of N, the son of N, diminish) occurs also the following, "Giṭṭin," 69b: "Or look for a dead man, who died on a Sabbath, lay his hand on the sick spleen and speak: Even as this hand shrinks, so may the spleen of N, son of N, diminish." Cf. supr., Ch. 8 D.

4. Executed persons. According to the Mishna "Sabbath," vi., 10, the hope of being cured induced many people to carry about with them a locust's egg [against pains in the hips] or a fox's tooth [if from a living fox, for facilitating waking up; if from a dead one, for insomnia] or a nail from the "Cᶜlûb" (cross, gallows) [for fever]. Cf. supr. p. 76. Besides, Cf. "Sabbath," 134 a: A new-born child, that will not cry, should be smeared with the after-birth belonging to it.—"Sabbath," 109ᵇ: R. Ḥanina said: If you take 40 days' urine, 1/32 of a *log* (taken inwardly?) helps against hornet's sting; 1/4 against scorpions'; 1/2 against the harmful effect of water which has stood uncovered; 1/1 even against sorcery. —Palest. "Sabbath," xiv., fol. 14ᵈ, line 3, mentions a child's dry ordure as an ingredient of a medicament against the mouth disease "Çaphdina" (scurvy?).

5. *So far as I see, human blood is only mentioned "Sabbath," 75 b, fin.: "Some say menstruation blood should be kept for the cat; others it should not be kept, because it is weakening." The blood is here regarded not as a means of cure or magic, but simply as a tit-bit. Moreover, Rashi remarks on the pas-*

* Cf. on the point, Pliny, "Nat. Hist." xxx., 6, l. 17!

sage: "Whoever gives such blood to a cat gets ill."—If it is true what Dio Cassius lxviii. 32 relates about the war against Trajan (115-7 A.D.*), the question does not turn upon a superstition, but only upon a reaction against the most outrageous maltreatment, though certainly a reaction of the grossest barbarity. The Jews are said to have killed 220,000 persons in Cyrene, to have sawn their enemies asunder, besmeared themselves with their blood, and eaten of their flesh.*

The following fact characteristically proves that the statements here gathered together have not the remotest connection with the Jewish *religion*. The blood of the sacrificed animals which ran from the altar of burnt offering through a subterranean pipe to the valley of Cedron at the time of the Second Temple was sold to gardeners for manuring, v. Mishna, "Joma" (day of atonement) V. 6; Talmud, "Pesachim" (Easter Festival) 22a.

C. Middle Ages. In "Sha'arê Çédeq," a collection of legal professional reports of the Geonim* (Salonichi, 1799, No. 22 b), we read, Book I., Ch. 5., §10: "The Jews in Babylon circumcise over water and wet their faces with the water; the Jews in Palestine circumcise over earth, v. Zachariah ix., 11."—§11: "Rab Kohen Cedeq: As regards your questions about the child's circumcision over land and water, there is no manner of prohibition, which would justify us ordering you to alter your practice. But we are used to boiled water, in which are myrtle and perfumes, which are pleasantly fragrant, and circumcise the child over the water, so that the blood of circumcision falls into the water, and all our young men wash

* Thus are called the most prominent of the authorities in the sphere of traditional Jewish religious law, who lived at Sura and Pumbeditha in Babylonia from the 7th century till the year 1040.

themselves therewith in remembrance of the blood of the covenant that exists between God and our father Abraham." *M. Brück* makes a mistake when he says in his "Pharisäische Volksitten und Ritualien," Frankfort a M., 1840, 25, that the Babylonians "held the blood of circumcision holy;" also Gaon's answer does not contain the statement of purpose advanced by Brück—"but in order that the public may be eager to snatch at this blood-water."—Cf. also *Jakob hen Asher's* "Tûr Jôréh Deāh, 265, and *J. Müller*, "Hillûph Minhāgîm," Vienna, 1878, No. 17. This custom is no longer referred to in the "Schulḥan 'Arûkh."

*In the "Buch der Frommen," by Jehuda ben Samuel the Pious, who lived c. 1200 in Regensburg, the following story is told to establish the conception that parents and children constitute a single body also from a physical point of view (Bologna, 1538, §232; Be., 1891, sq., §291): A rich man travelled with his servant over the sea, and took a large sum of money with him. Soon after he died in foreign parts. Thereupon the servant seized upon all the treasure, making himself out to be the son. But a short time after her husband's departure his pregnant wife, who remained behind, had borne a son. When this son grew up, he went to the Gaon Saadja [in Sura; flor. 892-942]. The Gaon advised him to go to the king. The king commissioned Saadja to decide the matter. Saadja bled both, and then laid a bone, taken from the father's grave, in the servant's blood; still the bone did not suck the blood up. This, however, actually happened when the bone was laid in the other's blood, because they were one body. So Saadja gave the son the fortune.**

* Cf. Geo. Al. Kohut, "Blood test as proof of kinship in Jewish folklore," in *Journal of Amer. Orient. Society*, vol. xxiv. (1903), p. 129-44.

"*Bahrrecht*" *(ordeal of the bier) (Cf. p. 49).* "*Buch der Frommen,*" *Bologna, §1143:* "*When the murderer approaches the corpse of the murdered man the wound begins to bleed, so that the murderer may be brought to justice; but this occurs also when anyone who has eaten bread dipped in soup, and then eaten no dry bread, approaches the corpse. Therefore murderers, after committing the crime, are wont to eat dry bread.*"—RUDIMENTARY ELEMENT OF THE BUILDING-OFFERING *(v.p. 31 sq.). Jehuda the Pious says in his* "*Testament,*" *§17:* "*Where a house has never stood, there let none be built. Should it, however, come to pass, the house should remain uninhabited for one year.*" *He probably considered the empty spot to be the happy hunting-ground of demons (Isai. xiii. 21). For that reason timid Israelites, even in the first half of the 19th century,* "*when they reared up a house in such a place, quartered in it a cock and a hen before they installed themselves there, and then had them killed. These propitiatory sacrifices were intended to avert the peril menacing the new inhabitants of the male and female sex,*" URQUELL, *1894, 158.*

F. Gregorovius, "Geschichte der Stadt Rom im Mittelalter," vii. (Stuttgart, 1870), 306 sq., relates about the death of Pope Innocent VIII. (July, 1492): "Surrounded by his greedy nephews, Innocent VIII. lay meanwhile dying in the Vatican. He was barely able to take any other nourishment than woman's milk. If the fine picture of the departing Medici, whom his doctor tried in vain to save by a potion of dissolved pearls, resembles a significant fable of the value of riches, by what name indeed should the scene be called, which is said to have been played at the death-bed of a Pope? His Jewish physician-in-ordinary lit upon the idea of instilling the life-blood of boys into the dying man; three boys of ten submitted to it for money, and they died victims of this criminal experiment. The dying man, it is true, did not give his consent; he thrust the doctor from him"* Assuming (not yet admitting) that the Pope really hesitated to accept the medicine offered him at the last, it is abundantly demonstrated as a conclusion from the first part of this work that the Jewish doctor did not advise such remedy as a Jew, but as a doctor living in the illusions of his period.

D. Modern Times. A great mass of varied material that properly belongs here is afforded by the numerous writings called "Book of Medicine" (Sēpher r^{e}phu'ôth or Sēpher r^{e}phu'ā^{h}) or "Book of secret cures" (Sēpher s^{e}gullôth),† which, partially belonging already to the Middle Ages in their material, even now stand in high esteem with those Jews, especially the Polish, who are little or not at all affected by modern culture. Before me lie four books, to which I limit myself, since they were even reprinted a few years ago, and we are here especially concerned with the relations that exist even now between Jews and superstition. 1. "Sēpher Tol^{e}dôth 'Adām," by Elia Ba'al Shem, firstly at Wilhermsdorf, 1734; in an undated new impression, names the same place of printing. 2. "Sēpher R^{e}phu'ôth," Kolomea, 1880, 18a-24a, secret remedies from *David Salomo Eybeschütz's* "L^{e}bushê ś^{e}rād." 3. "Sēpher Z^{e}khirā^{h}," by *Sacharja Plungian,* Hamburg, 1709, and often in the Warsaw edit., 1875. 4.

* "Judaeus quidem fugit, et Papa non sanatus est. The blood-money was a ducat for each poor child. No wonder that the fable of the Passover blood persisted. Infessura and Raynaldus n. xxi. The Florentine Valori, however, gives no information of the kind."—[Also Burkhard's diary has here a hiatus, as Gregorovius mentions in another place: The Manuscript in the Chigiana stops at the 14th July, 1492, and then begins the Pontificate of Alexander VI. with his elevation to the throne.]

† *J. A. Benjacob,* "Oçar-ha-sepharim," Wilna 1880, p. 407 sq ; 548-50 gives a fairly copious, but yet incomplete list.

"Sēpher Miph'alôth 'Elohîm," by the Kabbalists, *Joel Ba'al Shem* and *Naphtali ben Isaak Kohen*, and the physician *Simḥa*, Zolkiew (?), 1810; Sklow, 1821; according to the Lemberg edition, 1872 (128).*

Some samples. Tholedoth Adam prescribes for jaundice: "Let the patient take a yellow turnip, make water† into it, and hang it in the chimney," and "Let goose-dung be put in wine, and let the patient drink without knowing about it." Against fever: "Take some of the patient's urine, add milk and bread to it, and give it to a dog to eat." Against fever and other illnesses: "Let the patient bury a small mug of his water under an elder-tree, and say thrice: 'Consumption, jaundice, vomiting-illness, siebenundsiebzigerlei‡ ("seventy-seven kinds of") illness; it is better I bury you than you me.'" To stop the bleeding of the circumcision wound: "Take warm pig's dung, and lay it on the child's belly." To stop menstrual bleeding: "Pulverise a ruby, and drink it in water or wine." One's own blood helps against bleeding: "Boil the circumcision blood or blood from the nose till it becomes a dry mass, and sprinkle this on the circumcision wound or the nose;" or: "Write on the nose or the forehead with the still fluid nose-blood: 'tîb beṭîb penîm bedām,' or 'zēṭō' (זטו) = Gk. 'ζήτω' § 'let him live.'" Quite

* Similar writings have been utilised by *A. Grunwald*, "Aus Hausapotheke und Hexenküche," in *Mittheilungen der Gesellschaft für jüdische Volkskunde*, 1900, 1-87, and 1907, 118-45, (chiefly manuscript, in Hamburg and in Vienna).—*M. Ginsburger*, "Jüdische Volksmedizin im Elsass," ibid. 1907, 1-10, mentions a volume written in Alsace in 1777 by Joseph Lehmann, with recipes and prescriptions ("Segulloth u-rephu'oth"), whose contents are said to be very similar to those in "Albertus Magnus" [v. supr. p. 21]

† *Pliny*, Nat. Hist. xxviii., 6, 18; *Bergel*, "Medizin der Talmudisten," 63; *Strackerjan* II., 115; *Wuttke*[2] §182, 338, 477, 493 sq., 500, 505, 530 sq., 541; *Frischbier* 58; "Mélusine," III., 278 (Vosges).

‡ For the number "77" cf. the proverbs in *Frischbier* 54.

§ In the Palest. Talmud "Berakhoth" vi., fol. 10d: "If anybody sneezes at a meal, one must not cry out to him "זט" "ζηθ[ι]" (live! = be healthy!) because otherwise he might swallow the wrong way dangerously."

similar stuff in the Sepher Rephuoth (e.g. 4a. 14b. sq.) from which let also the following be taken. Externally applied: fox's blood and wolf's blood are good for stone in the bladder; ram's blood for colic, weasel blood for scrofula and podagra; wolf's blood in deafness; pigeon's blood in eye-ache; dry raven's blood, fresh hare's blood, and hare's gall in hemorrhoids. In excessive or improper bleeding let the woman bake some of the blood in bread, and give it a pig to eat. The coming-out of a tooth is effected by the laying-on of the tooth of a corpse. For the plague there is a tried and approved remedy 23a: lay the key of the house in a dead Jew's hand. In order to be protected from all evils, gird yourself with the rope with which a criminal has been hung, No. 20a (Cf. supr. p. 47 sq.).

B. W Schiffer (fictitious name for "Segel!") "Alltagglauben u. volktümliche Heilkunde galizischer Juden," *Ur-Quell*, 1893. Under the pillow of a person seriously ill is put a cloth which has previously lain on the grave of a pious person (119). If a woman after her first child wishes to have a boy, the afterbirth should be given to a dog to devour; if a girl, to a bitch. "'An efficacious, but godless remedy,' an old Jewish nurse remarked to me" [B. W. Sch.] (187). Washing with urine as a cure, rarely (211). For epilepsy: Kill a cock and let it putrefy (273).—*B. Benczer*, "Jüd. Volksmedizin in Ostgalizien," *Ur-Quell*, 1893, 42, 120 sq. (no blood).—*J. Spinner*, "Zur Volkkunde galizischer Juden," ibid., 1893, 95 sq. *J. A. Charap*, "Volksglaube galizischer Juden," ibid., 1894, 81 (No blood. Love magic: Hold an apple about an hour under the right arm, and then give it to the girl).—*B. W. Segel*, "Materyaly do etnografii żydów wschodnio-galicyiskich," Cracow, 1893 (72). Cf. *Ur-Quell*, 1894, 184.

For authentic proofs that these remedies are known to the people, v. URQUELL, 1894, 290 sq. (remedies for epilepsy and jaundice, collected in London among Jewish emigrants from Russian Poland: URQUELL, 1898, 33 sq. — "In order to get children, barren women drink water in which was boiled moss which had been plucked at the ruins of the Temple wall.—The Sephardim [Spanish Jews] prepare a remedy from the powder of bones which are found beneath the sand of the desert. These bones are mostly connected with the pilgrims for whom the simoon has ready a grave in the glowing desert-sand. The collected bones are reduced to dust and sold to the apothecaries. The powder is shaken up with mead, and it is given every now and then to the patient, who has been washed beforehand and wrapt in white linen." URQUELL, 1894, 225 (after Moses Reischer, "Schcarê Jerushalajim," Lemberg, 1875).

So far as regards the use of human blood, the superstitious Jew uses only his own blood, and particularly indeed for the stopping of bleeding.—Apart from this only menstrual blood (cf. supr. p. 51 sq.) is mentioned, and that too quite seldom. Against fire, "Sepher Zekhira," 130: Let a garment stained with such blood be hung at the fire on a long rod. Let the sufferer from quartan fever put on such a garment, "Sepher Rephuoth," No. 17 b. In order to be invisible, put water melons first in such blood, then in the earth; after the new fruits have ripened, one of them will make him invisible who carries it about with him, ibid. 23 b.* For podagra the smearing of the menstrual blood of a woman who has borne for the first time is a help. Tholedoth Adam, 96, and Miph'aloth Elohim, 96. If a midwife is visited by a menstruating woman, the child gets leprosy on the head and face. Cure for it: Bathe the child with the stained shift, *Ur-Quell*, 1893, 171 [v. sup. p. 141, line 19]. Otherwise as far as I perceive, in superstition among Jews blood is never mentioned as a cure for leprosy (cf. supr. p. 62 sq.).—Also, as far as my knowledge goes, there is nowhere the point, that animal blood or even human blood, in particular the blood of another

* Cf. *Wuttke*,[2] §482 sq.

man, should be drunk or swallowed dry for superstitious purposes.

Corpses as 'pain-removers' (Cf. Ch. 8): In the "Ḥatham Sophĕr" of the Pressburg Rabbi, Moses Sopher (1762-1839) is a technical decision on the following query put from West Hungary: A man of the family of the Aaronides, who must not touch a corpse [Cf. supr. Ch. 14 G], suffers severely from epilepsy. May he, to cure himself, take a dead man's hand and say: "Take this evil from me; you it will not hurt, and me you will benefit thereby?" (*L. Mandl, Ur-Quell*, 1895, 37). Cf. supr. Ch. 8 D.—When about three decades ago many Israelite children were carried off by an epidemic in a small West Hungarian town, an old man put a padlock [cf. sup. p. 68] into the grave of a child just buried, threw the key away and spoke: "With you shall everything evil be shut up." *L. Mandl, Ur-Quell*, 1895, 37.

CASSEL 34 says that "even recently Jewish bridal pairs in Silesia mingled blood from their fingers at the wedding." Nothing is known about it by the Christians and Jews I have asked; also in books nothing was to be found. If the statement is correct, the custom may be explained according to Ch. 3.

E. The attentive reader will admit that a considerable amount of the practices here alluded to are of non-Jewish origin. The reference appearing in but few passages to something specifically Jewish is obviously not aboriginal, as in the "Sepher Rephuoth," 19 a b: "In order to stop an enemy's tongue, take wax of an Atonement Day candle, put a spider into it, then stick it in your mouth and speak, 'As the spider endures in the wax, so may all enemies, who do evil, be in my hand and power, that I may be able to do them evil, but not they me.'" Quite as little, of course, do the concluding words, "In the name of the Father, and the Son, and the Holy Ghost! Amen" (e.g. supr. p. 57), used in many magic formulas, "sympathetic," and other superstitious attempts to cure by superstitious Christians, prove any connection between these superstitious forms and the Christian religion. The other popular-medical and purely superstitious ideas, which are propounded in the Jewish medical and secret-cure books, are, as is established in the first part of this work, common to the whole of mankind. Also the fact that there is but little of the kind to be discovered in the Talmuds, which are yet so comprehensive, corroborates the assumption that much was introduced later from non-Jewish circles.

F. Relying on the *Bernstein* case, which was much discussed in February and March, 1889, not a few papers at the time accused the Jews of ritual employment of blood. *H. Desportes*, 244-8, and many others repeated this charge in 1890.—A Jewish candidate for a Rabbiship, Max B., of Breslau, was on 21 February, 1889, condemned for doing deliberate bodily harm, by making a slight scratch* on the skin of the penis of Severin Hacke, a Christian boy, which had caused a few drops of blood to flow. The circumstance that B. had immediately soaked up the blood in two bits of blotting paper was from the start convincing proof to me that the "Christian blood" was not intended to serve any of the objects commanded or even allowed by Jewish religion, that it was much rather a case of "blood-superstition." This conviction was brilliantly confirmed by the official publication about the case. The *Vierteljahrsschrift für gerichtliche Medizin*, 1891, 207-35, published in regard to the B. case the supreme decision of the Royal Scientific Committee for the medical profession of 5 Nov., 1890. An autobiography of B. himself, printed there, states that B., tortured by pangs of conscience, owing to non-fulfilment of the ceremonial

* The accusation, which has been several times made, that there was "repeated tapping of blood," is untrue.

law, tried *beforehand*, in the case of two *Jewish* boys, to replace by a quite similar scratch the circumcision which had not been at all, or had been unlawfully carried out in their regard, in order to announce to God his repentance by such voluntary action. It then goes on further (220 sq.): "The performance of the acts of repentance lightened my spirits, but did not quite content me, so I made up my mind to free myself from sin. Now since, according to the Biblical doctrine, the soul is contained in men's blood, and since my sin-burdened soul could only be atoned for by an innocent one, I had to get blood I could use from a human being who was without sin. Then as I knew the boy H. was suitable, as his soul was sinless, I resolved to procure myself blood from him, and I dealt with H. as a few months before with the two others, but carrying out the circumcision on this occasion without intending to complete it, as it was useless to a Christian boy. It is possible those first two actions in my search for freedom from sin guided me. I kept the blood I got on a sheet of blotting paper, and shortly undertook my atonement with it. After it had itself become sinful by taking on itself my sins, I buried it in a cemetery, as it could not remain in the vicinity of men." (Cf. Leviticus xvi., 21: The high priest on Atonement Day lays the sins of the people of Israel on the goat, which is then to be driven into the wilderness). The Royal Scientific Committee for the Medical Profession did not investigate the connection of the superstition appearing in B. with other ancient forms of superstition, none of which have any specifically Jewish stamp, and therefore they did not use the general key to the explanation of B.'s method or action. On the other hand they, or rather the report agreed to by them, of the judicial expert, Professor Dr. Lesser, of Breslau, who was first consulted, gives an answer to the question whether such a superstition in a man of B.'s education was reconcilable with mental equilibrium. P. 210: "Not merely the mother's, but also the father's relatives were not intact in regard to the central nervous system; no fewer than seven of B.'s relatives, some on the mother's, some on the father's side, had died mad or were still alive in a condition of insanity. The deputation came to the conclusion (234 sq.) based upon personal observation of B. in the Charité Hospital at Berlin: "(1) that B. is diseased in mind, and suffers from religious madness, Paranoia chronica religiosa; (2) that he committed the deeds of bodily injury he was charged with, in a state of morbid disturbance of his mental activity, by which his free decision of will was excluded."—Thus the "Bernstein case" must be judged just like the occurrences described in Ch. 13.*

* I do not think it impossible that some medical superstition had also something to do with B.'s action. The consulted medical experts, as far as I know, did not go farther into this question.

XVI. IS THE USE OF CHRISTIAN BLOOD REQUIRED OR ALLOWED FOR ANY RITE WHATEVER OF THE JEWISH RELIGION?

That the question whether the use of the blood of a non-Jew, particularly the use of Christian blood, is requisite or allowed, perhaps for the preparation of the Easter loaves (Mazzoth) or for the Easter wine—that this question is to be answered in the negative, is already sufficiently obvious from the collective whole of the previous researches. Yet I think I should adduce some further reasons for the negation.

If the use of Christian blood were commanded, or even only allowed, there would be bound to be passages referring to it in the Halakhish literature of the Jews, which is positively colossal in its comprehensiveness, and enters into every detail of both religious and domestic life. But neither the zeal of the experts among the controversialists of Christian faith nor the hate-sharpened penetration of those proselytes, who wished to show their reliance on the new religion by fanatical enmity towards the Jews, has been able to extract anything out of all those writings which could in the lease serve for corroboration of the notion. It is also not to be expected that such passages shall yet be discovered in MSS. of the Talmud and the other ancient Jewish literary productions; the learned Spanish Dominican, Raimundus Martin (second half of the 13th century), whose "Pugio fidei adversus Mauros et Judaeos" has taken all its numerous quotations from Talmud and Midrash MSS., knows absolutely nothing of the charge here in question. There is also absolutely nothing to be found in the collections of the passages struck out by the cenorship in the later editions of the Talmud and in the big collection of variants, "Diqduqê Soph^e^rîm," by *R. Rabbinowicz,* that could afford any sort of corroboration of the "blood-charge."

B. Those proselytes, who have given voice to the accusation in question against Judaism, have been throughout both malignant and ignorant enemies of the Jews, on whose statements, as no proofs are afforded, no weight can be laid, e.g.: *Samuel Friederich Brenz*, author of "Jüdischer abgestreiffter Schlangen-Balg," Nuremberg, 1614 (again printed in *J. Wülfer's* "Theriaca Judaica ad examen revocata," ibid. 1681, 4°), or *Paul Christian Kirchner,** author of "Jüdisches Ceremoniel Frankfurt, 1720," or *Paulus Meyer*, whom the Berlin Anti-Semites had hired to libel me in 1892, and who then on account of his book† "Wölfe in Schafsfell, Schafe in Wolfspelz! Enthüllungen über die Judenmission und eine Abrechnung mit Professor Strack. Alle Rechte vom Autor vorbehalten!" L.,

* What sort of a fellow this *Kirchner* was, *Joh. de le Roi*, "Die Evangelische Christenheit und die Juden" I. (1884), 405, and *S. J Jugendres,* the preparer of a second, improved edition of the "Ceremoniel," Nuremberg, 1734, 150, have shown. The latter at the same time gives the reason why *Kirchner* "should have remained at home with this accusation." That Kirchner deliberately uttered falsehood can be inferred from a letter of the learned Pastor Chr. Theoph. Unger (ob. 1719) to Joh. Chr. Wolf (v. his "Bibl. Hebr." III., 914): "Miror, qua fronte Kirchnerus talia scripserit. Nam ipse mihi non rogatus, cum in sermones de Christianorum criminationibus, Judaeis imputatis, incideremus, coram adfirmavit sancte disertis verbis; Judaeos quidem omnes et singulos esse Christianorum hostes infensissimos; eo tamen ipsis injuriam fieri, quod a nonnullis incusarentur, ac si Christianorum sanguinem ad certos usus adhiberent.

† "Wolves in Sheep's Clothing. Sheep in Wolves' Clothing! Revelations about the Jew mission and a reckoning with Professor Strack. All rights reserved by the author!"

1893 (94), was condemned by the Royal Court of Sessions at Leipsic, in November, 1894, to a year and ten months' imprisonment for "libellous insult." About his "operations" in Vienna Cf. Ch. 18 for the year 1893 (p. 224). As to the denial given by numerous proselytes, v. Ch. 19, B.

C. About the middle of the 8th century, A.D., arose the sect of the Karaeans, of whom even now the survivors, not very numerous indeed, dwell especially in the Crimea, in Poland, and in Cairo. The Karaeans are essentially, apart altogether from anything else, differentiated from the other Jews, the so-called Rabbanites, by the fact that they reject the Talmud, while the latter acknowledge it. A violent enmity existed, and still exists, between Rabbanites and Karaeans, which has also found vent in numerous writings. Now, no one has ever believed that the Karaeans use Christian blood for the purposes of their ritual. If, then, there were such a ritual among the Rabbanites it would be perfectly unintelligible that this difference is nowhere touched upon in the Jewish polemics, that neither the Rabbanites reproach the Karaeans with the non-accomplishment of this rite, nor the Karaeans reproach the Rabbanites with this murderous and cannibalistic savagery.

D. The Sabbathaically-disposed Frankists, fanatical believers in the Sohar, asserted in the presence of the Bishop Nik. Dembowski of Kamienec Podolsk, 1756 and 1757, not only: that according to the Sohar, the Godhead consists of three persons alike one to another, which form at the same time a trinity and a unity, and that the Godhead has continually assumed human form, in order to show himself visibly to all, but also: that the Talmud contained the most abominable things, inculcated the slaughter of Christians as a religious ordinance, and the adherents of the Talmud used the blood of Christians. And in 1759 they declared to the Archbishop Wratislaw Lubienski, that they panted for Baptism like the hart for the water-springs, and offered to prove "that the Talmudists shed innocent Christian blood, even more than the heathens, lusted after it, and made use of it." At the same time they asked to have dwelling places assigned them east of Lemberg, in order to be able to live by the work of their hands, "where the Talmudic brandy-farmers nurtured drunkenness, sucked out the blood of poor Christians, and marked it up with double chalk." In May two deputies of the Frankists pronounced in the name of all of them before Canon Mikulski the confession: The cross was the symbol of the Holy Trinity, and the seal of the Messiah. It concluded "The Talmud taught the use of the blood of Christians, and whoever believed in it, was bound to use the blood." At the discussion carried on in July in the Cathedral of Lemberg, under Mikulski's presidency, the Frankists tried to show "that the Sohar taught the trinity, and that one of the persons in the Godhead had become flesh. . . . That such ideas occurred in the Talmud," the Talmudists "could not deny. They had, indeed, been able to repel with all decisiveness the fictitious assertion as to the use of the blood of Christian children, and the blood-thirstiness of the Talmud, and to appeal to the testimony of Christians and even to statements of Popes. But they were ignorant about their own history of suffering, and their ignorance has avenged itself upon them. It is, indeed, credible that the Talmudic spokesmen returned home ashamed and confused after three days' discussion. Even the blood accusation remained sticking to their confession." Soon after the disputation, about a thousand Soharites had themselves baptized, on the pressure of the polish ecclesiastics; in November also Frank himself, who had brought it to pass that the King was inscribed as his godfather (Jakob Frank called himself, after that, Joseph). As it became evident that the baptism was to him merely a means to an end, and he allowed himself in secret to be worshipped as God Incarnate and "Holy Lord," he was confined in March, 1760, in the monastery of Czenstochow. After thirteen years' confinement he was set free by the Russians, and played for many years more the part of an impostor in Vienna, Brünn, and in Offenbach; he died in 1791.

The preceding is taken as far as possible verbatim from H. GRÄTZ, "*Geschichte der Juden,*"[2] *X., 425 sq., 430 sq. Grätz, however, is mistaken, when trusting the exceedingly one-sided Jakob Emden "Hith'abbekûth," Altona, 1726 sq., 35), he writes that the Hamburg Rabbi,* JONATHAN EIBESCHÜTZ, *had remained "dumb" to the imploring entreaty of the Polish Jews that he should "meet the accusation of the use of Christian blood."*—As this sentence has left an impression on Christians, that there might after all be something in the blood-accusation, I will here put the facts of the case clearly. Eibeschütz not only himself elaborated a detailed, professional report in December, 1759 (probably for despatch to the Danish Government), but also repeatedly urged Christian scholars to express their views. E.g. in 1760 (he was impelled to do so precisely by the lies of the Frankists) the well-known Professor of Theology in Halle, Chr. Ben. Michaelis, and John. Sal. Semler, v. "Jüdische Volks- und Haus-Kalender für das Jahr 1893," Breslau, Jahrbuch, p. 79-109. Semler's pregnant exposition closes with the sentences: "But from it all comes the irrefutable inference that people who impute guilt to the Jews and want to prove from the books of their law that they use Christian blood, must*

* "Christentums" in Grätz is obviously a printer's error.

be either very illiterate simpletons or malignant hostile spirits. . . . and that the Jews could not be accused before any equitable magistrate upon such frivolous wretched charges, but far rather such simple or malignant accusers might be repulsed, and probably even held to an apology." Jonathan Eibeschütz himself writes at the beginning of his work: "I have had to hear, not merely with the greatest exasperation, but also with the greatest sorrow, how a few godless people, forgetful of honour, who a long time ago were expelled from the Jewish Synagogue, have banded together, and in order to conceal their viciousness have tried to diminish the Jewish nation in the sight of the Christian high authorities, and to affirm with baseless, even altogether lying sentences taken from Jewish books, that the Jewish nation has need of Christian blood for its chief ceremonies. BUT THIS ACCUSATION IS SO GODLESS THAT ONE HAS FAIRLY TO WONDER HOW THE EARTH CAN BEAR SUCH PEOPLE ON ITS SOIL."—*The manuscript which contains these three documents has been transferred out of the property left by Dr. B. Zuckermann to the Jewish Theological Seminary at Breslau.—And already in 1736, likewise at the request of Eibeschütz, Prof. F. Haselbauer, of Prague, delivered a pronouncement against the blood accusation, v. inf. Ch. 19 E.*

E. It is generally admitted that those Jews who held fast at all to their religious law, or now hold fast, have always been ready, or still are ready, to give up their lives rather than to become unfaithful to that law. If, then, there were any phrase whatever that ordained the use of Christian blood, such blood would be annually requisite, would therefore also be shed; in that case, however, a considerable number of instances must doubtless have been alluded to, especially during the period of the last hundred years, at least in those law-governed States of Europe in whose midst the Jews live in scattered groups. Yet such proofs are altogether wanting.—Again, the accusation of the ritual use of blood would be bound to have been declared and to be declared everywhere; also, it would be bound to have been referred to in every century since the establishment of the Christian religion; or, at any rate, since the Christian religion has become the ruling one in the old Roman Empire. But there is no "everywhere" nor "at all periods" to be found in this case. It is especially noticeable that the decree by which the "Catholic Kings" Ferdinand of Aragon and Isabella of Castile, on 31st March, 1492, commanded all the Jews of Spain, Sicily and Sardinia to emigrate within four months on pain of death, does not mention the blood accusation.

F. In order to make the assertion of the ritual use of blood plausible, people talk readily about "Schächtschnitt* (Jewish butcher's cut), and the employment of a "Schächtmesser" (Jewish butcher's knife); also "Schächter" (Jewish butchers) are accused, by preference, of killing Christian children. It is on that account very notable that Joseph Theomim, a Rabbi of Lemberg and Frankfort a. O. (ob. 1793), in his extremely prized Hebrew commentary, "P^eri m^egadîm" (Be., 1772, sq.), on the first two parts of the "Schulḥan 'Arukh, Jore De'a," 8, relates the following:—A "Schächter" bought a knife which an executioner had used at an execution, and wanted to use it for his own professional purposes. Rabbi Joseph declares this forbidden; because human flesh was forbidden, and the human flesh absorbed by the knife would combine with the animal flesh in slaugh-

* "Schächten" is the verb used in German for "to butcher" in the Jewish manner; the usual Gentile butcher "schlachtet," not "schächtet."—Translator.

tering, and thereby make the latter also forbidden. Whoever affirms the ritual killing of Christian children by "Schächtung" (Jewish butchering) is bound to assume that the "Schächter" have *two* sets of "Schächtmesser," one for the animals which are to be slaughtered, the other . . . would not such an assumption exceed the extremity of foolishness?

G. Every experienced criminalist, especially every investigating judge who carefully handles criminal cases, knows that the detailed information of public journals about "interesting cases" has often acted as a provoking influence on the imaginations of men, who were not firmly established in the good or were already disposed to the bad. The fact that men who make attempts on crowned heads, even when the bullet or the dagger has not reached its mark, are, at least temporarily, notorious through the daily Press, has provoked many a fresh attempted murder of the kind.* Accordingly, it might be *imaginable* that precisely the unceasing repetition of the idea that the Jews want Christian blood might have suggested or might suggest,† somewhere, at some time, to a subject not quite mentally responsible who happens to have been born a Jew, just to try whether Christian blood was really a quite different fluid from Jewish blood. An incident of the kind could not be laid to the charge of the Jewish religion.

* The imitative impulse altogether plays a great part in criminology, v. e.g. *Lombroso*, II., 289-91, 86, 106.

† *O. Stoll*, "Suggestion und Hypnotismus in der Völkerpsychologie," L. 1894 (523).

XVII. THE AUSTRIAN PROFESSOR AND CANON AUG. ROHLING

The Imperial-Royal Austrian Professor Aug. Rohling, of Prague, became in 1883 the mainstay of the blood accusation levelled against the Jewish religion. To the scientific world, indeed, his name has never been worth anything. His polemic against the Talmud and his "proofs" of the reality of the Jewish blood-ritual were of such a kind that one could only be in doubt whether, owing to his malignancy, the penal law ought to be invoked, or owing to his spiritual obfuscation the doctor ought to step in. It unfortunately happens, however, when one looks at the result, that it is often far less important whether an assertion is true than whether it is believed. Therefore, as Aug. Rohling, in consequence firstly of the praise of very numerous partisan newspapers, secondly, of the irresponsible patronage, even favouritism, on the part of the then Austrian Ministry of Education, was blindly believed in very wide circles, not only of Austria, but also of Germany, nay, even of France and other countries, I wrote in September, 1892, in the fourth edition of this book:—

"I PUBLICLY ACCUSE HEREWITH THE IMPERIAL ROYAL AUSTRIAN PROFESSOR AND CANON AUGUST ROHLING OF PERJURY AND GROSS FORGERIES. *I further publicly ask those who, after reading this book, protect the aforesaid Aug. Rohling, whether they are not making themselves guilty of aiding in the continuance of the aforesaid crime or delinquency. Finally I declare that Aug. Rohling has given numerous proofs in his judgments on Jewish literature and Jewish religion of his disgraceful ignorance, and that he got the copious quotations from Talmudic and Rabbinical literature which blind the lay mind, partly copied out of Eisenmenger's "Entdecktes Judenthum," partly guided by others, especially by Ahron Brimann.—I am ready to establish this grave accusation in the presence of any Court of Justice."*

Although this edition sold to the extent of 9,000 copies, and numerous papers, especially Austrian, quoted my words and made them widely known, neither Rohling nor the Austrian Ministry of Education took action against me. Rohling kept silent, in the hope that his reputation among the racial Anti-Semites, whose feelings of justice are dulled by hatred, could not be damaged by anything whatever, and that the great majority of people partly possess a short memory, partly had remained ignorant of my accusation. At any rate, I will to the best of my ability prevent Rohling from being again in the future regarded as an expert. For that reason I have here repeated my accusation, and bring forward some points, at least, to substantiate it.

Rohling became most known through his book (which was ALMOST ALL COPIED OUT OF EISENMENGER*) "Der Talmudjude," Münster, 1871; in 6th edition, 1877 (126). The "Entdeckte Judenthum," of Eisenmenger, owing to the one-sidedness with which the author has made his compilation, offers no accurate picture of the Jew who holds fast to the Talmud; yet the reader is able, at least to a certain degree, easily to check his [i.e., E.'s] assertions because Eisenmenger everywhere gives the Hebrew or Aramaic wording of the original,* *and indeed frequently long extracts.* Rohling, however, only quotes those words which exactly suit his purpose, without any consideration of the context, and indeed only in the German language (according to E.'s translation), so that his exposition is not merely a caricature of the truth, but even the contrary of it.— The most important counterblast is that of* FRANZ DELITZSCH, "*Rohling's Talmudjude,*" *L., 1881 (64); 5th impression enlarged by a continuation, 1881 (87). Among writings of Jewish authors I only name:* JOSEF NOBEL, "*Kritisches Richtschwert für Rohling's 'Talmudjude,'*" *Totis (Halberstadt), 1881 (87).– Rohling rejoined in "Franz Delitzsch und die Judenfrage,"*[2] *Prague, 1881 (155). With how little knowledge and veracity,* DELITZSCH *has showed in the 7th edition of his already-mentioned work, L., 1881 (120); Cf. also* DELITZSCH'S "*Was Dr. Aug. Rohling beschworen hat und beschwören will,*" *L., 1883 (39).*

Rohling followed up with "Meine Antworten an die Rabbiner. Oder: Fünf Briefe über den Talmudismus und das Blut-Ritual der Juden," Prague, 1883 (106), and "Die Polemik und das Menschenopfer des Rabbinismus," Paderborn, 1883 (108).—Rejoinders by Delitzsch: "Schachmatt den Blutlügnern Rohling und Justus," Erlangen, 1883 (43), and: "Neueste Traumgesichte des antisemitischen Propheten," Erlangen, 1883 (32).—JOSEF BLOCH, *Rabbi at Floridsdorf, near Vienna, also wrote very severely against the "Antworten," in the* WIENER ALLGEMEINE ZEITUNG, *22 Dec., 1882; 6, 10, and 24 January, 1883, which articles are reproduced in "Acten und Gutachten in dem Prozesse Rohling contra Bloch," I. (Vienna, 1890), 5-89. This book of*

* Cf. *A. Th. Hartmann,* "Johann Andreas Eisenmenger und seine jüdischen Gegner," Parchim 1834 (40).

25 sheets contains altogether an abundance of conclusive evidence against Rohling.

Rohling was repeatedly and publicly accused by Franz Delitzsch and others not only of gross ignorance and malignant distortions, but also perjury. R. went on lying and kept on indulging again and again in false swearing, in the comforting conviction that the authorities over him would not make up their minds to take steps against him, or even allow the actual state of affairs to be expertly examined into. At length R.'s attempt to influence the Hungarian court of justice of Nyiregyhaza (Tisza-Eszlar trial) caused the aforesaid *J. Bloch* to accuse Rohling ("Acten," I., 109-20) of offering perjury in the *Wiener Morgenpost* of 1st to 4th July, 1883, in such strong terms,* that R. could not but take action, and, in fact, instituted an action "for insult to honour." Bloch pronounced himself ready to produce the proof of the truth of what he wrote. He prepared this proof in an uncommonly thorough-going manner, so that the judicial proceedings could not be commenced before 18th November, 1885, and the twelve following days. *Just*

* A few examples: "His lying Talmudic quotations he has already often solemnly sworn to . . . An Imperial Royal professor with repeated false swearings is in itself a unique fact in the variegated changeful history of Austrian Universities . . . . But a forum must at last be found before which lying, which has lost conscience and shame, habitually carried on, is judged according to truth and law . . . . . If, meanwhile, naked mendacity and fraud prostitute themselves before the whole world in barbaric nudity free from shame, it must be named by its true name and recalled to decency and morality. . The professor, however, is ever ready and greedy to swear, especially then when he puts forward assumptions, and propounds assertions about which he is sure, that, being without the slightest shadow of truth, they would be harshly repelled by all experts . . The Professor of Hebrew Antiquities at Prague carries on lying like a handicraft."—Cf. also Bloch's "Rohling und kein Ende" in the *Oesterreichische Wochenschrift*, 12 August 1892, No. 33 (R. is there repeatedly termed the "perjury-canon"), as well as the article, "Meineid" in *Jüdische Presse*, 1892, No. 30-3, 35.

before the proceedings Rohling simply withdrew the charge! Cf. also *Joseph Kopp* (a Catholic, and a well-known barrister-at-law in Vienna), "Zur Judenfrage nach den Akten des Prozesses Rohling-Bloch,"[3] L., 1886 (199).

According to R.'s statement—and here he seems to have uttered the truth for once—the Ministry commanded him, after the appearance of the "Antworten" and the "Polemik," "to leave the Jewish question alone on his part." This command afforded him the welcome opportunity to write *under a false name* a justification of his whole conduct and a laudation of his own erudition, and so to create the *impression* that there was a Christian scholar and expert in the Talmud who had tested *and* approved of R.'s assertions! "Prof. Dr. Rohling, Die Judenfrage und die öffentliche Meinung. Von Abbé Dr. *Clemens Victor*," L., 1887 (83). Victor is nobody, but Rohling himself, although R. has obstinately denied it. So far as this writing shows wide reading in Jewish literature, it does not proceed from Victor-Rohling, but from a convert (probably from notes of Brimann, which R. has in part entirely misunderstood)—and so far R. has indeed a certain right to deny his authorship; in all main points, however, the same ignorance and mendacity come to light as in the writings describing the aforesaid Rohling as their author.

At any rate, two examples, intelligible to any reader, may be adduced of Rohling's *ignorance*. He translates "dam b^ethulîm" not "sanguis virginitatis," but "sanguis virginum," which in Hebrew would be "dam b^ethulôth." The very frequent expression "'Am ha-'āreç," "the mass ignorant of the law" (John vii. 49, "this people who knoweth not the law"—in particular, the "tradition of the elders" —or also "the individual Jew ignorant of the law," he translates "non-Jew!" and thus he renders a saying of the Rabbi Eleasar: "It is permitted even on the Day of Atonement, when it falls on the Sabbath, to stab a non-Jew." That the sentence, which is formulated with real Oriental coarseness, is not to be taken literally, but is merely a proof of the fanatical hatred dividing those learned in the law from those ignorant of it, is shown by the opposite saying of the Rabbi Aqibâ, not quoted by R., which has been handed down on *the same* page of the Talmud, Pesaḥîm 49b—"When I was an 'Am ha-āreç, I said: Give me a learned man that I may bite him like an ass."

Between most of the others, especially the older advocates of the "blood-charge" and Rohling, there is in particular this difference, which is, indeed, only secondary as far as results go, that R. does not so much assert the partaking of Christian blood, but rather the effusion of Christian blood by the murdering of Christians as an object of the Jewish ritual.

Now what are the *proofs?* Firstly, the unproved and unprovable assertion of the existence of a *tradition* about the blood-ritual or ritual blood-murder, *orally* handed down from generation to generation. I think I may declare there is at the present moment absolutely no domain of the Jewish ritual, however remote in appearance, which has not been dealt with in more than one *printed* book.

Rohling makes particularly much ado* about a

* Cf. R.'s writing, dated 10th July, 1892 (during the Xanten proceedings) to the District Crout at Cleve: "If *the facts of history* cannot be denied, it is indeed unintelligible that, in spite of the *castration* of certain Rabbinical works there are still *texts* here and there, which point to the subject . The Talmud hints at the matter even in the castrated editions [about "Kethubboth" 102^b v. infr. p. 162 sq.]; Sefer halkutim and Zohar speak more definitely, as is stated in my work, "Polemik and Menschenopfer des Rabbinismus" (Paderborn, 1883). This statement is to-day still completely convincing to me . . . . But since my

passage in the "Sėpher ha-liqquṭin," written down after the discourses of the Kabbalist Isaak Luria (b. 1533, d. 1572, in Safet), the Jerusalem edition of which R. used, I have had since 1884, and about some passages of the "Zohar." Against the crazy interpretations of R. cf. *Franz Delitzsch*, "Schachmatt," and *Ad. Merx*, "Wissenschaftliches Gutachten über den wahren Sinn der Stellen aus dem Sohar und aus Vital's liqqutim, auf die Herr Professor Rohling seine Blutbeschuldigung grüden will," Vienna, 1885 (repeated in *Bloch*, "Acten," I., 125-38). The original phrasing of these presumably so bloodthirsty passages is also to be found in "Acten," I., 353-7. To this may be added the following: *Rohling made the acquaintance of these passages through Brimann* and blindly believed his interpretations. Brimann, however, writes* in his work bearing the date 1885, dedicated to Prince-Archbishop Eder, of Salzburg, "Die Kabbala" (Innsbruck, 58),† p. 44: "How

holy conviction (! !) was officially branded a frivolity before a court of law (by the judicial expert, Prof. Th. Nöldeke), I held it to be my duty to inform you that, in *view of death and my eternal Judge I cannot speak otherwise, and must confess that the blood-accusation is the truth.*"

* *Dr. Justus* [pseudonym of Ahron Brimann], "Der Judenspiegel," 4th edition, Paderborn 1883, 80. About Rohling's dependence on Br. v. also "Acten" I., 205, 207.

† The work certainly appeared without a name; I know, however, from an absolutely sure source (through a Christian theologian descended from a Christian family), that Br. is the author. And Br.'s testimony must be decisive for R.: for even in 1887 (I will not here touch upon testimonies from the year 1883) *Rohling-Victor*, 10, writes: "*Brimann* . . is . . . *an altogether honourable*, strong *man*, who always studies honourable conduct, and is entirely worthy of every confidence."—I have good reason for the belief that Br. adhered later on, too, to his depreciatory judgment of R. (the letter of Br. communicated by Rohling Victor, 14-6, is either a forgery or was extracted for Br. by some stratagem). And, besides, I am convinced (till *proof* of the contrary), that the fifth edition of the "Judenspiegel" which appeared in 1892 was produced *without* the author's express consent. Possibly Br. sold his author's rights in return for a single payment or for some other cause he could not resist; but he did *not* collaborate in that edition.

many there are, unfortunately, who from *ignorance* believe or from *malice* wish to make others believe that the Kabbala contains nothing but murder and conflagration, slaughter of virgins, assassination of Kings. . . . What a *disgrace.* . . to our century. . . . that there are still such fools as to lend ear to such malignant calumniations." In the Kabbala one could "find true pearls, which will afford such an apologia for Christianity as could hardly have been expected." And p. 41: "How unskilfully Messrs. the Jew-eaters or the so-called anti-semitic scholars exploit quite harmless passages in their *amazing ignorance,* can be seen from the truly *laughable interpretation* of this Sohar text in [Rohling's] 'Polemik und Menschenopfer,' etc., p. 62!"

For a considerable time R. was of the opinion that ritual blood-murder was taught indeed in oral tradition as well as in the books of the Kabbala (the Jewish mysticism), but that it could not be pointed out in the Talmud. But as he sought and wanted to find, he found. He first of all gave information of his find in the *Antisemitische Correspondenz,* No. 171, of 22 November, 1891. He then disseminated (as a contribution to the *Neue Deutsche Zeitung*, of 16 March, 1892, evening edition, and in other ways) a pamphlet "Eine Talmudstelle für rituelles Schächten." Beneath this superscription he put firstly, "Confidential," in order to give the impression of something mysterious, secondly, "Pamphlet for connoisseurs," so as to flatter the noodles who would be caught in his snare. The main sentences run:

> "*It might be interesting to know that the Talmud itself, although the fact long remained unnoticed, testifies to the Jews' blood-ritual. The Talmudic passage occurs in the treatise Kethubboth, 102b (infr.). It is there announced that even a Jew boy, a minor, was* KILLED ON THE EVENING BEFORE THE

EASTER FESTIVAL *by his brothers or* [*!*] *was going to be killed. The Talmud states that people (on the part of the Jewish authorities) did not desire this slaughter, and therefore let the minor grow up with his mother, and not with his brothers, who were avaricious, and wanted at the same time to inherit the boy's property; it was not allowed because the dead father had bequeathed the boy to the mother, and so they wanted in this case to show respect for his last will.—In this affair, logic* [*!!*] *forces on everyone the conviction, that (1) even a Jew boy, whom his father's last will did not protect, can be slaughtered as an Easter lamb. . . . (2) If Jews sought for* [*!*] *Easter lambs even among the minors of their own people, how much more will they ritually* [*!*] *slaughter the non-Jews (esteemed low as the beasts?)—The memorable passage runs. . . . according to the Amsterdam edition of the Talmud "Babli" as follows:* "מי שמת והניח בן קטן לאמו יורשי האב אומרים יהא גדל אצלנו ואמו אומרת יהא בני גדל אצלי מניחין אותו אצל אמו ולא מניחין אותו אצל ראוי ליורשו. מעשה היה ושהטוהו ערב הפסח." *That means: If a person dies and leaves behind a son, not yet of years, for his mother, and the father's heirs (the brothers) say: "Let him become big (grow up) with us, but the mother says: "Let my son become big with me"—he is left with his mother, and he is not left with those entitled to his inheritance: the case comes to pass (it might occur in analogous cases, Cf. Berakhoth 2a),* THAT THEY WOULD SLAUGHTER HIM ON THE EVENING BEFORE THE EASTER FESTIVAL *(14th Nisan, on 15th is the actual Easter Festival."*

This passage in the Talmud had been known to me since 1885; I did not, however, mention it in the first edition (1891) of this book of mine, because I did not think it possible for anyone, who had read even a single page in the Talmud, to come upon the idea of using these sentences for proof of the accusation that *Christian blood* is employed by Jews for *ritual* purposes. As, however, they had been quoted by Rohling, I give the correct interpretation in the fourth edition (1892). First of all an exact translation of the whole extract.

> *Mishna xii., 1 (101b): If anyone takes a wife, and she arranges with him that he should rear up her daughter [from a previous marriage] five years, he is under obligation to rear her up for five years. If she marries another man [after being divorced from that one] and arranges with him, that [also] he should nurture her daughter for five years, he is [likewise] under obligation to nurture her five years. Let not the first one say, 'Only if she comes to me, will I rear her up,' but he brings her her maintenance* THERE WHERE HER MOTHER IS."

The Gemara, 102[b] attaches the following elucidation to the last sentence:—

> *Rab Ḥisda says: "This Mishna teaches, the daughter must be with her mother."* (QUESTION)—"*Whence does it follow that it holds good of a grown-up daughter? Perhaps it holds good of a little daughter, and the Mishna refers to a fact which has once occurred* for a doctrinal tradition says: 'If any one has died and leaves a little son to his mother, and the father's heirs say: Let him be brought up with us—and the mother says, my son shall be brought up with me—he is left with his mother, and not with anyone who might inherit from him, for it once happened that he was murdered (shāḥáṭ) on the day*

* Rashi declares: It has namely to be feared (on account of the occurrence mentioned in the doctrinal tradition), that the brothers might murder her (hārág) in order to inherit the tenth of the fortune due to her. But in the case of a grown-up daughter murder (reçiḥā) is not to be feared; whence one might continue thinking that she might live with the brothers.

before the Easter festival.'" (ANSWER)—"*In that case* it would be said in the Mishna: 'There where* SHE *is."*† *But why does the Mishna say: 'There where* THE MOTHER *is'? Thence you can infer that the daughter should be with the mother without distinction, whether she is grown up or little."*

To understand this it may be remarked: The wife is not the heiress of her husband; altogether women only have the right to inherit in a very limited way, if males entitled to inherit are present. (Cf. *M. Bloch*, "Das mosaisch-talmudische Erbecht," Budapesth, 1890); so the small children (the daughters, and, according to the doctrinal tradition quoted in the question, also the sons) are safe with the mother, but this is not equally the case with the males entitled to inherit.

The reader will ask in wonder: How is it possible to find in Kethubboth 102[b], the ordaining or even merely the permission of the ritual slaughter of Christians? In this sphere everything is possible for R. when he pleases.—Firstly, e.g., he translated "Shāḥáṭ," by "religious, ritual slaughtering." This meaning, however, is only proper to the verb when animals are in question. When human beings, "Shāḥáṭ" stands for the meaning of a violent death, e.g. the word "slew," in Jerem. xxxix., 6, and lii., 10: The King of Babylon slew the sons of Zedekiah, and the chief Jews; Jerem. xli., 7: Ishmael, the son of Nethaniah, slew eighty Israelites; II. Kings x., 7: The inhabitants of Samaria slew 70 of Ahab's descendants; Judges xii., 6; Jephthah's followers killed 42,000 Ephraimites; Cf. also Numbers xiv., 16: "The heathen will say of God, He slew Israel in the wilder-

* Rashi: "If namely there was a distinction to be made between a grown-up and a little daughter."

† Rashi: "A grown-up daughter, where she is, and a little daughter, where she is."

ness," and I Kings xviii., 40; Elijah slew the priests of Baal. With regard to the human sacrifices which were offered up on the part of the idolatrous Israelites, the word Shāḥáṭ is twice contemptuously used, Isai. lvii., 5; Hezek. xxiii., 39. It need not be pointed out that in all these passages, and in Genesis xxii, 10, Jewish ritual slaughter cannot be alluded to.—In agreement therewith is the Talmudic use of language, v. "Nedarim," 22a, "Megilla," 7b; "Ḥullin," 56b, infr. Of violent death at the hands of the Romans: "Sanhedrin," 110b, and "Pesaḥim," 69a. In the ritual blood-murder was taught assuredly in oral Midrash on Jerem. ii., 2, it is related that Nebusaradan, in the place where Zachariah was killed, killed, "shāḥáṭ," the members of the great and the little synedrium, the young priests, the school children; but the Talmud, "Giṭṭin" 57b, says of the occurrence, therefore quite synonymously, 'harág.' The two verbs are likewise used, "Sukka," 52a, supr.

Secondly: The "doctrinal tradition" advanced by Rohling alone closes with the sentence: "For it once happened," etc. These words ("maʿaśeʰ hajāʰ"; literally, "fact [or occurrence] has been") are so interpreted by R. that a reader ignorant of Hebrew gets the doubly false impression: that such actions happened repeatedly, and the Talmudic ordinance (the child shall stay with the mother) had the object of preventing religious butcherings from taking place on the day before the Easter festival. In reality, however, the ordinance is not intended to forbid religious slaughtering on the day before the Easter festival, but to assure the lives of young heirs and heiresses. And furthermore it is only a matter of a single event that happened once. The latter follows from the permanent use of the word "maʿaśeʰ," Cf. Mishna Sabbath iii., 4; xvi, 7 sq.; xxii., 3; xxiv., 5, etc.; moreover, in the old collection of Jewish law traditions called

"Tosephta," Zuckermandel's edition, 273, where the same thing is related, the words are; "ma'aśeh hajāh beeḥād," "it came to pass with one man, that they killed him on the day before the Easter festival." The phrase "ma'aśeh hajāh," or the Aramaic (of identical meaning) "hawā 'obadā," often points to a previous case, which gives occasion for the establishment of a decree of the law. Cf. "Qiddushin," 85b. fin., and especially "Kethubboth," 60b. It is stated in the latter passage, in the addendum to the doctrinal tradition brought forward 60a fin., according to which a suckling woman, whose husband dies, can neither be betrothed or marry before the lapse of 24 months: "If the child dies, the new betrothal or marriage is allowed; if she has weaned it, she must await the expiry of the 24 months. Mar, the son of Rab Ashe, said: 'Even if the child has died, the prohibition holds good, that she may not kill it so as to marry. The fact once happened, that she strangled it.' But that is worth nothing, because that woman was a fool; women, after all, are not wont to strangle their sons."

Thirdly: From the words "the day before the Easter festival"* no inference can be drawn about the *ritual* character of the killing. Far from it. The choice of the day (if altogether there is need to think of anything else than a purely historical assertion) is connected with the circumstance that on this day there was least fear of discovery of the cause of death. Everyone is occupied with the preparations, and no one enters the house of a dead person, unless obliged, because he would then be unclean for seven days, and therefore miss the whole of the festivities, cf. Tosephta "Ahiloth," iii., 9 (Zuckermandel, 600).

* The conjecture expressed on the Jewish side in consequence of R.'s "find" (they wanted to deprive the "Antisemites" of a point of attack), that the statement of the time rested on an error in the text, is quite untenable.

According to Talmud "Ḥullin," 83a, this day of preparation belonged to the four days on which many entertainments at meals and rejoicings took place.

Fourthly. The reference to the Christians is introduced by R. into the passage in the Talmud by the following audacious conclusion:—"If Jews sought for Easter lambs, even among the minors of their own people, how much more will they ritually slaughter the non-Jews (esteemed low as the beasts)?" But in the whole passage there is no word about Jewish children as Easter lambs. As far as the words, "non-Jews (esteemed low as the beasts)," are concerned, the uncompromisingness of the utterance must be, and is intended to provoke in all, who are not professional experts in the subject, false ideas.

The Austrian Reichsrat Deputy Schneider had this "newly discovered, amazingly important passage from the Talmud" photographed, according to the imprints of Venice, 1526 sq., and Amsterdam, 1644 sq., and made it the subject of inflammatory dis-
No. 190) and pamphlets. Moreover, too, he had the
courses (v. e.g., *Staatsbürger-Zeitung*, 23 April, 1892,
effrontery to say at the sitting of the Reichsrat, 10th November, 1899: "Now there are quite a number of Jews who state that there is no written passage in the Talmud about the use of Christian blood. Well, I have here a photograph, which I have taken personally. . . . . So no explaining away is possible. . . . . There is no falsification in regard to this passage in the treatise Kethubboth."

Be it observed in conclusion, that the passage in "Kethubboth," 102b, if it really meant what according to Rohling and Schneider it does, would have been deleted by the Christian censorship, or at any rate altered. All the impressions produced in Germany, however (e.g. the Berlin edition of 1862), give exactly the same text as those photographed by Schneider.

XVIII. THE PRETENDED EVIDENCE OF HISTORY FOR JEWISH RITUAL MURDER

"*Personne ne la racontera sans que la plume n'hésite et que l'encre, en écrivant, ne blanchisse de larmes.*" (J. Michelet, "*Du Prêtre, de la femme, de la famille,*" *3rd edition, Paris, 1845, on the history of the Waldenses).*

The first writer in recent times,* who busied himself to prove, by instances from history, the actual existence of the doctrine of ritual murder among the Jews was, as far as I perceive, *Konstantin Cholewa de Pawlikowski*, "Der Talmud in der Theorie und Praxis," Regensburg, 1866. He enumerates 73 "human sacrifices" (p. 245-308), which the Jews had brought about, or at least had tried to bring about, "in order to eat the blood in their unleavened bread." —*Geza v. Onody*, "Tisza-Eszlár in der Vergangenheit und Gegenwart," authorised translation by G. v. Marcziányi, Budapesth, 1883 (215) devotes a chapter of 91 pages to "Ritual murders and blood-sacrifices."—*Rohling* referred to the "verdict of history" in "Meine Antworten," 53 sq. in "Prof. Dr. Rohling, die Judenfrage u. die öffentliche Meinung," 22-6, and further in the letter of 10th July, 1892 (v. supr. p. 114). He

* Eisenmenger II., 220-7, gives a long list of Christians (especially children), who are said to have been murdered by Jews. In relation to the use of blood, he says at the end: "Every one can guess that not everything is bound to be untrue. But I leave it undecided, whether the matter is so or not."

copied out some articles that appeared in the *Civiltà Cattolica* in 1887 and 1882.—*H. Desportes*, "Le mystère du sang chez les Juifs de tous les temps," Paris, 1890, has devoted almost 200 pages to the "facts of the case."—Anonymous: "Die Juden und das Christenblut," L., 1892 (46), a plagiarism, especially from Pawlikowski, Desportes, and Onody, superabounding in ignorance.—The book of *Carl Mommert* (a Catholic priest), "Der Ritual-Mord bei den Talmud-Juden," Leipsic, 1905 (127 p.), a contemptible mixture of malignancy and ignorance, is almost entirely stolen from the writings just mentioned.—Similar books about "ritual murders," not a single one of which rests on original work, have often been printed, cf., e .g., *Athanasius Fern* [pseudonym], "Die jüdische Moral und das Blut-Mysterium," L., 1893, 32-45.

In March and April, 1892 (Nos. 8438-8473) the Milan paper, *Osservatore Cattolico* published 44 articles on "Certezza del ritualismo nelle uccisioni giudaiche" ("certainty of the ritual character of the murders practised by the Jews"), including lastly a comprehensive "list" of 154 cases "of perpetrated or attempted ritual murders."

This long list has received attention among many people, partly because of the bold impudence shown by its author. But it was undeserved, because he *is an ignorant plagiarist, who does not even observe the simplest rules of historical criticism.*

First of all, a few examples of the disgraceful *ignorance* of the *Osservatore Cattolico*. Copying a printer's error of Desportes, it declares, case 106, Dublin to be the capital of a Russian government! Copying two other mistakes of Desportes, it believes "Steyer-Marck" and "Karntey," case 96, to be towns! Eisenmenger II., 223, correctly has "in Steyermarck, Kärnten." Likewise the town of "Thorn," in the

"Belgian Province of Lüttich," case 103, is merely a printer's error (for Theur?) copied from Desportes. The Emperor Joseph II. died on 20th February, 1790, but the *Osservatore Cattolico*, case 102, makes out the Jews, condemned for a murder committed in 1791 in Transylvania, to have been pardoned by this "Freemason!" Desportes, the *Osservatore Cattolico's* authority, read perfunctorily Onody's account, and thereupon misunderstood it!

The *Osservatore Cattolico* conceals the fact that it is *plagiarising*, by very often naming not *Desportes*, but the authority mentioned by him, and in doing so not infrequently copies wrong numbers, and wrong or inaccurate quotations. In case 4, e.g., occurs the wrong number, 1071 (instead of 1171) as in Victor, Desportes, and the Leipsic anonymous writer.—Case 22, "Florent de Worcester, p. 222." In an Italian paper the name ought to have been given either in Latin, according to the title of the book, or in English, according to the country of the author, or in Italian, but not in French. Desportes forgot to give the number (II.) of the volume, so it is also missing in the *Osservatore Cattolico*. The page number is missing in both: in case 91 and 111.—In case 113, Desportes has the incorrect page number, "355" instead of "356;" so also the *Osservatore Cattolico*.—Desportes *and* the *Osservatore Cattolico* have wrongly: "Wizzens" instead of "Weissensee," case 36; "Zirgler" instead of "Ziegler," case 77; "Orkul" (in Hungary) instead of "Orkuta," case 102; "Pecho" instead of "Pico," case 61.—In the name "Colmenares" the letters "en" are are not clear in Desportes's book, which has been produced by stereotyping. To this circumstance the author "Colmohares" owes his existence in the *Osservatore Cattolico*. The exact title of the book, which Desportes also did not look for, runs: "Historia de la insigne ciudad de Segovia," Madrid,

1640, fol., v.p. 400, 1649 sq.; the author, who is not named on the title page, is Diego de Colmenares.—Also the quotation taken from Desportes, "Onody, Tisza-Eszlar passim," in cases 132-5 betrays the plagiarist, because Onody, 137, mentions these four cases in two immediately successive lines.—The *Osservatore Cattolico* has also plagiarised from *Rohling*. Firstly in regard to his book, assumedly written by Victor, 25 sq., for in cases 22, 29, 42, 46, 47, 69, 73, 74, there are the same mistakes or inaccuracies in the quotations. Secondly, in regard to "Meine Antworten," 55 sq. Both "authorities" have the following errors in common: Case one is attributed to the year 425 under appeal to Baronius, whilst the "Annales Ecclesiastici" of that industrious compiler have "415;" for case 39 these annals are brought forward for the year 1325 instead of 1305; that the Jew Salomo killed the boy Konrad, case 66, is stated in the Annals for the year 1476 not in No. 20, but in No. 19. Incidentally, whoever looks closely into the matter, can easily recognise that Rohling did not derive information from the authorities themselves in the domain of history any more than in that of Jewish literature.

Likewise those quotations of the *Osservatore Cattolico*, which are neither in Desportes nor in Rohling-Victor, so far, at any rate, as concerns dates up to 1840 inclusive, are copied without verification from other sources (mostly indeed from the *Civiltà Cattolico*; cf. e.g. case 8: "Pagi n. 15," and case 17: "Blancas. Arag. Comment." with *G. de Mousseaux*, "Le Juif," Paris, 1869, 191).

A large number of the cases are impossible of examination because Desportes and his copier, the *Osservatore Cattolico*, *neither adduce an authority nor give otherwise sufficiently precise information*, e.g. case 30: "1289, Suabia, ritual murder."

At least four times the same case is counted double.

Case 23, "Northampton, 1279;" case 24, "London, 1279." The chronicler Florence, of Worcester ("Florentii Wigorniensis manochi Chronicon ex Chronicis," de. B. Thorpe, II., London, 1849), 222, whom Desportes and the *Osservatore Cattolico* quote, but have not looked up, says quite distinctly: "Apud Northamtonam die Crucis adoratae [14 September] puer quidam a Judaeis crucifixus est; ipso tamen puero non tunc penitus interfecto. Cujus quidem rei praetextu multi de Judaeis statim post Pascha [2 April] Londoniae equis distracti et suspensi sunt." (Moreover let the word "praetextus" (a pretext) be taken into consideration).—Case 25 "Munich, 1282," is identical with case 27, "Munich, 1285," as Desportes and his copier must have seen, if they had not merely quoted but also read *Matth. Rader's* "Bavaria Sancta," II. (Munich, 1624), 315 sq. The Leipsic anonymous writer uses the same passage in Rader even for a third case, "Munich, 1286."—Case 74, "1503, Waltkirch," and case 75 are one and the same. The *Osservatore Cattolico* did not look up either the "Acta Sanctorum," which Desportes mentioned as his authority, nor the work of *Joh. Eck* ("Echio!"), which he found quoted in an Italian book. —Also case 12, "1235, Norwich," is identical with case 15, "1240, Norwich." It is true, Matthew Paris mentions in both years in his "Chronica Majora" (ed. H. R. Luard, London, 1876 sq.) the circumcision of a Christian boy; but the account of *D'Blossiers Tovey*, "Anglia Judaica" (Oxford, 1738), 96-101, based upon the original documents, leaves no doubt that it concerns only one occurrence.

Yet worse than these faults is that *there is no criticism whatever exercised as regards the credibility of the reports.* All accusations are regarded as correct, without consideration as to when and by whom they were made, and without testing the question, whether they are probable or even possible.

Even were it assumed—but not admitted—that all the cases announced by the chroniclers and other reporters had actually happened, and indeed happened just as they are said to have (followed by miracles, etc.), *very many cases* would nevertheless not belong here, because they *have no ritual character whatever even according to all these reporters*.

In several cases, always assuming the credibility of the tradition, it would be a matter of *popular-medical belief*, and therefore hardly of anything ancient Jewish, and quite certainly not specifically Jewish. According to the Marbach annals, the Jews of Fulda (when tortured, of course), confess in December, 1235, that they had murdered the miller's children, "ut ex eis sanguinem ad suum remedium elicerent." Here should be placed the confession forced from the Jews at Tyrnau, in 1494, with which the statements of J. Pfefferkorn and F. A. Christiani (v. Ch. 19 B) should be compared. The case of Poesing, in 1529 ("at the marriage festival,") points perhaps to a popular belief of a similar kind.

Thomas Cantipratanus (called after the monastery of Cantimpré, near Cambray, b. about 1201, d. between 1270 and 1272) believed that the Jews use Christian blood as a means of cure. (Note the words, "importune fluidam," and "verecundissimo cruciatu.") In "Bonum universale de apibus," II., 29, §23 ed. Colverenius, Douay, 1627, 304 sq.; cf. *W. A. Van der Wet*, "Het Biënboec van Thomas van Cantimpré," 's-Gravenhage, 1902, 221, 222), he examines the question, why the Jews annually shed Christian blood: "It is namely quite certain that they cast lots every year in every province, which community or city shall produce Christian blood for the other communities. When Pilate washed his hands and said:

'I am innocent of the blood of this just person,' the excessively godless Jews cried out: 'His blood be upon us, and on our children!' (Matthew xxvii.) St. Augustine appears to allude to this in a discourse, which begins "In cruce;" that in consequence of the curses upon their fathers, the criminal disposition is even now transmitted to the children by the taint in the blood, so that the godless posterity suffers torment inexpiably through its violent coursing through their veins till they repentantly admit themselves guilty of the blood of Christ, and are healed.* Besides, I heard that a very learned Jew, who was converted to the faith of our times,† said that a man, who was reverenced among them as a prophet, had prophesied to the Jews at the end of his life: 'You may be firmly convinced, that you can only be cured by Christian blood of this secret torment, with which you are punished.'‡ This utterance was caught at by the ever-blind and godless Jews, and they hit upon the plan that every year Christian blood should be shed in every province, so that they might be healed by such blood. And he [the proselyte] added: They all interpreted the utterance by understanding the blood to be that of any Christian whatever; whilst yet that

"Quod ex maledictione parentum currat adhuc in filios vena facinoris per maculamsanguiuis, ut per hanc importune fluidam proles impia inexpiabiliter crucietur, quousque se ream sanguinis Christi recognoscat poenitens et sanetur."

† [Perhaps *Nicholas Donin*, of La Rochelle, who in 1239 presented Pope Gregory IX. with a complaint against the Talmud, containing a good many calumnies, which led in 1242 to the burning of a mass of Talmud MSS. which filled 24 waggons, Cf. *Js. Loeb* in *Revue des Etudes juives* I. (1880), 247-61; II. (1881), 248-70; III., 39-57, and I., 293-6. In 1240 a Disputation between *N.D.* and Jechiël, f Paris, and three other Rabbis about the Talmud. Thomas, of Cantimpré, was in Paris 1237-42, and relates in the "Bonum universale" I., 3 §6; van der Vet, "Biënboec," 230 about the Talmud-burning; so he was personally acquainted with Nicholas.]

‡ "Certissime vos scitote nullo modo sanari vos posse ab illo, quo punimini verecundissimo cruciatu nisi solo sanguine Christiano."

blood was meant, which is daily poured on the altar for the forgiveness of sins; everyone of our people who, converted to belief in Christ, receives this [the blood of Christ in Holy Communion], as is proper, is soon healed of the curse inherited from his fathers.'·

It is a question how those cases should be judged, in which the desire for blood is mentioned without a statement of its object, e.g. Pforzheim (1261), Weissenburg (1270), Krems (1293). The actual or presumable motive may either have been the above-mentioned (popular medicine or absolute superstition connected with folklore), or that which will presently be mentioned.

Numerous other murders might, if not be justified, at least be explained as a *reaction against* the far more numerous *deeds of blood and violence practised against Jews*, especially in the Middle Ages, *by Christians*, and indeed not only by private but also by official individuals.*

The first incident that is relevant here is that related by the Ecclesiastical historian Sokrates, vii., 16. In the Syrian town of Inmestar the Jews, who had got drunk on the occasion of a festival, began to scoff at the Christians, and then at Christ Himself. They next tied a Christian child to a cross, and made mock of it. Finally they so ill-treated the child that it died. The Jews were severely punished for this outrage committed in their insolence. The Jewish festival was presumably the feast of Purim, and the child was supposed to represent Haman (*H. Grätz*, "Geschichte der Juden," 2nd ed., iv., 393; *J. G. Frazer*, "The Golden Bough," 2nd ed., iii., 173 sq.)

* No Christian will be able to read without pain and without shuddering the fifty-page chapter on "Sufferings" in *Zunz's* "Die synagogale Poesie des Mittelalters" (Be. 1885). (Cf. also *A. Neubauer* and *M. Stern*, "Hebräische Berichte über die Judenverfolgungen während der Kreuzzüge," Be. 1892).

The hatred of Jews for Christians, the Christian religion, and its founders, [odium Christi et Christianorum] corresponded to the hatred of Christians for the Jews and the Jewish religion. The crucifixions of Christian children, more rarely of grown-up Christians, at Easter, frequently reported, especially in the 12th and 13th centuries, so far as they are really historical, would give expression to this hatred, e.g. William of Norwich,* 1144, Harŏld of Gloucester, 1168, Blois, 1171, William of Paris, 1177, Richard of Paris, in Pontoise,† 1179, Robert, in Bury St. Edmunds, 1181, Winchester, 1182, Prague, 1305 (v. infr.) Christians were treated as Jesus was once treated, and as they would gladly have treated all those by whom they were hated, persecuted, and killed. Also, whoever assumes all these reports to be exact accounts of actual happenings, has no right to speak of ritual actions. Such ideas are simply contradicted by the fact that the reports referring to the more remote periods speak of the *Christian*, not of the Jewish Easter festival.—The combination of the crucifixions, and the other so-called "ritual murders" with the *Jewish* Easter I hold to be something quite secondary. It is utterly perverse to imagine these assumed or actual murders to be sacrifices of atonement. If they had that character, they would have frequently been mentioned about the time of the Jewish Day of Atonement, i.e. the end of September or in October.

* This accusation is the oldest after 416 A.D., and appears to be an imitation of what happened at Inmestar. Cf. A. Jessop and M. R. James, "Life and Miracles of St. William of Norwich," Cambridge 1896 (91 and 303 p.); S. Berger in "Mélusine, Recueil de mythologie," etc., vol. viii. (Paris 1896-7), col. 169-74.

† Louis VII. of France (1137-80) subsequently admitted that the Jews were not guilty of the murders in Blois and Pontoise, v. *A. Neubauer* and *M. Stern*, 34 (p. 149 of the German translation).—That false charges were often brought, can be seen by the Jewish ordinance of the Bohemian King, Ottokar II., in 1254 (v. Ch. 19 D).

Again, it should be carefully noted, that *even in the case of the twelfth century, the utilisation of Christian blood* by the Jews *is not mentioned by any ancient writers,* much less its utilisation for ritual objects. According to the Marbach annals, it was in 1236 the Emperor Frederick II. first inquired whether, as a wide-spread idea was current, the Jews needed Christian blood ("utrum. . . . Christianum sanguinem in parasceve necessarium haberent,") and he received a negative answer from the expert commission appointed by him (v. Ch. 19 B).

The long list of "ritual murders," which terrifies the ignorant, will shrink very much in size in the judgment of anybody who seriously weighs all the facts here presented. It is at once nullified, if one critically examines every single "case" which is described in sufficient detail. Whilst referring the reader to a series of articles called "Die Blutlüge" (the blood-lie), published by *Dr. H. Hildesheimer* in the *Oesterreichische Wochenschrift* (Vienna), 1899, No. 44 sq., I shall mention here at any rate the majority of those older cases which are often brought up, and a portion of the accusations belonging to the most recent times, and indeed in chronological order. Fulda, 1235; Valréas, 1247; Trent, 1475; Tyrnau, 1494; Pösing, 1529; Damascus, 1840; Tisza-Eszlar, 1882; Corfu, 1891; Xanten, 1891; Polna, 1899; and Konitz, 1900 are the most "famous" cases.

1235. *Fulda,* Cf. supr., p. 176 sq. It is related in the Erfurt Annals ("Monumenta Germaniae, Scriptores," xvi., 31): "In this year [1235] on 28 December, at Fulda, 34 Jews of both sexes were put to the sword by crusaders, because two of the Jews had, on holy Christmas Day, cruelly killed the five sons of a miller who lived outside the city walls, and was at the time at church with his wife; they had collected their blood in bags smeared with wax, and had then, after they had set fire to them, gone away. When the truth of this occurrence was made known, and confessed to by the guilty Jews themselves, they were punished, as stated above." Here, too, no witnesses; here, too, merely confession produced by torture, therefore valueless. At any rate, there can be no question here of a ritual murder; because (1) the Jews' confession concerns only the use of blood for curative purposes (Marbach Annals, v. supr. p. 176 sq.); (2) the expert commission appointed by the Emperor Frederick II. declared the untenableness of the accusation that the Jews were obliged to have human blood for any object whatever, and the Emperor in consequence "fully acquitted the Jews of Fulda of the crime attributed to them, and the rest of the Jews of Germany of such a serious charge" (v. Ch. 19 B); (3) on 25th September, 1253 (v. Ch. 19 C), Pope Innocent IV. likewise declared against this accusation: "Since many Jews at Fulda and in several other places have been killed owing to a suspicion of the kind, we forbid," etc.—Cf. *R. Höniger*, "Zeitschrift für die Geschichte der Juden in Deutschland," I. (1877), 136-51, and *M. Stern*, ibid. II. (1888), 194-9. The names of the victims are given in the Nuremberg Register, v. *S. Salfeld*, "Das Martyrologium des Nürnberger Memorbuches," Be., 1898, 13. 122 sq.

1247. *Valréas* (a little town in the present department of Vaucluse). Meilla, a girl two years' old, disappears on 26th March, the Tuesday in Passion week. The following day she is found dead in the town ditch, with wounds on her forehead, hands, and feet. The child has been seen previously in the Jews' street; for the rest, torture was employed here also as a substitute for all evidence. The confession ran to the effect that Christian blood was used as a kind of sacrifice ("quasi sacrificium.") Cf. *A. Molinier*, "Enquête sur un meurtre imputé aux Juifs de Valréas" (in "Le

Cabinet Historique. Nouvelle Série," II., Paris, 1884, 121-34), and *M. Stern*, "Beiträge," II., 46-62. This "case" gave rise to two bulls (not known to Molinier at the time) of Innocent IV. to the Archbishop of Vienne, 28 May, 1247. I translate the one which is most important here, according to the first impression in *E. Berger*, "Registres d'Innocent IV.," Vol. I., Paris, 1884.

I., No. 2815: "If the Christian religion were carefully to weigh, how inhuman and contrary to piety it is, to torment with divers oppressions, and exasperate with manifold grave injuries, the survivors of the Jews, to whom, as the remaining witnesses of His redemptory suffering, and His victorious death, the goodness of the Saviour has promised the grace of salvation, then would it not only keep its hands from doing them injustice, but would also, at least for the sake of the semblance of piety, and out of reverence for Christ, impart the consolation of humanity to those who to a certain extent pay tribute to it. Now a petition of the Jews of Vienne to us states that the nobleman Draconetus, after the Jews of Valréas had been accused of having crucified a girl who was found dead in a ditch, despoiled three Jews, without their having been convicted or having confessed, nay, without anyone having accused them, of all their property, and consigned them to terrible imprisonment, refused them legal redress and justification of their innocence, had some of them cut to pieces, others burnt. The genital organs were torn off the men, and the breasts off the women, and they were tortured with all manner of tortures until they admitted with their mouths what their conscience knew nothing about, because they preferred to die once in agony than to live and be continually tortured. In order to increase*

* "Donec ipsi id quod eorum conscientia non didicit ore, sicut dicitur, sunt confessi, uno necari tormento potius eligentes quam vivere et penarum afflictionibus cruciari."

the agonies of the tortured, the Bishop of Trois-Châteaux and some magnates of the province had seized this opportunity to rob all the Jews dwelling in their districts of their possessions, and to imprison and torture those whom the Apostolic See has taken under its protection, by various forcible methods and oppressions. They have therefore humbly entreated us, mercifully to be solicitous for their innocence. As therefore, when there has been no antecedent crime, no one shall suffer punishment, and also no one may be punished for another's crime, we, filled with fatherly sympathy for them, command you, if things are so, to cause the Bishop and the others to restore to the aforesaid Jews their freedom and belongings, to give them compensation, and to allow them to live unhampered."

II., No. 2838: "*It proves an unpraiseworthy zeal or a repulsive cruelty, when Christians, acting contrary to the clemency of the Catholic religion, which permits Jews to dwell among them, and has ordained that they may live in their own rites, despoil, mutilate and kill the Jews out of avarice or blood-thirstiness, without a trial. The Jews of your province are now making bitter complaint to us, that some prelates and nobles of those parts, in order to have a cause for raging against them, charged them with the death of a girl, who is said to have been secretly murdered near Valréas, and on that account inhumanly delivered some of them to the flames, without their having been legally convicted, or having confessed,* deprived several of all their property, and banished them, and that they are compelling their sons (con-*

* "Quod quidam prelati et nobiles . . . . . ut in ipsos haberent materiam seviendi eis cuiusdam puelle, que apud Valria furtim perempta *dicitur*, interitum imponentes quosdam ipsorum *non convictos legitime nec confessos* flammis ignium inhumaniter cremaverunt."

*trary to the manner of the free mother, who bears her children to freedom) to become baptised. Since we do not intend to tolerate this, as indeed, under God, we cannot, we command that you restore everything again to legal conditions as regards these Jews, and do not allow them to be unjustly oppressed by anybody whomsoever henceforth, on account of these or similar accusations, by using the compulsion of ecclesiastical punishment, without granting appeal, in the case of those who oppress them.**

1261. *Pforzheim.* Thomas Cantipratanus (about him v. Ch. 20, ad init.), "Bonum Universale," Douay, 1627, 303 sq., gives the story according to the accounts of two Dominicans, who are said to have been at Pforzheim three days after the incidents: A thoroughly bad woman, on friendly terms with the Jews, was said to have sold them a girl of seven years. The Jews inflicted many wounds on the child, and carefully collected the blood on a folded piece of linen placed under her. They then weighted the corpse with stones, and threw it into the river. A few days later some fishermen noticed a hand raised up to the skies, and find the dead child. The populace at once suspected the Jews. When these are brought to the corpse, the wounds begin again to bleed (v. supr. Ch. 3, p. 49. When they are brought before the dead child a second time, her face flushes, and her arms rise up, as had already happened before in the presence of the Margrave of Baden, who had hastened to the spot. There were in addition statements by the woman's little daughter ("filia parvula,") and ("quia a puero et ebrio extorquetur veritas,") because the truth is extracted from children and drunken people, the Jews were broken on the wheel after various tor-

* "Non permittas, ipsos de cetero super his vel similibus ab aliquibus indebite molestari, molestatores hujusmodi per censuram ecclesiasticam appellatione postposita compescendo."

turings; two of them strangled one the other. A proper judicial examination did not take place; the miracles taken together with the child's statements sufficed. It is curious that the same miracles are reported apropos also of other "ritual murders" (Werner, of Oberwesel, etc.). If proof were necessary that the Pforzheim "case" was also a judicial murder, it is forthcoming in the manner of its narration in the Nuremberg Register (Salfeld, 15. 128), and in the synagogal poems. Cf. *Osterreich. Wochenschr.* 1899, No. 45, p. 850 sq., where in my opinion it is justly assumed, that the woman should be regarded as the murderess.*

1270. *Weissenburg.* The Leipsic anon. writer, Desportes and *Osservatore Cattolico*: "1260. The Jews of Weissenburg kill a child," following the minor annals of Colmar, "Monum. Germ. Script." xvii., 191. But year and day of the death are established by the Jewish authorities and Hertzog's "Edelsasser Chronik" (Strasburg, 1592, 198 sq.): Peter and Paul Sunday, 29 June, 1270. Heinrich Menger, a boy of seven, was on that day left alone by his father in a field near the town. When the father returned, the child had vanished. His cap is found on the brink of the Lauter, which flows near at hand; on Tuesday his mangled corpse in the river near a mill. There is no investigation as to whether the wounds have been caused by the mill-wheels, but the Jews are accused, because the wounds bleed afresh as soon as the corpse was carried into the town. Count Emicho IV. of Leiningen, who is summoned, postpones judgment till the following Friday. As the wounds bleed on that day also, although, according to the accusation, the Jews

* (Salfeld, 128-30, holds the year to be 1267; but Thomas's book, so far as we know, was ready as early as 1261, and that date is given both in the above-mentioned edition of the Latin text and also in the Middle-Dutch translation, v. van der Vet, "Biënboec," 222.

had hung up the child by the legs, and opened all his veins, in order to extract all the blood, any further examination into the actual circumstances was thought superfluous, the former torturing of the protesting Jews was even omitted, and they (seven of them) were brought by the wheel from life to death. Cf. *Oesterr. Wochenschrift*, 1899, No. 47, p. 888 sq.; Salfeld, 21 sq., 148-151.

1283. *Mainz.* Leipsic anon.—"A child is delivered over by its nurse to the Jews of Mainz, who killed it." In April, 1283, the body of a child was found near Mainz. Archbishop Werner, of Mainz, befriended to the best of his abilities the Jews who were accused without proof, but could not even accomplish the introduction of a regular trial; the rabble, exasperated by a relation of the child's, fell upon the Jews on the 7th Passover Day (19 April), slew ten of them, and then started plundering. Cf. K. A. Schaab, "Diplomatische Geschichte der Juden in Mainz," Mainz, 1855, 32 sq., Salfeld, 20. 144 sq., *Oesterr. Wochenschr.* 1899, No. 45, p. 851.

1285. *Munich* (Cf. supr. page 173). An old woman, caught kidnapping, accused the Jews when tortured. The fury of the populace cannot in any way be restrained, either by the authority of the magistrate nor by the command of the prince ("nec magistratus auctoritate nec principis imperio ulla ratione cohiberi potest,") M. Rader, "Bavaria Sancta," II. (Munich, 1624), 315 sq. There was no waiting for judicial proceedings and pronouncement of sentence ("non expectato judicio vel sententia," Hermann von Altaich, "Mon. Germ. Hist., Scriptores," xvii., 415), but on 12th October the mob storm the synagogue and burn it down, together with 180 Jews who had taken refuge in it. Cf. also Salfeld 21. 146 sq.

1286. *Oberwesel.* "The good Werner." Leipsic

anon.: "At Oberwesel am Rhein, the fourteen-year-old Saint Werner is slowly tortured to death by the Jews for three days." Neither the brief Worms Annals ("Monum. Germ. Script." xvii., 77, for the year 1286), nor Baronius (for the year 1287, No. 18), say anything about blood, or even of a ritual purpose. The sole evidences against the Jews were the "miracles." The corpse swam upstream to Bacharach, gave forth a halo, healed sick people. And yet there were between 1286 and 1289 persecutions of Jews in Oberwesel, Bacharach, Siegburg, and numerous other places, v. Salfeld, 24 sq., 155 sq. The Emperor Rudolph I. of Habsburg, to whom the oppressed Jews had turned with prayers for protection (would they have done so had they been really guilty?) commanded Archbishop Heinrich to announce solemnly in his sermon that the Christians had done the Jews the greatest injustice, and that "the good Werner," who was commonly described as having been killed by the Jews, and was worshipped by some simple-minded Christians as a Saint, should be burnt, his ashes scattered to the wind, and brought to nothing (Colmar's "Chronik," for the year 1288, in "Monum. Germ. Script." xvii., 255. Cf. *Oesterr. Wochenschr.* 1899, No. 44, p. 832 sq.)

In spite of these being the actual circumstances, F. S. HATTLER, "Katholischer Kindergarten oder Legende für Kinder" (4th edition), Freiburg i. B., 1889 (606) ventures to inform Roman Catholic children in detail, that the Jews of Oberwesel first hung up the boy Werner by the legs, because they thought they would in that way get hold of the consecrated wafer [v. supr. p. 58 sq.] of which he had partaken beforehand, and then opened his veins and cut him with scissors, in order to collect his blood. Tales are told about Andreas, of Rinn (1462), and Simon, of Trent (1475) in a similarly mendacious manner! Does this work rightly commence with the statement: "With approval of the right rev. vicarship of the Chapter of Freiburg?"

1293. *Krems* (Lower Austria). "The Jews in

Krems had a Christian sent from Brünn, and killed him in the most cruel way, in order to get his blood." Thus Zwettl's "Klosterchronik," the only original source, "Monum. Germ. hist. Script.," ix., 658. But it was written nearly three centuries after the occurrence. Who believes that the Jews at that time were able to "send" each other living Christians, and in addition, over so long a distance? Besides which, the chronicler adds that after two Jews had been already broken on the wheel, Duke Albert I. (as King of Germany, 1298-1308) and the nobility interfered in favour of the rest.

1294. Rudolph of Berne. Leipsic anon. for the year 1287: "The Jews rob St. Rudolph at Easter, put him to fearful tortures, and finally cut the child's head off. The chief offenders were broken on the wheel, their accomplices banished." The best examination of the actual facts has been made by the Bernese clergyman, *J. Stammler*, in "Katholische Schweizer-Blätter," Lucerne, 1888, 268-302, 376-90, which I follow here.* The Roman Ritual Congregation had indeed in 1869 approved the mention of the boy Rudolph in the Diocesan Supplement (brieviary and missal), and in the Diocesan Calendar of the bishopric of Bâle (17 April); "but that certainly did not imply any declaration of the truth of the whole contents of the story of his life, but merely a permission of its use in the breviary or choir prayer. It is altogether not forbidden Catholic knowledge, to test the correctness of the historical part of the breviary" (269).—All later mentions go back to the Chronicles of Konrad Justinger, who died in 1426. The Jews

* His predecessors in correctly judging the affair were *J E. Kopp*, "Geschichte der eidgenössischen Bünde" II., 399; *W Fetscherin* (in "Abhandlungen des histor. Vereins des Kantons Bern" II. (1851) 61 sq.; *G. Studer* (in "Archiv des histor. Vereins von Bern" 1863, 536); and *C. v. Wattenwyl* ("Geschichte der Stadt u. Landschaft Bern" I., 146, Schaffhausen 1867).

were alleged to have horribly martyred and murdered the boy Ruof in the house and cellar of the rich Jew, Jöli. "Die morder wurdent gevangen, ein Teil uf reder gesetzet, die andren usgeslagen und wart da einhellenklich von einer gemeinde bern gelopt und verheissen, daz kein jude niemerme gan bern komen solte" ("The murderers were caught, some broken on the wheel, the others banished, and it was there unanimously sworn and proclaimed by a meeting of the Bernese community, that no Jew should ever again come to Berne.") King Rudolph of Habsburg is said to have waxed very wroth about it, and to have appeared before Berne with an army of 30,000 men at the end of May in the same year, 1288. But the real cause of the King's wrath was the refractoriness of the town, and the dealings of Berne with Savoy, which were dangerous to the kingdom. The King repeatedly besieged the town in 1288 without, however, taking it; his son, Duke Rudolph, defeated the Bernese in 1289, and peace was concluded in the same year. "The Jewish persecution narrated by Justinger" was "not even a complementary cause" of the fighting, "and indeed for the simple reason that the persecution can be proved to have taken place only later on" (284). The Bernese quarrel with the Jews, and the murdering of the child belong, according to the original documents, to the year 1294, i.e. to the time of King Adolphus of Nassau. A boy of the name of Rudolph was found dead in the year mentioned, and public opinion accused the Jews of having killed him out of hatred for Christians. The man Jöli, described by Justinger as the chief criminal, appears alive in the original documents of June and December, 1294, so he was not broken on the wheel; there is also nothing recorded about the execution of one or several other Jews. The words "ut dicitur" (as people say) in the quittance of the magistrate of

December, 1294, prove "that no judicial finding of guilty took place, and accordingly also doubtless no breaking on the wheel" (293 sq.). Moreover, the contemporary annals of Kolmar for the year 1294 merely announce: "As people say, the Jews of Berne killed a boy," and King Albert, in the year 1300, speaks only about "excesses which, as people say, have been perpetrated by the Jews." In 1294 the Jews were maltreated by the Bernese before 30th June. The Jews turned to their liege-lord, King Adolphus. The judgment of his ambassadors said nothing about the guilt of the Jews, did not especially mention the death of the boy, but levied a heavy money-bail on the Jews: they were obliged to remit all debts of all the inhabitants of Berne, and pay besides to the community 1,000 silver marks, to the magistrate 500 silver marks (according to the present value of money about £4,000 and £2,000). This can only be explained if it was not a question of blood-guiltiness, but bitterness prevailed owing to the fact that very many persons owed the Jews money (297).—Not before the 18th century comes the statement of *J. R. v. Waldkirch*, "Einleitung zu der eidgenössischen Bundes-und Staatshistorie" (Bâle, 1721), I., 135, that the Jews "crucified" the child, and *J. Lauffer*, "Beschreibung helvetischer Geschichte" (Zurich, 1736), III., 108, is the first to know that the Jews "distilled all his blood out of him, in order to practice their damnable superstition!"

1303. *Weissensee*, in Thuringia. The contemporary Presbyter, Siegfried von Klein-Balnhausen, "Monum. Germ. hist. Script.," xxv., 717 relates that the Jews before the Passover had drawn all the blood out of a schoolboy named Konrad, after opening all his veins, and put him to a cruel death. No further proof of the guilt of the Jews apart from the miracles (the Jews are supposed not to have been able to bury the corpse, etc.) is brought forward. There was no judicial investigation; but on the 14th March the Jews were nevertheless slaughtered in heaps ("turmatim.") The Nuremberg Register has preserved the 120 names, v. Salfeld 59. 215-17. The Jews in other parts of Thuringia, with the exception of the town of Erfurt, were visited by the persecution of that period. Cf. *Oesterr. Wochenschr.* 1899, No. 49, p. 929 sq.

1305. *Prague (Osservatore Cattolico* wrongly "1325.") Crucifixion of a Christian at Easter time. Oldest authority: Johannes Dubravius, who wrote two and a half centuries later, in his history of Bohemia. In this case, too, the rabble, without waiting for judicial proceedings on the King's part ("non expectato judicio regis") put the Jews to death in a horrible fashion ("exquisitissimis suppliciis.") These hasty proceedings become comprehensible, when it is considered that Wenceslaus II. (1283-1305) had confirmed Ottokar II.'s Jewish Ordinance a few years before, and therefore no condemnation of the Jews without proofs was to be expected from him. If the accusation was well-founded, it was a question of one of the crucifixions mentioned supr. p. 125 out of hatred against Christ ("odio Christi.")

1317. The Jews of *Chinon* (in Touraine) complained to the French Parliament that four of them had been arrested and tortured because of a suspicion they were guilty of a child's death. Two of them, under force of torture ("vi tormentorum,") had confessed, and been hung; two had resisted, and were still in prison. The Parliament named plenipotentiary commissaries of investigation (*Boutaric*, "Actes du Parlement," II., No. 4827, 5 May, 1317). The investigation quickly took place, and led to the arrest of a number of Christian men and women, who had come to be suspected of being the real murderers (ibid. No. 4936, 12

July, 1317). "In order to determine the commissaries to these arrests they had to have very strong evidence; above all the innocence of the Jews had to appear quite clear to them," *Molinier*, "Cabinet Historique," new series II. (Paris, 1884), 127.

1329. Savoy. Children had disappeared in Geneva, Rumilly, Annecy, and elsewhere. A Christian, Jaquet, of Aiguebelle, was under suspicion; when arrested he admitted the kidnapping, but declared that he had sold them to some Jews through the medium of a Jew called Acelin, of Tresselve. Acelin confessed voluntarily ("sponte,") i.e. according to the language of that period, "after the first degree of torture," he had resold five children to his co-believers, Jocetus (Jose) and Aquinetus (Isaac). These, he said, had killed the children, and compounded out of their heads and entrails a salve or food, "aharace,"* so as to give some of it to all the Jews; "and the Jews eat of this food at every Passover instead of a sacrifice ("loco sacrificii,") and prepare it at least in every sixth year," because they believe they are saved thereby ("credunt se esse salvatos.") The accusation was soon levelled also against the Jews of other parts, in fact, throughout the whole of Savoy. Count Edward of Savoy thereupon set on foot a thorough investigation of the matter. This led to the result that the accusations were heaped upon the Jews by deliberate misrepresentations and deceptions on the part of some adversaries of theirs, so that they might be robbed of their property, contrary to God and justice," v. *H. Hildesheimer* in *Jüd. Presse*, 1892, No. 18, p. 211, and *Oesterreich. Wochenschrift*, 1899, No. 51, p. 963, and Edward's whole original documents of 20 July, 1329, in *Stern*, "Beiträge," I., 7-14.

* i.e., "ḥaroseth," the sauce, in which the bitter herbs (endive, etc.) were dipped on the first Passover Evening.

1332. *Ueberlingen* (in the present Grand-Duchy of Baden). A boy was found dead in a well. John of Winterthur relates in his Chronicles,* that the parents had "observed by definite surmises and clear proofs, especially by incisions in the bowels and veins, that he had been killed by the Jews." In addition to this proof occurred "the renewed flowing of wounds when he was carried in front of the Jews' houses." The Jews (as is said, more than 300), were enticed together into a house, and this was set fire to from below, without consulting the Emperor Ludwig [1314-47] and without paying attention to the judgment of his Imperial Governor." Cf., besides, *Oesterr. Wochenschr.* 1899, No. 51, p. 964 sq.

1345. Munich. It can only be gathered from Rader's "Bavaria sancta" that the lacerated body of the boy Heinrich was found, and the guilt for the deed was laid on the Jews. Nothing is said about using the blood, and as little about a judicial investigation. Even John von Winterthur (Wyss, 232; Freuler, 334), relates that Ludwig, the Bavarian, forbade worship of the boy.

1462. *Rinn.* The boy Andreas Oxner, of Rinn, near Innsbruck, is said to have been sold by his godfather to Jewish merchants, to have been cruelly killed by them on the "Jew-stone" ("Judenstein,") in the neighbouring birch-wood; they had carefully, it is alleged, collected the blood in vessels. *Adrian Kembter*, "Acta pro veritate martyrii corporis et cultus publici B. Andreae Rinnensis," Innsbruck, 1745; *J. Deckert*, "Vier Tiroler Kinder, Opfer des chassidischen Fanatismus," Vienna, 1893, 87-119; also a

* "Johannis Vitodurani Chronicon," published by G. v. Wyss, Zurich 1856, 106sq.—"Die Chronik Johann's von Winterthur," done into German by *B. Freuler*, Winterthur 1866, 145-7.—In regard to the date (J. v. W. says "1331"), cf. *M. Stern*, "Die israelitische Bevölkerung der deutschen Städte; I., Ueberlingen am Bodensee," Frankf. a. M. 1890, 3 sq.

bibliography in *Daumer* II., 263. The tradition was not committed to writing before the beginning of the 17th century, and then especially by the physician Hippolyt Guarinoni, in Hall, who died in 1654. He also found beneath the wall decoration, dating from 1575, near the pulpit in the Rinn Church, pieces of an older inscription, in which the Jews are indeed accused of the murder, but there is nothing said about the extracton of blood. That the inscription cannot be regarded as historic in the strict sense of the word, is clear from the two following statements contained in it: that the money given to the godfather changed into leaves, and a lily grew on the child's grave. There was no judicial examination into the facts of the case; nothing is even said of an inspection of the corpse by the authorities. The Jews are said to have bought the child on their return to their homes, on the pretext that one of them wanted to adopt him. But how, then, is it intelligible that they did not delay the sacrifice, which took up time on account of the collecting of the blood, till they had crossed the boundary which was near at hand? The careful reader may perceive even in Deckert's excessively biassed account that a "ritual murder" is nothing less than proved.

1468, Regensburg, v. 1476.

1474, *Regensburg*. *C. Th. Gemeiner*, "Regensburgische Chronik," III. (Regensburg, 1821), 532 sq., narrates as follows, according to the official documents: "A master of the Jews [Judenmeister] living here, too, Israel, of Prunn [Brünn], was acquitted of such inhuman dealing. For a time there were only rumours about it in the community, till it was said aloud that Hans Veyol, a baptized Jew, had really asserted about the Judenmeister and himself given information that he had sold him a boy seven years old. Then nobody doubted any more that the lawless deed had truly been done." As King

Wladislaus pronounced from Prague and the Emperor from Nuremberg a very decided prohibition of Israel's execution, the council resolved to try again the baptised Jew, about whom it was probable that he had only made such assertions through hatred of Israel, and who was destined to the death penalty on account of other crimes. This man, "in the certain expectation of death, confirmed his earlier statements [about his own crimes], and he only recalled the accusation brought against the master of the Jews, and declared him innocent. His recantation was the more readily believed, since, in spite of all searching, nobody had been able to discover the parents from whom the child was said to have been stolen."

1475 Murder of Simon of *Trent*, a child of two and a half years, on Good Friday night. Bibliography: "Acta Sanctorum, March IX," 24 March; Bonelli, "Dissertazione apologetica sul martirio del Beato Simone da Trento," Trent, 1747; *Civiltà Cattolica*, 1881, sq.: Onody, 83-99; Rohling, "Meine Antworten," 58-80, 96-101; Desportes, 132-63; *J. Deckert*, "Ein Ritualmord. Aktenmässig nachgewiesen,"[3] Dresden, 1893 (39); *J. Deckert*, "Vier Tiroler Kinder, Opfer des chassidischen Fanatismus. Urkundlich dargestellt," Vienna, 1893, 1-72.—I here use the results of the archival researches of *Dr. Moritz Stern*. Trent, 1475, and Damascus, 1840, are the two chief bulwarks of the blood-accusations, when it is a question of proof by adducing "historical facts." But unjustifiably, because both in Trent and in Damascus the confessions desired by the examiners, but untrue, were extorted by torture. All Jews were for several days subjected to inhuman torments, and only confessed after repeated torturing, increased in agony each time. Bishop Hinderbach, of Trent, admitted this himself in his letters to the Pope.

The assertion that a ritual murder in the proper

sense of the phrase, i.e. a murder for procuring Christian blood to be ritually used, took place, is proved impossible merely by the date of Simon's death. The Jewish Passover in 1475 fell on Maundy Thursday, 23rd March, so it began on the evening of 22nd March. The partaking of the "mazza" (the unleavened Easter bread) and the four cups of wine is prescribed by the religious law precisely for that initiating evening, the so-called "Seder" evening. But the boy first disappeared on Maundy Thursday, and so the charge states, was murdered on Good Friday night. How on earth could the Jews on the 22nd March bake into the Easter bread and put in the wine the blood of the boy who was staying in his parents' house, still hale and unharmed? And, after all, according to the accusation confirmed by "confession," they were obliged to have "*fresh* Christian blood" precisely in that year as in a year of Jubilee! Incidentally: The year 1475 was celebrated with quite extraordinary pomp by Pope Sixtus IV. as "annus jubilei," but since the destruction of Jerusalem in 587 B.C. the Jews have no longer commemorated the Year of Jubilee (Leviticus xxv.) Thus have the accusers made constructive charges arising out of their own peculiar point of view, and then had them confirmed by the Jews by means of torture!

About the kind of torture practised, the documents, which Hinderbach sent to Rome for his justification, and therefore prepared for publication, afford even then more than sufficient revelation (Vienna, Codex, 5360):

> *On 30th March, Samuel, the most respected of the incarcerated Trent Jews, was "tried" for the first time; at the conclusion he was led back to prison "in order to recover" ("animum repetendi," i.e. in the judicial language of that age, he had fainted). The following day he is stripped naked, bound hand and*

foot, and drawn up high by a rope, so that his limbs, drawn down by the weight of the body, were wrenched out of their sockets. As he protests his own and the other Jews' innocence, he gets "una cavaleta," a "jump," i.e. he was quickly let drop, in order that he might be pulled up again equally quickly; they then "move," i.e. strike the tense-stretched rope on which he was hanging, and made him "jump" several times more. A swoon prevents the continuation.

Torture is resumed on 3rd April, and first of all, with the repetition of all the grades already applied. As he asseverates he can pledge his word for the innocence both of himself and of all Jews, the rope is "vigorously moved," and he is made to "jump" twice from twice the height of his arms. Run up again, the poor wretch cries: "Where has your Worship learnt that Christian blood has importance and use for us?" The reply is, he had learnt it from other Jews like Samuel† The "jumping" procedure is then twice repeated, each time twice or thrice the height of his arms, and as even this martyrdom does not force any confession he is let float up aloft for two-thirds of an hour, till a swoon again overpowers his senses.*

The fourth day of torture (7th April) begins with a repetition of the previous grades. As Samuel not only disputed any guilt, but called out: "Were I to

* "Corda fuit pluries squassata." Innsbruck "Akten"; "also rueret man das sail ettwas vill." (Lit. "then one moves the rope rather much."—Trlr.).

† "Quod didicerat illud a Judaeis similibus sicut ipse Samuel," i.e., from the statements procured by torture in previous trials. This answer of the city prefect, who was conducting the examination, confirms what is established by other documents (Cf. "Archiv für katholisches Kirchenrecht," vol. 50, p. 46), that Bishop Hinderbach furnished the protocols connected with other trials. No wonder that the confessions of the Trent Jews partly tallied with those of their companions in suffering in other trials.

confess I had done any evil, I should be lying," they tied to his leg as he floated in the air a piece of wood (which wrenched the limbs yet further apart and substantially increased the pains); next they took an iron pan filled with burning material, on which sulphur was thrown, and held it under his nose. In spite of the stinking sulphur gas, fatal to all breathing and feeling, and the pressure of interrogations ("cum pluries interrogaretur,") he abides by his denial of any guilt. Accordingly they "move" the rope several times, and thereupon tie the piece of wood between the shin bones (whereby the weight became yet heavier, and the pain greater), and let the poor wretch hang thus for a quarter of an hour. When the "jumping" process was now again repeated, Samuel's power of resistance was broken; he "confesses" that he and Tobias "put a pocket-handkerchief round the boy's neck and drew it tight, so that the boy was strangled." Apart from this "statement," which directly contradicts the accusation of extracting blood, nothing could be got out of him. When the question is put to him, how and by whom the wounds were inflicted on the boy, he declares he knows nothing.

There is now a pause of nearly two months in Samuel's "examination." During this interval occur the torturings and "confessions" of the rest of the Jews, which now form the basis for his further interrogation. About the 6th June the protocols concerning Samuel only report about the first degrees of the torture (stripping, binding, hoisting up); but as they add that he was taken back into the prison "animum repetendi," the tortures must have been substantially greater. He probably RECANTED *already on 6th June his "*CONFESSION*"* OF 8TH APRIL, *as he did on 7th June. The protocols report verbatim as follows regarding the tortures on this day:—*

"*In the torture chamber. When invited to tell the truth, since he did not need to hide* WHAT ALL HIS ACCOMPLICES HAD ALREADY ADMITTED, *he replies that* IF THEY HAVE ADMITTED ANYTHING, THEY HAVE NOT SPOKEN THE TRUTH. *As the aforesaid town-prefect had been told that the drinking of* HOLY WATER *brings to confession rogues who do not wish to confess, he gave Samuel a spoonful of such water. Then being invited to tell the truth, he said he had told it. Whereupon two* BOILING HOT EGGS *were taken and put under his armpits. Once more invited to tell the truth, he answered he was willing to tell it; he wished that only the Hon. City Captain, and the Hon. City Prefect should be present at his* CONFESSION. *The captain and prefect then ordered all those present to leave the torture-chamber, and Samuel now declared, as the Captain afterwards informed me, the Notary, that he was willing to speak the truth,* ON CONDITION *that the captain and the prefect* PROMISED *him* TO HAVE HIM BURNT, AND NOT TO PUT HIM TO ANY OTHER DEATH."

The report speaks a deeply-moving language: although Samuel learns that his companions in suffering have already confessed, he disputes any guilt till the abominable tortures force him to acknowledge the hopelessness of further resistance, the certainty of fresh, augmented martyrdom, and place him at the disposal of his tormentors. In dull resignation he has but one wish, to be liberated by the quickest death possible from his agonies, which had now lasted almost four months and a half: after all it had been promised him that he would ONLY *(!) be burnt!*

At first he only makes the "confession" to the two officials named; he then, we assume, repeats it to a third party (Odoricus de Brezio), whilst he only says to the other councillors, who have been recalled to the torture-chamber, "he WANTED *to tell the truth." Since the*

Captain and the prefect, however, saw that he "was well disposed to tell the truth," they did not make him do so immediately on the spot, as he is said to have done a short time before; but he is brought into the City Captain's house, and there he is said to have delivered his "confession," "sitting on a kind of cathedra,"† before a number of witnesses. In spite of his self-accusations his torturers were not yet satisfied; because he is again "tried" on 11th June, again in the City Captain's house. He is invited "to tell the truth* BETTER,"‡ *whilst he is threatened with a hoisting on the rope in case he does not tell the truth. Samuel answers he wants to tell the truth; after confessing to the murder of the boy, he would also confess the rest.—Further denials would have been futile in the position of affairs, would only have resulted in a renewal and enhancing of the tortures, and accordingly he "confesses" everything they want to hear from him. On 21st June the poor wretch was burnt.*

Thus do the documents of the proceedings, the documents PREPARED *by Bishop Hinderbach for submission to Rome, describe the manner in which the "declaration" of Samuel, the chief accuser, was compassed! And* ALL *the other victims in this tragedy were treated likewise, even those who let themselves be baptized. Typical of it is what Israel, the son of the Mohar from Brandenburg, has certified. The latter was taken prisoner on 27th March, was tortured from 12th to 21st April, desired baptism on 21st April, is set free in consequence and is now called Wolfkan (Wolfgang). But on 26th October he is again imprisoned, repeatedly tortured from then till 11th January, 1476, and on 19th January broken on the wheel. This*

* "Bene dispositus ad dicendum veritatem."

† "Dum sederet super quadam cathedra."

‡ "Quod melius dicat veritatem."

subsequent punishment accrued to him because he bore witness at Roveredo before the Papal Legate, the Bishop of Ventimiglia, about the torturing of the accused Trent Jews. At his "examination" at Trent, on 23rd November, 1475, Wolfgang says he answered the aforesaid bishop's inquiry: "That fire with sulphur was held under his (Wolfgang's) nose, by which his face was burnt . . . and that the other Jews were tortured in many ways, that fire with sulphur was held under their noses, so that their faces and breasts were burned, and that boiling-hot eggs were placed under their armpits."

The Jews had already in this first trial pointed to the Swiss Zanesus as the murderer. This man had lost a lawsuit against his neighbour Samuel, and was therefore a mortal enemy of the Jews. In the second trial, conducted at Sixtus IV.'s command, by G. B. dei Giudici, Bishop of Ventimiglia, at Trent and Roveredo, in 1476, Anzelinus, too, a citizen of Trent, accused Zanesus of the murder. It was besides established, firstly, that the "confessions" of the Jews were only forced from them by cruel torturings, secondly, that the clerks of the court of Bishop Hinderbach in Trent had committed gross forgeries. At the third trial, which took place in Rome in 1477-8, the guilt of the Jews was not the point of issue, but only the question whether the first trial had been conducted with formal regularity. To save the face of Bishop Hinderbach the Pope, on a bed of sickness, allowed himself on 20th June, 1478, to be implored into giving the decision that "processum *ipsum* recte factum," i.e. the trial as such. In the same document, however, he ordered the bishop to take heed, that no Christian should venture, on account of the Trent episode, or for any other reason, to kill any Jew without permission of the authorities, or to mutilate or to wound or unjustifiably to extort money from them, or to hinder them from continuing to observe their rites which were allowed by law ("ritus suos a jure permissos continuare.") The ritual of the Jews is here positively placed under Papal protection, which is again a proof that the Pope considered the Jews innocent who were done to death on account of the boy Simon. The careful reader can recognise that this was the state of the case, even in Deckert's biassed account.

The fact that Pope Sixtus V., more than a century later, in 1588, allowed the Mass in honour of Saint Simon, proves nothing as to the guilt of the Jews; from the standpoint of the Roman Catholic Church this permission seems justified by the miracles which were admitted by the Church. Similar proceedings took place in respect of the boy Lorenzino of Marostica (ob. 1485), v. "Bullen," 113 (note by *M. Stern*).

1476. *Regensburg. Gemeiner* III., 567 sq. Proceedings arising from the Trent "confessions," because of a murder which the Regensburg Jews are supposed to have committed eight years previously, i.e. 1468. New light is thrown upon it, and consequently upon the Trent occurrences, by *A. Osiander*, 22 sq. (for title v. Ch. 19 E): "So too, many years ago at Regenspurg, in the case of seventeen Jews, and among them the most respected and wealthy, it had to be acknowledged that they had never done [the deed], and when the commissaries of His Imperial Majesty had heard the evidence, they came to the conclusion that one of the Jews, namely Jossel Jud, on the day, on which he was said to have committed the murder at Regenspurg, had indisputably been at Landsshut, engaged in great and important business with, and in the presence of, the same commissaries, and so it was discovered, that everything the seventeen Jews had confessed was untrue, and had simply been extorted by threats and violence." Jossel was the chief of the accused, and had described himself as a murderer, under torture.

1490. The child at *Guardia*, near Toledo. Isidor Loeb, "Le saint enfant de la Guardia" (in "Revue des Etudes Juives," xv., Paris, 1887, 203-32) points out, that there was no search either for the remains of the body nor for the clothing of the child, nor for the instruments of the crime, also that neither the place nor the time of the crime have been established; there was not even an inquiry whether a child had really disappeared. In the same sense *Henry Charles Lea*, "El santo nino de la Guardia." (in *The English Historical Review*, IV. [London, 1889] 239-50). Loeb and Lea follow the work of the Jesuit Father *Fidel Fita*, which is based on careful study, "El Proceso y Quema de Jucé-Franco (in "Boletin de la Real Academia de la Historia," xi., July-September, 1887, Madrid).

1494. *Tyrnau. Anton Bonfin*, "Rerum Hungaricarum decades," Decad V., Book 4, Edition of C. A. Bel, Leipsic, 1771, 728:

"*In the same months several Jews of Tyrnau suffered the penalty they deserved. Twelve men and two women strangled a Christian youth of high rank, whom they had secretly caught and brought into the nearest house, and drew his blood from him whilst he was dying, by opening his veins. This blood they partly drank at once, partly kept for others; the body, which was cut to pieces, they buried. As the youth did not make his appearance, and it was sufficiently established that he was last seen on the previous day in the Jews street, a judicial examination is set on foot against the Jews. The servants of justice sent into the house find fresh traces of blood, and arrest the master with his whole family. The women, dragged to judicial examination, confess, under compulsion of the fear of torture (" metu tormentorum adactae "), the whole story of the extremely unworthy deed. Through their evidence the rest are convicted, and then they are all burnt, at the command of the Count Palatine, who was the chief authority of the town, after a big wood-pile had been raised for the purpose in the market-place; others, who seemed less guilty, were mulcted in a large sum of money. When the reasons for the perpetration of such a horror were ascertained from the old men by the agony of tortures ("per tormentorum cruciatum"), it was found there were four reasons why the Jews at Tyrnau at that time and elsewhere had often made themselves guilty in a criminal way. Firstly: They were convinced by the judgment of their ancestors that the blood of a Christian was a good remedy for the alleviation of the wound of circumcision. Secondly: They were of opinion that this blood, put into food, is very efficacious for the awakening of mutual love. Thirdly: They had discovered, as* MEN *and women among them suffered equally from* MENSTRUATION, *that the blood of a Christian is a specific medicine for it, when drunk. Fourthly: That they had an ancient but secret ordinance by which they are under obligation to shed Christian blood in honour of God in daily sacrifices in some spot or other; they said it had happened in this way that the lot for the present year had fallen on the Tyrnau Jews."*

Bonfin is, so far as I know, the only Christian authority.* No examination of witnesses. The men in their prime and the youths confess nothing; the fear of torture opens only the women's mouths, the torture itself opens the old men's mouths. And the

A Hebrew elegy on an empty sheet of a Hebrew MS. in Cracow bewails the death of the innocent slain, cf. *S. Kohn*, "A Zsidók Története Magyarországon" [History of the Jews in Hungary] I., Budapesth, 1884, 241-4. Had a ritual extraction of blood taken place, the poet, who was sure no Christian would read his verses, would have boasted of the fact.

confessions thus extorted are so silly, contain partially such impossible stuff * that one recognises that the accused spoke what was expected to be heard from them; they thought an end of terror was better than a terror without end. In a very large number of cases of "blood-accusation," the sequence of events, alas! is simply as follows: A Christian child is murdered or has vanished; no witness is in a position to state anything; suspicion is directed against the hated Jews; the suspicion suffices to raise the accusation; the accused are tortured, and at length confess, preferring any death, however, painful, to the agonies which are worse than death. *Such judicial transactions yield no proofs of the positive occurrence of ritual murders.*

1504. *Frankfort a. M.* A shoemaker, Henrich Bry (also called Henrich Bry's son) beat his step-child with leather thongs, so that it died. Immediately at the first hearing he made a candid confession; also at the second he confessed, likewise without torture, that he was the murderer, but added that he had stabbed the child, gathered the blood in a vessel, and taken it to the Jew Gompchen (who had lent him money against security). The latter even under torture asserted he knew naught of the deed, and begged, but in vain, to be conducted to the evil-doer, that he might confront him eye to eye. The latter's guilt was then made evident by the statement of the

And yet the Bollandist, Gottfried Henschen ("Acta Sanctorum," April II., 501, Paris 1866) give these four confessions according to Bonfin, as the grounds why the infamous Jews commit murders of children! What impossible and at the same time horrible statements have been wrung by *torture*, can be seen especially in the ghastly instances afforded by trials of witches (intercourse of female werewolves and witches with the devil, etc.); Cf. e.g., *De l'Ancre*, "Tableau de l'inconstance des Mauvais Anges," Paris 1613, and *Boquet*, "Tableau des Sorciers," Lyons 1608 (some extracts in *W. Hertz*, "Der Werwolf," Stuttgart 1862, 100 sq.); *W. G. Soldan*, "Geschichte der Hexenprozesse," Stuttgart 1843; *Jakob Sprenger* and *Heinrich Institoris*, "Malleus maleficarum," passim.

servant; Gompchen acquitted. A few days before his sentence was pronounced, the criminal admitted having falsely accused the Jew, and repeated this again a short time before his execution. *L. Neustadt*, "Eine Blutbeschuldigung in Frankfurt a. M. im J. 1504. Auf Grund der Prozess-Akten des Frankfurter Stadt-Archivs," Magdeburg, 1892 (26).

1529. Pösing in Hungary, ritual murder of a kidnapped boy. *Osservatore Cattolico* and Desp., following Eisenmenger, wrongly: "1509." Onody, 103-7, relates the case in detail according to a very old printed sheet of eight pages: "Ain erschrockenlich geschicht vnd Mordt, so von den Juden: zu Pösing, ain Marckt, in Hungern gelegen: an ainem Neünjärigen Knäblin beganngen, wie sy das jämerlich gemarttert, geslagen, gestochen, geschnitten, vnd ermördt haben: Darumb dann bis in die Dreyssig juden, mann und weybs personen vmb jr misshanndlung, auf Freytag nach Pfingsten, den xxi. tag May, des M.D.vnd xxix. Jars, verbrennt worden seind," and the *Staatsbürger-Zeitung*, 1st July, 1892, No. 302, did the same.—"After enduring the agonies of torture [I quote from Onody verbatim], the tortured ones at last confessed," one "that they sucked such blood out of the little child with quills and small reeds," another that they "afterwards took the blood into the synagogue, whereupon they had great rejoicing," a third "that the Jews must have Christian blood, wherewith Jews of the highest rank besmear themselves for their wedding feasts, and the Jews term such in Hebrew 'komandy (?) pentsche.'"—The fairly careful reader, on merely reading the above-mentioned account, must feel extremely doubtful as to the credibility of the statements made. In this case, however, we do not require any internal evidence for the *valuelessness of confessions extracted by torture: the child alleged to have been slaughtered by the Jews was stolen by the prosecutor himself, and later on was discovered alive.*

G. WOLF, "*Historische Skizzen aus Österreich-Ungarn,*" *Vienna, 1883, 296-8, fixes the actual circumstance according to the documents ("Examen vnd Vrtel vber die Juden zu Bösing in Ungarn") in the Imperial Finance Ministry at Vienna as follows: "Count Wolf of Bösing owed money to the Jew Esslein Ausch of that place, and besides to several Jews at Marchegg in Lower Austria. He wanted to free himself of those debts by getting his creditors out of the way. A pretext for doing the Jews an injury was soon found. Count Wolf induced an old, half-imbecile woman to leave B. with a Christian child not belonging to her. Whereupon . . . Count Wolf raised the charge against the Jews. . . . Esslein Ausch was taken in custody and tortured. . . . He declared everything they wanted him to say, among other things also, that the Jews in Marchegg were his accomplices. Thereupon all the Jews, who had not saved their lives by absconding, were burnt to death. Count Wolf then wanted to continue his work in Marchegg. The Jews then applied . . . to the Emperor Ferdinand, with the request that the matter should be looked into . . . Whilst the proceedings were going on, some Viennese Jews, who were travelling on business, discovered the woman and the boy who was alleged to have been murdered, whereupon the proceedings came to an end, as a matter of course. The fate that befel Count Wolf, even supposing anything happened to him, is not ascertainable from the documents here [in Vienna] deposited."—Cf. also the work of Andreas Osiander mentioned in Ch. 19 E.*

1764. *Orcuta*, in Hungary. The son of Joh. Balla, a boy of ten, is discovered dead in the brushwood on 25th June, "with the signs of ritual murder" (*Osservatore Cattolico.*) *Dr. S. Kohn*, of Budapesth, who some time ago went through the legal documents in the provincial archives, writes in a letter that was before me: "I remember well, that the *judges* in this trial were at last condemned, and that lengthy legal proceedings were instituted because of the child, who was forcibly converted in prison." Cf. also *P. Nathan*, "Tista-Eszlár," 29-31.

1791. *Tasnad*, in Translyvania. February. Murder of a boy of thirteen, Andreas Takal. Desportes and his copiers affirm that the guilty and condemned Jews were pardoned by Joseph II. [ob., 20th February, 1790!] At the Tisza-Eszlár trial the anti-semites produced documents to prove that in 1791 certain Jews were condemned to death, because they had murdered a Christian boy and extracted his blood. It resulted, however, from the findings of the courts of higher instance, that the Jews were finally acquitted, and the functionaries of the court of first instance were called to account for practising tortures, etc., v. *P Nathan*, "Tisza-Eszlár," 266.

1834. During the night of 13/14 July, a boy of six was murdered near *Neuenhoven*, in the Government district of Düsseldorf. "Circumstances came to light in connection therewith, which seduced a portion of the credulous mob with the delusion that the boy's blood had been drawn off in an outrageous manner, whence it was then further concluded that Jews and Jewish fanaticism had necessarily had something to do with it." In consequence of this, during the night of 20/21 July an attack was made by "a numerous crowd on the dwellings of two Jews living at Neuenhoven, and they were almost entirely laid waste together with the furniture and goods in them, whilst at the same time the Synagogue at Bedburdyk was stormed and likewise completely destroyed" (*Elberfelder Zeitung*, 26 July, No. 205). A few days after, on 26 July, a decree of the Kgl. Ober-Procurator at

Düsseldorf, proclaimed (*Amtsblatt der Kgl. Regierung zu Düsseldorf*, No. 48): "The murder of a child of Christian parents in the Grevenbroich district has awakened a superstition sprung from the barbarism of centuries long past, and occasioned wild deeds of violence against Jews living in the neighbourhood and the places of their religious gatherings.—The judicial establishment of the facts of the murder has completely banished any thought of the reality of the silly tale, and the ringleaders of the attacks directed against the Jews are in the hands of justice." Cf. the brochures of *Binterim* and *Wiedenfeld* (Ch. 19 E.)

1840. Murder of the Capuchin Father Thomas and his servant in *Damascus*, February. Chief work: *Achille Laurent*, "Relation historique des affaires de Syrie, depuis 1840 jusqu'en 1842, et la procédure complète dirigée en 1840 contre les Juifs de Damas," Paris, 1846, 2 vols. (After this: Pawlikowski, 284 sq.; Onody, 116 sq.; Rohling, "Meine Antworten," 84 sq.; Desportes, 188 sq., etc.) Achille Laurent was never a Professor, and is not to be confounded with Professor François Laurent, of Ghent, the Jurist and Historian. He asserts, II., 399: "As all documents referring to the proceedings taken against the Jews of Damascus are deposited with the Ministry for Foreign Affairs, the [possible] inaccuracy of the protocols, etc., in this part can be easily established." This assertion is either *untrue* (because the aforesaid Ministry, when L. wrote, allowed nobody to look into its archives; it is only since 1874 that permission has gradually been granted to use documents extending to 1830), or Laurent used the documents *illegally*. In either case his credibility may be regarded as open to suspicion. But even if the words are correctly reproduced, the correctness of the contents does not therefore follow, because the prejudice of the then French

Consul, Ratti-Menton, is universally admitted by those who have looked closely into the matter.—The confessions are forced from the accused by tortures equally barbaric and refined; two of the accused died in prison of their maltreatment. I particularly allude to the reports of the missionary *Pieritz*, a convert, who was sent to Damascus by the great London Jewish Mission Society, and who, as he says himself, was "in no respect a friend or defender of Rabbinism." "Persecution of the Jews at Damascus. Statement of Mr. G. W. Pieritz," London, 1840 (21), and his work addressed to the Jews of Alexandria on 13th May, 1840, in which it is said (v. *Löwenstimm*, "Damascia[2]," 203 sq., in which book there is still further material for the confutation of Laurent):

"*I will not here describe what my feelings were when at Damascus I found the whole charge against the Jews there a vile fabrication, that all means and right of legal defence was denied them, whilst the most cruel tortures were employed to extort from them false confessions of guilt, which some were cowards enough to make. . . . The tortures employed were—1st, flogging. 2nd, soaking persons in large tanks of cold water in their clothes. 3rd, the head machine by which the eyes are pressed out of their sockets. 4th, tying up the tender parts, and ordering soldiers to twist and horribly dispose them into such contortions that the poor sufferers grew almost mad from pain. 5th, standing upright for three days without being allowed any other posture, not even to lean against the walls, and when they would fall down, were aroused up by the sentinels with their bayonets. 6th, being dragged about in a large court by the ears until the blood gushed out. 7th, having thorns driven in between the nails and the flesh of fingers and toes. 8th, having set fire to their beards till their faces are singed. 9th, having candles held under their noses so that the flame arises up into their nostrils.*"

It may incidentally be remarked that Desportes's assertion, which he made twice, and which was repeated by others, to the effect that the documents disappeared during the time of the Crémieux Ministry, is untrue. An official document of the Ministry of Foreign Affairs of 5th May, 1892, says verbatim: "Les pièces concernant le meurtre du P. Thomas à Damas en 1840 n'ont nullement été dérobées ou détruites par Crémieux en 1870. Ces pièces se trouvent, en effet, complètes au ministère."

1844, On 17th April, the Jews of Tarnow addressed a petition to the Emperor Ferdinand of Austria, that he would oppose the blood-accusation which was continually being levelled against the Jews in Galicia. Out of this petition I extract the following according to *G. Wolf*, in Wertheimer's "*Jahrbuch für Israeliten*, 5623," Vienna, 1862, 30-9:

"*The first attempt of this kind was made by fanatics in 1829 in the village of* BOLESLAW *(in our district), on the river Weichsel. There came a girl and informed against the Jews dwelling there . . . that three weeks before the Jewish Easter holidays they bought her child off her for a fixed paid price, for the purpose of killing it and using its blood for the Easter festival. On the basis of this . . . charge the magistrate, without further examination, arrested four of the Jews mentioned, and chained them to the walls of the prison, and thus they languished for several weeks.*" *Then the accuser confessed* "*she had murdered her child with her own hands, through want of means to support it, and hid it in a pool, and by the advice of the provost of the place made her above-mentioned accusation. Thereupon the Commission went with this murderess to B., where, in the presence of the magistrate of the place, the child was drawn out of the depths of the pool, without any external injury, with a stone tied to its neck. The murderess was then condemned to the penalty she deserved. . . .*

"The second attempt was maliciously made in 1839 in the village of Niezdow, in the Bochnia district, where similarly a girl called S., who drowned her child in March of the same year, accused the Jews of the place . . . of a similar crime, the buying and murdering of the child for the Jewish Easter festival, before the magistrate, who, after undertaking a search through their houses, had them at once arrested and chained. The Government councillor at Bochnia being put in possession of the facts, at once appointed a criminal commission, whilst the innocently-suffering Jews were set free. The traducer was convicted of the murder of her own child, concerning which the legal documents in possession of the worthy district officer of Bochnia as well as of the Royal Imperial Court at Wisznia can give the authoritative proofs.

"On 25th March, 1844, W. Ritter von D., barrister of the Royal-Imperial District Court in these parts, brought the charge before the worthy magistrate here that he had gone from the village of Gtobikowka in the district into the Jews' street with an orphan boy, called J. G., who was in his service and was eight years old, and when he made the same wait for him there till he had made his purchase, this boy had disappeared in the Jews' street, and was already two days missing, whom the Jews had kidnapped in order to get blood from the same for their approaching Easter festival. In consequence of his information an official inquiry was ordered, which was undertaken on the evening of the same day at about 7 o'clock by many officials appointed for the purpose, the entrances and exits of the Jews' street being barred, in all the Jewish houses in the town and the nearest

neighbourhoods, with the help of 80 men of the military provided with loaded arms, besides the finance and police watches . . . in the course of which all rooms, chambers, cellars, chests and drawers were most strictly examined, and in several cellars even the earth was dug up. D., however, not yet satisfied with this, made charges in this connection also before the Imperial-Royal criminal court at Rzeszow, when he adduced as proof the bloody stories of the Damascus and other murders. This worthy penal court at once ordered an investigation. Ten days went by, and the boy had not yet been found. Hatred and demand for revenge became continually louder among the Christian public. We lived through an anxious time; disgrace and shame, fear and despair lay heavy upon us; full of care and anxiety we saw each day dawn, which showed us again there was no trace of the missing lad. We were scoffed at, and could not encounter a single Christian, however good friends he might be, without hearing reproaches about our cannibalistic methods. It was simply with a shudder that we looked forward to the approaching Easter Festival."

At last it was found possible to ascertain beyond doubt that the boy (who was, by the way, 12 not 8) had run away from D. owing to ill-treatment and bad food, and is bringing him back alive to Tarnow.

1873. *Enniger.* The (then) Berlin paper *Das Volk*, 13 March, 1892, No. 62, has the following information from Ravensberg: "So far as I know, a Jewish ritual murder or blood-murder has not hitherto been reported from Westphalia. But there has* already been such a one here. About 1860 or 1870 a young girl was murdered in the village of Enniger, near Ahlen. The Jews, of whom there was a large num-

* The word "has" should be noticed, in contradiction of the following "no proofs."

ber there, were universally accused of the deed. It was asserted the Jews wanted to use the blood of the girl, who had a reputation for genuine piety, for the consecration of the new synagogue [building sacrifice, v. supr. p. 31]. The judicial inquiry certainly produced no proofs of the charge; but public opinion spoke vigorously enough to drive all the Jewish families out of Enniger. The synagogue has never been used, and not only time, but also the hatred of the inhabitants, has treated it ill, as is related: horror dwells in the empty window-holes."—Attorney-General *Irgahn*, of Hamm, said in reply to my request for information about it, "that certainly an investigation was carried out on the part of the Royal Court at Münster on account of the murder of an unmarried person, Elizabeth Schütte, which was committed near Enniger on 23rd April, 1873. The person who did it was not discovered. The motive of the deed, however, is from the beginning not doubtful to the persons entrusted with the enquiry, and is exclusively to be found in the *satisfaction of the sexual appetite*."

1881. Franciska Mnich, alleged to have been murdered by the Jewish publican, Moses Ritter, and his wife in *Lutscha* (Galicia). The accused were acquitted by the supreme Court of Judicature. Cf. *J Rosenblatt*, "Prozess Ritter" (in *Das Tribunal. Zeitschrift für praktische Strafrechtspflege*, Vol. I. and II., Hamburg, 1885 and 1886).

1882. *Tisza-Eszlár*. On 14th April [Friday] there disappeared at Tisza-Eszlár, on the Theiss (Hungary), the young servant, Esther Solymosi. Suspicion turns against the Jews, several of whom are arrested by Bary, the investigating judge, who was only twenty years old. Moritz Scharf, the son of the temple servant, Joseph Scharf, declared at the first hearing that he did not know Esther, and likewise knew nothing about her disappearance;

at the second hearing he made precise statements about the alleged "religious butchering" of E. S. in the Synagogue, which he said he had observed through the keyhole, and this declaration he repeated on the first day of the trial, 19th June, 1883. But on the 17th July it was established by an inspection on the part of the court of the premises, that Moritz could not possibly have seen what he said he had. One of the judges said: "We ought to have begun with this inspection of the place of the deed; we should not then have needed to deal with the matter for five weeks." The verdict, which corresponded with the pleadings of the State Attorney and the defence was to the effect "that there was not the least ground for the assumption that E. S. had been murdered, and all the accused would be acquitted." This sentence was confirmed by both the courts of higher instance. A body which floated to the bank on 18th June, 1882, some twenty kils. below Tisza-Eszlăr was in all probability that of E. S. Cf. Paul Nathan, "Der Prozess von Tisza-Eszlár," Be., 1892 (416). Onody and Desportes, 212-43, wrote on the racial anti-semitic side.

1891. Corfu. In the night, between 12th and 13th April, a girl of eight was murdered. The magistrates have unfortunately omitted to publish an official report on the inquiry. It is usually asserted it was a Christian woman, Maria Desylla, who was murdered by Jews and deprived of her blood. It is in reality as good as certain that the murdered woman was called Rubina Sarda, and was a Jewess, the daughter of the Jewish tailor, Vita Chajim Sarda de Salomon; Cf. particularly the following document, which has lain before me in the original:

"CERTIFICAT: *Je, soussignée, religieuse institutrice de l'Ordre des Soeurs de Notre Dame de la Compassion de Marseille, actuellement au Couvent et Orphelinat de cet ordre établi à Corfou, certifie: Que la petite Rubina Sarda, Israélite, après autorisation préalable de sa Grandeur Monseigneur Boni, Archevêque latin de Corfou, a été admise dans la classe gratuite que je dirige, au commencement du mois de Juillet de l'anneé mil huit cent quatre-vingt-neuf (1889); qu'elle a quitté notre école au mois d'octobre de la même année, pour suivre, m'a t'on dit, les classes d'une école fondée vers cette époque, à Corfou, par le Gouvernement italien. Je déclare en outre: 1° que cette enfant, fille de père et de mère israélites, professait, à ma connaissance, la même religion que ses parents; 2° qu'elle a toujours été connue à l'école sous le nom de Rubina Sarda, et que, jamais je n'ai entendu parler d'une nommée Marie Desylla; 3° que ladite petite fille a toujours été très douce et très sage tout le temps qu'elle a fréquenté ma classe, et qu'enfin, elle n'a nullement manifesté le désir de changer de religion.—Et à la demande du Consul de France en cette ville, je signe le préscrit que j'affirme sincère et véritable. Corfou le 22 Juin, 1891. Signé: Joséphina Martin, en religion Soeur Marie Loetitia.*

Le consul de France à Corfou certifie véritable et bien conforme à l'original déposé aux archives de la Chancellerie, la copie de la déclaration çi-dessus.

Corfou, le 22nd Juin, 1891.

Le Consul de France,

(L. S.) (Signed) A. DANLOUX.

In a communication of M. Danloux to M. Pariente, the Director of the Israelite Schools in the Orient (Corfu, 23rd June, 1891), the murdered woman is expressly called Rubina Sarda, and the sentence occurs: "Nobody can tell me whence the name of Marie Desylla comes, about which it is asserted it was the victim's name."—On the respective side (known to me by a photograph) of the register, which is kept by the Rabbi in Corfu, there are nine entries, Nos.

28-36, in the period between 29 March till 18 April, 1883. No. 35, of 16th April, runs: "Rubina di Vita Sarda e Lucie Eliezer," i.e. Rubina, daughter of the [Chajjim] Vita Sarda and Lucie Eliezer.—Cf., too, M. HOROVITZ, "*Corfu,*" *Frankf. a. M., 1891 (15).*

1891. *Nagy-Szokol,* Tolna County, Hungary. Esther Fejes, a young servant of an Israelite, Jonas Grünfeld, disappeared in June. The charge of ritual butchery was raised, and as the father and the authorities searched for the girl in vain, Grünfeld was put under police supervision. Half-a-year later Esther was seen at Buda-Pesth by another girl from Nagy-Szokol, and told her she had left her home secretly because her parents did not live at peace and her mother had taken all her money away. Besides, a strange gentleman had persuaded her she should not remain at the Jew's, else it would happen to her as it did to Esther Solymosi; and he had given her ten gulden for travelling expenses. She was now in service at Moritz Fischl's, Karls-Ring 17. *Oesterr. Wochenschrift,* 1892, No. 3, p. 40, following the *Magyar Hirlap* of 7th January.

1891. *Xanten* (Rhine province). Cf. "Der Xantener Knabenmord vor dem Schwurgericht zu Cleve, 4-14 July, 1892. Vollständiger stenographischer Bericht," Be., 1893 (509).* On the evening of Monday, 29th June, the corpse of a boy of five and a half years, Johann Hegmann, was found with a gaping wound in his neck on loose-lying chaff in the barn belonging to a publican, Küppers. In connection with the fact ("Report," 384) that the medical practitioner, Dr. Jos. Steiner, in the protocol of the inspection of the corpse, which was drawn up on the

* The three defending barristers corroborate the trustworthiness of this report in prefatory autographic writing, and the three shorthand writers similarly give assurance that they have worked reliably to the best of their ability.

evening of 29 June, had written, "The trace of blood appears as an after-bleeding," it was declared in wide circles that undoubtedly a Jewish ritual murder had been perpetrated for the sake of obtaining blood, and people soon talked also about a Jewish butcher's cut ("Schächterschnitt," Cf. supr. p. 108). Some of the inhabitants threw suspicion on the butcher and former "Schächter" of the Jewish community, Adolf Buschhoff. Firstly, as far as concerns the species of the neck-wound, it was irrefutably established that there could be no serious question of a "Schächterschnitt," by the protocol of the dissection ("Report," 461 seq.) prepared on 30th June by the district physician, Dr. Bauer (Mörs), and the district surgeon, Dr. Nünninghoff (Orsow), and by the expert report (478 sq.) drawn up by the medical college at Coblenz on 4th April, 1892: "The cut was not prolonged below the Adam's apple, the knife was applied much higher up—namely, in the region of the upper margin of the Adam's apple. Thus the air-pipe was not only divided, but the cut went also—which is expressly forbidden under penalty in the "Schächterschnitt"—through the gullet instead of through the œsophagus. . . . Further, whilst the "Schächter" so conducts his cut as to cut evenly through the soft parts on both sides of the neck, we see that in the case before us all the soft parts on the right side were divided up to the spinal column; whilst on the left side, on the other hand, not even the sterno-cleido-mastoid muscle and the big blood-vessels were touched. Next, the "Schächter" carefully avoids penetrating with his knife into the spine, so as not to injure the spinal marrow. Here the cut had pierced two centimetres deep into the spine ("Report," 488, cf. 48). Cf. also the declaration of the Prussian Minister of Justice in the Chamber of Deputies in Berlin on 9th February, 1892: "The manner of the cutting of the throat [was] not such as is observed in the butchering of animals according to Jewish ritual." It was further proved beyond doubt that the place of discovery (Küppers' barn) was also the place of the deed ("Report" 40, 45), so that the child could not have been killed in Buschhoff's house. Thirdly, it was settled beyond any doubt that so much blood was found in the chaff under the body, on and in the body of the murdered boy, and in his clothes, that there was not the very least ground for assuming that any blood had been removed.* Cf. "Report" 39-48, 388, 478 sq. The Attorney-General Hamm declared: "It is therefore beyond dispute that the deed took place in the barn. That is established beyond the possibility of doubt. I shall lose no words about the initiatory and repeated remarks that a large amount of blood was missing, that there was only a little blood there, whereas there ought to have been a great deal more. Such remarks are all utterly confuted." Prof. Köster ("Report" 374) stated besides that the murderer would have plied his knife deeper if he had been concerned about obtaining blood. It seems to me Dr. Steiner's statement before the Court on 9th July was especially important. "On 29th June [1891] I was . asked to take up the case of the finding of the corpse. I could not then touch the wounds more particularly; I could only look at them. I could also not undress the body, etc. It was dark at that time, 9 o'clock at night, and the inspection of the corpse took place by the light of a petroleum lamp. . . . The experts have now . . . explained to me how much blood a man has altogether, and how much he can lose so as to bleed to death; I have also learnt the opinion of the experts about the chaff and earth, and have, for the first time, been able to inspect the clothes, as you

* *J. Marcus*, "Etude médico-légale du meurtre rituel," Paris 1900 (107 p.), pp. 22-48: Xanten; p. 49-76: Polna.

have here seen them. At that time I did not dare to take the clothes away. I have now come to the conviction that all the blood which the child could lose has been discovered, and . . . so it is a matter of course that the place of the discovery is also the place of the deed" ("Report" 297).

The Attorney-General Hamm, moreover, said in his pleading ("Report" 399): "It is proved that Buschhoff could not have done the deed, and the court must come to the conclusion to pronounce a sentence of 'not guilty' with regard to the accused." And the Chief Attorney Baumgard ("Report" 417): "I must observe that in my long experience of criminal cases no single instance has yet come to my notice in which there has been brought forward such clear, circumstantial proof that the accused cannot have perpetrated the deed as in this case." The Editor-in-Chief of the *Staatsbürger-Zeitung* (Berlin), O. Bachler, again disseminated at least four *deliberate untruths* when he allowed it to be stated on the 19th September, 1899, in No. 438 of his paper: "On 22 [read "29"] June, 1891, the bloodless [1] corpse of the boy Johann Hegemann [read "Hegmann"], of Xanten, was found behind the ground-property of the Jewish 'Schächter" [2], Buschoff [read "Buschhoff"], with a 'Schächtschnitt" [3] in his neck, whilst the blood, which had streamed away from the small body, was nowhere to be found [4]."

1892. *Eisleben.* As this case seems especially valuable to the *Osservatore Cattolico*, No. 8,454, and also the Leipsic anon. and others have made a fuss about it, I will, as far as possible, make the matter clear.

On 1st February, 1892, Herr G. Krüger, President of the Reform Association at Eisleben, held a discourse on "Rituelle Morde der Juden und der Knabenmord in Xanten." The EISLEBENER ZEITUNG *of 7th Febru-*

ary, 1892, No. 32, reported in regard to the discussion: "A citizen of our town, who had appeared as a guest, and well deserves his claim to credibility, stated. . . . that he had opportunity for keeping up intercourse with Jews during his sixteen years as a handicraftsman in a small town in Posen. The friendship between him and them became so intimate owing to their meeting every night, that he gladly and repeatedly accepted the Jews' invitations to accompany them into the temple. He was there handed by the Jews all kinds of dainties and sweet drinks. When he had visited the temple several times he received one Friday evening—it was the time before the Jewish festival—an invitation to accompany them again into the temple. The Jews who accompanied him there, first of all left him standing at the outer door, with a view to bringing him in later on. Scarcely had he approached nearer when he was informed that he would only then be allowed to stop in the temple any longer, if he was 'pure,' and that he must be subjected to a testing for the confirmation of the assumption. Then there immediately appeared an older Jew, who was hung round with a big white cloth, and wore a black head-gear, and he bade him strip his left arm. As he dreamt of no ill befalling him, he did what was desired of him. Hereupon the same Jew made a cut with a small sharp knife into the inner elbow joint of the guest, who is an Evangelical Christian, and collected the blood flowing from the wound in a vessel which already stood prepared, whilst during the operation the other Jews sang songs (certainly Hebrew) which were unintelligible to him. The wound caused was bound up, and healing followed in about eight to fourteen days. The scar can even now be seen[!]".

As *early as the next number (33, 9th February) there appeared a declaration signed "Walther Simon, Max Zweig," that these statements "rest upon lies. At* *any rate they may be referred to a morbid desire for bragging on the part of the person in question. We do not hesitate to pronounce the supporter of the Reform Association to be simply a malignant slanderer."*—THE STAATSBÜRGER-ZEITUNG, *No. 68 (10th February) introduced its report of the meeting with the words: "We are able in the following to bring forward a fresh example . . . as regards the question of ritual extraction of blood," and it remarked at the conclusion: "That was an occasion for two genuine Jews of those parts . . to publish a notice in which they represented the honourable citizen with truly Jewish shamelessness as 'a liar and malignant slanderer.' As the man who has been so grossly insulted will not let the matter rest as it is, it is good news that the affair will be decided* BEFORE A COURT OF LAW." *But the "honourable citizen," W. Schneider, the miner, did* NOT *bring an action!* THE STAATSBÜRGER-ZEITUNG, *so far as I know, has not robbed its readers of the expectation that W. Simon and M. Zweig would have to atone for their crime in prison.*

1892. INGRANDES *(department of Vienne, France). The (clerical) paper that appears in Tours, the* JOURNAL D'INDRE ET LOIRE, *published on 27th March, No. 74, an article headed, "Un meurtre rituel," which treats of the discovery of a child's shockingly-mangled corpse. "Justice has set on foot the customary investigations, but has reached no result up to now. That is perhaps because a wrong road has been taken, although the mutilation which the victim has endured points sufficiently to the real criminals. . . . A murder for motive of gain or out of revenge does not bear that stamp. That the murderer cuts off his victim's head so that it may not be recognised is not out of the way. But why the other mutilations? [The genital organs and the limbs were also cut off]. . . .*

We find ourselves in the presence of a ritual murder achieved by the Jews; everything proves it. . . . The body was found in a new sack, therefore the blood was drawn off from it beforehand. . . The murder could not have been committed at the place of discovery, but in a perhaps distant part, certainly at a place, where it was quite convenient to draw off the blood from the yet living victim, and to cut the body in pieces, which could readily be made to disappear. . . . It is easy to understand the interest of the murderers in the disappearance of the limbs: the point was to get rid of the marks on the neck, on the arms, on the femoral artery, on the limbs which were finally crucified, of the extraction of blood, which would have been terrible and irrefutable accusers on the count of ritual murder. And if there had been found on the body the marks of circumcision, which is ordained for the obtaining of the circumcision blood, a panacea in the eyes of the Jew—who then does not understand the interest of the sacrificers in the disappearance of the traces?"—The Paris paper LE TEMPS, *of 5th August No. 11,397, reports about the result of the affair: "The investigation showed that the child was the son on an unmarried woman named Marquet, who let herself be called by the name of a former lover, Widow Joubert. During the searching of the house there were found in the privy the entrails and the half-burnt cap of the poor little boy. The mother was arrested. She declared in her own defence that she wanted to suffocate herself with her son, when she was awakened by violent pains; the child lay on the ground, and one of his legs had been half-charred by the overturned coal-pan. She had then made up her mind to cut the corpse to pieces, and to throw the larger portion into the water in a sack. The prosecution, however, is of opinion that she only proceeded to this mournful operation after she had strangled her own son, and had attempted to burn him. The jury of Vienne has just condemned the unnatural mother to 20 years' hard labour.*"

1892. *Bacau* (Roumania). An Israelite, Eisik Suler, had a young gipsy girl, Florea, in his service. The girl's parents, who knew of the accusation that Jews used Christian blood for their unleavened Easter cakes, made her secretly leave her master, and hide in their hut. They then, accompanied by a crowd of half-drunk gipsies, demanded their child back with great outcry; Eisik had killed their child in order to get its blood. The chief of police quickly ascertained the baselessness of the charge. He therefore arrested the parents, and threatened them with severe punishment if they did not point out where their daughter was staying. Next day they confessed where the girl was, and that their sole intention was to extort money from the Jew. Monthly Report of the "Alliance Israélite Universelle," 1892 (Cologne), p. 84 sq.

1893. *Kolin* (Bohemia). At the beginning of March, Marie Havlin, a girl in whom melancholy had shown itself for a considerable time, and who was in service with the Jewish family of Brett, was missed. Not until over a month had elapsed was the dead body found in the Elbe, whilst sand was being drawn up from the river. The Young-Czech, anti-semitic journal, *Polaban*, announced in leaded type, that stabbing wounds had been noticed on her body, so that suicide was out of the question. The accusation that a ritual murder had been committed was bruited through the town, and led to serious excesses against the Jews, so that the military were summoned from Kuttenberg. On the 15th of April, the burgomaster, A. Civin, issued the following proclamation, in the section of the Royal Imperial County District in his charge: "At the dissection of the body of Marie Havlin, which was held by the Commission of the

Royal Imperial District Court, consisting of the judge and the official physicians, Dr. Sil and Dr. Stappan, it was confirmed that there were no marks of an injury or assault found on the corpse. It was on the contrary established that Havlin came to her death by drowning, and in fact by suicide, and that the body must have lain already five weeks in the water, because remains of red clay, such as the then high water carried with it, were found on the clothes. . . . All rumours which were set afloat about the girl's murder are untrue and without any foundation. Therefore the further dissemination of these rumours is to be punished as a malicious deception of the people." Cf. *Jüdische Presse*, 20 April, 1893, No. 16. Also in the Bohemian Landtag, the Statthalter, Count Thun, declared on 3rd May, in consequence of an interpellation: The judicial inspection of the corpse had proved, that there were not the slightest traces of violence found on the corpse, but that it was rather a case of suicide. On the grave a memorial tablet was placed with the following inscription: "Here rests Maria Havlin, who died a martyr's death before the Jews' Easter. May God reward them for it!" Owing to complaints from the Israelite religious community it had to be removed. Otherwise the tablet would certainly in a few years have been used as an original, monumental proof of the reality of ritual murder. *Jüd. Presse*, 12th October, 1894, Nos. 41-42.

1893. *Holleschau.* On 9th, or on 15th June, 1893, the servant Karoline Schnula and the peasant-woman Katharina Schönbaum were condemned by the Court at Ungarisch-Hradisch to 13 or 15 months' imprisonment with hard labour, because they had made the accusation against David Tandler, and also two other Jewish inhabitants of Holleschau, that these had wanted to slaughter them for ritual purposes. The barrister asked for severe punishment, so that cases might not recur in the future, by which honourable citizens of the state would, in consequence of an absolutely stupid fairy-tale, be menaced in their honour, life, and property. The actual authorship of the libel was alleged to be due to an unknown third person; that person must be very powerful, since both of the condemned women shrank from giving him up. *Jüd. Presse*, 22nd June, 1893.

1893, *Prague.* Jaromir Huschek, the editor of the Czechish journal, *Nove Zajmy*, had announced that in August, 1893, the "Schächter," Hermann Löwy, of Chotzen, had for ritual purposes extracted blood from a worthy, industrious Christian named Joseph Horky, and then given him two gulden, that he might recover from the loss of blood. Inquiry showed that Horky, a toper, suffering from hallucinations, had invented the whole story. He was punished by the Court at Hohenmauth for spreading agitating news; Huschek was condemned by the Prague Penal Court on 3rd April, "in contumaciam," to 14 days' imprisonment, emphasised by two days' fasting. (*Neue Freie Presse*, Vienna, telegram from Prague, v. 4 April).

1893. The trio, *Paulus Meyer, Josef Deckert, Franz Doll.* Paulus Meyer (born 1862, at Wlozlawek, Russian Poland; baptised, alas! in 1887), was expelled from Berlin by the police in September, 1892, because he had made himself "troublesome." Next he produced in Leipsic the material for the libel mentioned supr. p. 148. He was on that account arrested on 25th May, 1893, at the request of the Leipsic Assize Court, in Vienna, where he was in the pay of the Catholic Priest, Josef Deckert, in order to collect from Jewish literature proofs of Jewish ritual murders. Aug. Rohling had recommended him! He had already written a letter to Deckert on 20th April (Leipsic is named as the place of composition), in which he asserted that in 1875, before the Jewish Easter festival in Ostrowo, Government of Lublin, he had been the witness of the ritual slaughter of a Christian boy. Ten Israelites were said to have been present at this holy transaction, of whom the names were given of the Rabbi "Jehoschua Ben h'Rab Schlohme Leb m'Lentschna" [son of the Rabbi Salomo Leb at Lentschna], and the Synagogue servants, Moische Berriches and Srul [Israel] Partzewar. A portion of the blood is said to have been poured into flasks, and to have been sent to the parishes subject to the Rabbi named; another portion was kept in a silver goblet for baking into the unleavened Easter loaves. A Jewish landed proprietor, Schmiel [Samuel] Tarler, was said to have procured the victim from Levertof, a place three miles distant. Deckert had already triumphantly referred to this letter on 5th, 7th and 10th May in the Viennese journal *Das Vaterland;* on 11th May its publication followed in No. 129. Numerous anti-semitical papers copied it with delight. But the joy was premature. Three of the persons accused by name of ritual murder were still alive; the fourth, Rabbi Jehoschua, had been dead more than two years *before* the crime falsely imputed to him, but his daughter Rahel and her husband, the Rabbi Jankiel (Jacob) Rabinowitz of Biala (Russian Poland), were still alive. They brought an action, with the result that on 15th September Meyer was condemned to four months' arrest (in which the long remand in custody during the inquiry was taken into consideration), Deckert to a fine of four hundred gulden, and the Editor of the *Vaterland* to two hundred gulden. The whole contents of the letter were a lie. But also in the case of Jos. Deckert two deliberate untruths were pointed out (by Meyer's official defender); Cf. *Neue Freie Presse* (Vienna), Nos. 10,040 and 10,041 (15th September evening and 16th

September); *Oesterreich. Wochenschrift*, Vienna, No. 38, pp. 731-65 (shorthand report). The well-known Pastor F. v. Bodelschwingh of Bielefeld gave his opinion of Meyer on 27th Sept., 1892: "A limitless amount of cynical ingratitude towards all his benefactors, who finally perceived his true character and did not desire to gratify his immoderate pretensions! About his behaviour here I need not tell you anything, and compress it briefly when I say that in my whole life I have never known such an example of deep degradation, malice, mendacity and arrogance, altogether of bottomless sordidness, as this fellow!"

1894. *Berent* (West Prussia). On the 5th of April the town was excited by the rumour that a girl of nine had been kidnapped by the Jews for purposes of ritual. It was due to the following circumstances: —A Jewish butcher, Werner, had bought a small she-goat from a Roman Catholic widow, Hermann. The mother sent her daughter to deliver the animal and receive the rest of the money. The child, however, sold the goat otherwise, and did not return home. So when Werner came to ask about the goat, Mrs. H. began to scream out: "My child has gone; the Jews have put her to death." She then hastened to W.'s house in order to demand her child back. A crowd of people soon assembled there with menacing gestures, and, in particular, some witnesses turned up who alleged they had *seen* that the child went into W.'s house in the morning. The woman at length ran off to the Burgomaster, and asked that her child should be released. Soon after the girl turned up again. The woman declared that she had often read in the newspapers that the Jews were obliged to have Christian blood. *Jüd. Presse*, 12th April, 1894, No. 15.—Mrs. H. was condemned to two weeks' imprisonment for gross contumacy.

1896. *Mährisch-Trübau.* As a "contribution to

the use of blood by the Jews," a story went the round of the papers, especially the Austrian, at the beginning of 1896, that the merchant Moriz Moller had extracted blood at the joints of the arms and legs of his former servant, Philomena Waclawek, at night, by pricking them with needles. The gossip had proceeded from the two present servants of M., Emilie Schwab and Sophie Nemluwil, who appealed to the utterances made them by Waclawek. The preliminary examination conducted against M. was stopped after a short time for want of any details or facts. Thereupon M., who had had to suffer under the false accusation, brought an action against the mendacious servant for insult to honour. The affair was decided on 22nd May before the Assize Court of Brünn. On the proposition of the Public Prosecutor, the woman W. was condemned for libel to three months' strict imprisonment, which was to be rendered more severe every fortnight by a day of fasting. *Oesterr. Wochenschr.*, 1896, No. 18, p. 357, and No. 22, p. 436; Cf. also *Gemeinde-Zeitung* (Prague), 15th April, 1896.

1898. SKAISGIRREN *(Niederung District, East Prussia).* STAATSBÜRGER-ZEITUNG, *16th February, 1898: "The rumour of a* RITUAL MURDER *set the inhabitants here in excitement, and causes a great deal of talk even now. Some time ago the* SERVANT GIRL OF A JEWISH MERCHANT IN THE PLACE DISAPPEARED WITHOUT LEAVING A TRACE; *the search inaugurated has so far resulted in no explanation of the girl's mysterious disappearance, but certainly given rise to the above-mentioned black rumour. We hope the matter will soon be cleared up."—According to the official material lying before me, the police authorities had no cause whatever to make enquiries. The servant girl, Wilh. Picklapp, had illegally left other places previously, and had done the same thing in the case of the merchant Markus Grodszinsky; and she had first gone to her sweetheart, and then to the foster-mother of her illegitimate child at Plicken near Mehlauken.*

1899. Polna (Bohemia). On 1st April, on the Saturday in Passion Week, the corpse of the nineteen-year-old sempstress, Agnes Hruza, who had been missing from Klein-Wieznitz since Wednesday, the night of 29th March, was found in the Brezina forest between Polna and Klein-Wieznitz. Suspicion of having committed the murder fell upon Leopold Hilsner, a Jewish cobbler's apprentice of twenty-two, who had often roamed about in the aforesaid forest. On 12th September the affair came before the District Court at Kuttenberg for trial. To the first question put to the jury, "Is Hilsner guilty of having, in association with others, murdered Hruza?" they answered, on the 5th day, 16th September, "No," with eleven votes. On the other hand, the second question, "Is Hilsner an accomplice in the murder?" was answered in the affirmative with all the twelve votes. The Court of Justice consequently pronounced judgment for H.'s condemnation to death by the rope. The Assize Court at Pisek, on 14th November, 1900, convicted him also of the murder of Marie Klima, who had disappeared on the 17th July, 1898.

It is universally admitted that H. was a man who shrank from work, and was not on good terms with the truth. He repelled the offer that on the day of Atonement (10 Tishri=14th September) i.e., on a day which even Jews, who care almost nothing at all about their religion, hold sacred, the trial should be postponed. And he contrived after his condemnation to point out as accomplices two innocent men, Josua Erbmann and Salomo Wassermann. Both were speedily found and arrested, but had to be set free after a short time, as they were able perfectly to prove an alibi. At the recantation of his "confession" Hilsner asserted that in spite of his innocence he had been dreadfully frightened by the news that the gallows were already being erected for him, and he had given the false information in order to get a postponement.

The unsympathetic nature of his personality, however, should not seduce us into declaring H. to be the murderer or an accomplice without convincing proof. Still less should "ritual murder" be asserted without convincing proof. And yet the public prosecutor, Schneider-Swoboda, put forward this assertion, in veiled words it is true, and the barrister, Dr. Baxa, representing the "Anti-semites," after describing desire for revenge, jealousy, lust as motives to be excluded, even said (Viennese NEUE FREIE PRESSE, 17th September, No. 12,597): "But we demand to know why Agnes Hruza was murdered! (Stormy cries of "Viborne" in the audience.) The body of the murdered woman tells why she was murdered. The body speaks to the whole world; it shrieks out why a poor, innocent Christian girl had to die. (Storm of applause in the auditorium.) The circumstance that Agnes Hruza was first caught with a noose shows plainly the motive of the deed, shows plainly why she was butchered. Up till now we knew the most diverse motives for murder, even political murder; but this motive, as it is exposed here, was unfortunately till now not yet believed in by everybody. Hruza was murdered for the sole reason that a Christian virgin had to be murdered. . . . The highest circles in the State will have to take heed of the fact that there is a society of human beings among us who only murder our Christian fellows in order to get our blood. The State must rise up against this class of persons, who want our blood, who want the blood of Christian girls; that is an inevitable duty, whether it is a sect of this people or the whole *race. We do not know where the blood went. That will have to be cleared up presently. But Hruza was murdered by a society that lives among us with the sole object of taking our blood from us. . . . Hilsner, with two other persons, tried to extract as much blood as possible from this girl, this Christian virgin. (Great sensation.) It is quite certain that everything was prepared beforehand for the murder in that synagogue where the blood-stained breeches were found; there the actual proof of the ensuing murder, the grey, blood-stained breeches, was actually taken. This synagogue is both the beginning-point and the ending-point of the Polna murder. No blood was found. That means everything. . . . The murderer wanted the blood. Therefore—according to the opinion of the experts—the blood was not found. (Prolonged sensation)" And after that Baxa said: If the defender declared he had proofs contradictory of a ritual murder, "I have proofs in favour of it. Perhaps the defender knows the books of the Rabbi Eleasar, perhaps also that of the Rabbi Mendel"* (STAATSBÜRGER-ZEITUNG, *Berlin, 19th September, No. 438.*)*

And both before the legal proceedings and after them the "anti-semite" newspapers spoke in the same sense. DAS BAYERISCHE VATERLAND, *Munich, 20th September: "The Court of Justice . . . has answered in the affirmative [the question if it was a Jewish*

* The mentioning of Rabbi Mendel is based upon a gross falsification of A. Rohling's, as I, as early as August, 1883, pointed out in a letter to Prof. W. Bacher, of Budapesth v. *Judisches Litteratur-Blatt*, Magdeburg 1883, no. 34). Cf. also *J. Kopp*, "Zur Judenfrage,"35-7, and *J. Bloch*, "Acten" I., 157-60. There is certainly, apart from Hartwig Wessely's Hebrew book of synonyms "gan naûl" ["closed garden," v. Song of Songs, iv., 12] another book of this name; but it is not by Rabbi Mendel, but by Abraham Abulafia, and it is not "in some twenty editions" (as Rohling lies), but a not even yet printed commentary on the Book Jeçira (Cod. Hebr. fol. 58 of the Royal Library at Munich).

ritual murder]; *it implicitly assumed that it was a* RELIGIOUS CUSTOM OF ORTHODOX JUDAISM *to drink the blood of Jewishly butchered* CHRISTIAN PERSONS. . . . *Anna Hruza was therefore simply butchered like any cattle, in order to draw off her blood!* . . . *Hilsner filled the position of a* JEWISH SLAUGHTERER [*untrue!—H. Str.*], *which is among Jews a kind of* RELIGIOUS OFFICE, *and into which the* RABBI INITIATES THE CANDIDATE AFTER SEVERE TESTING. . . . *All the facts point to a* RITUAL MURDER, *in connection with which it has also to be considered that Hruza was slaughtered immediately before* [*untrue!—H. Str.*] *the* JEWISH EASTER FESTIVAL, *at which, as is asserted, the Talmud prescribes the consumption of* CHRISTIAN BLOOD [*untrue!—H. Str.*]"

The assumption of an actual "ritual murder" (for using the blood at the Jewish Passover) is decisively disproved by the simple fact that Agnes Hruza was, till the evening of 29th March, still in Polna with the sempstress Prchal, whilst the Jewish Easter began on 26th March. Furthermore, the accusation and condemnation are essentially based on the opinion that Hruza was murdered in the forest in which her corpse was found. This view, however, is false. Cf. the works of the Prague Professor Th. G. Masaryk, "Die Nothwendigkeit der Revision des Polnaer Prozesses," Vienna, 1899 (31), and "Die Bedeutung des Polnaer Verbrechens für den Ritualaberglauben," Be., 1900 (94).

I take the following from him:—The corpse was found lying in such a way on the belly that the lower portion of both legs were bent upwards in an acute angle, and the trunk was somewhat curved to the right. This bending of the legs and this curving of the body could only have been effected after the setting-in of the *rigor mortis*, or otherwise the body would not have remained curved and the legs would have sunk down again. But *rigor mortis* only begins some hours after death. Therefore the corpse was brought where it was found, only after the appearance of *rigor mortis*. One alternative is that it was carried so that the legs were bent over the right shoulder of the carrier and held by one of his hands, whilst the other hand drew the trunk of the dead body to him by means of a rope placed round her neck. It would also be explained in this way why only the right side of the neck showed a strangulation furrow. Had the girl been strangled with the cord before death, the furrow would have been visible right round her neck. The other alternative is that the corpse was brought into the forest in a wheelbarrow. In that case the legs would have been bent, otherwise the wheelbarrow would have been hampered by the length of the body. It was important to the murderer or murderers that no blood should drip on the ground during transport. That explains why the head was wrapped up in the shift and petticoat. The murder probably happened in a house, and, indeed, at a late hour of the night, when Hruza was already partially undressed. The following circumstances point to it: Firstly, the body was clothed only with gaiters, stockings, and the remainder of a shift (the statement about the breeches are contradictory); secondly, her hair was undone; thirdly, there was only blood, not dirt, on the palms of the hands and behind the nails of both hands, although, according to the charge, the murder took place in the forest on ground soaked with rain; fourthly, the cleanness of the corpse, no blood-stains on breast or stomach (the murdered woman was perhaps washed); fifthly, on dissection numerous remains of food, especially milk, were found in the stomach (A. H., who began her return home after 5 o'clock, seems, before she was murdered, to have had an evening meal). Six metres from the place of the crime two cloths belonging to A. H. were found, "folded together." Had the murderers, who, according to the charge, did the deed in the greatest haste, time to fold up these cloths? Hilsner was seen in Polna a short while before the time of the murder (about 6 p.m.), as fixed by the charge, in the evening he was at home. The Viennese *Juristische Blätter*, September, 1899, also pronounced a new trial necessary: "He was accused without proofs, condemned without proofs, and that is a judicial murder in the eyes of lawyers. . . . An important piece of counter-evidence, that the criminal alone would not have been able to overpower the strong girl, led to the accusation and condemnation for being an accomplice, without any intelligible reasons for thinking there were accomplices being given." It observes about Hilsner's denials: "It is well known to every practical man that persons belonging to the populace deny everything, even the most harmless, as soon as they are aware they are under accusation."

Dr. Arthur Nussbaum ("Der Polnaer Ritualmordprocess. Eine kriminalpsychologische Untersuchung auf aktenmässiger Grundlage." Be., 1906, 259 pp.) has now convincingly shown: (1) That Agnes Hruza's neck-wound was not a Jewish butcher's cut, but more probably inflicted after death in order to remove the rope tied round the neck; (2) that the amount of blood to be expected under the circumstances was present; (3) that the reasons given for Hilsner's guilt are entirely null, that the statements of the witnesses for the prosecution not merely became definite only gradually and in the course of time, but that they also contradict each other, i.e., are in themselves unworthy of belief; (4) that throughout no probable motive was adduced by which Hilsner could have been impelled to murder A. Hruza (either as the result of blood-thirstiness, or as a deed of perverse sexuality, or for the purpose of robbery).

In regard to the Klima case Hilsner's alibi is proved to be credible; concerning the manner in which Marie K. met her death, the inspection of the skeleton found on the 27th of October, 1898, in the forest north of Polna, no longer afforded a solution. The identity of the perpetrator, or, as the Public Prosecutor asserted, of the perpetrators, was not proved in any way in either case.

The Court of Justice did not allow the execution of Hilsner, who had been condemned for the double murder, but changed the punishment to life-long imprisonment. That is a clear sign that they did not trust in the truthfulness of the sworn witnesses.

1900. *Konitz* (West Prussia). On 11th March, 1900, Ernest Winter, a public school youth ("gymnasiast") of eighteen and a half, left his lodgings in the house of Lange, a master-baker. In the afternoon he was seen by several people. In the afternoon of the 13th of March Winter's father (a builder in Prechlau) and the master-baker found in the water by the bank of the Mönchsee a parcel, the wrapper of which consisted of packing-paper; it contained in a sack the upper part of Winter's body, without head or arms. Quite close by they found the lower portion of the trunk. On 15th March the right arm was found in the Evangelical Churchyard; on the 20th of March the left upper leg in the Mönchsee; and, lastly, on 15th April, in a pit two kilometres from Konitz, the head wrapped in paper.—The anti-semites again raised the charge that here was a case of ritual murder committed by the Jews. Not even the shadow of a proof of this could be adduced. The Royal Medical College of the province of West Prussia and the Royal Scientific Medical Committee (in Berlin) who carefully examined the parts of the body and the articles of dress which were found, arrived, in two detailed expert reports, at the following conclusion (which was indeed very painful to the feelings of those who had celebrated Ernst W. as a hero in virtue, especially at the funeral of the parts of his body):— "(1) The death of Ernst Winter was the result of suffocation. (2) There is no scientific foundation for the assumption that the cut in the neck discovered on the mutilated corpse of Winter was perpetrated during his lifetime, and thus caused death from bleeding. (3) The death took place on 11th March, 1900, within the first six hours after he had enjoyed a meal. (4) The evidence of seminal spots on the outside of his trousers and shirt renders it probable that Winter was performing the act of coitus, or was trying to do so, shortly before his death." Cf. "Die Gutachten der Sachverständigen über den Konitzer Mord," Be., 1903 (87).

XIX. CONTRADICTION OF THE "BLOOD-ACCUSATION" BY PIOUS JEWS AS WELL AS CHRISTIANS

My intention has been to collect not as many testimonies as possible, but those that really carry weight.

A.—JEWS

ISAAK ABRAVANEL, *a well-known Bible exegetist (born in Portugal 1437, died in Italy 1508), on Ezekiel xxxvi., 13.*

SAMUEL USQUE, *in his Portuguese book printed in 1553, "Consolations for the oppressed among Israel" ("Consolaçam," etc., v. Wolf, "Bibliotheca Hebraea," III., 1071-5.)*

JEHUDA KARMI, *"De charitate," Amsterdam, 1643, v. Wolf, Bibl. Hebr., II., 1131-5.*

MANASSE BEN ISRAEL *(born in Lisbon 1604, lived later in Amsterdam; intercourse with Queen Christina of Sweden; brought about permission for the Jews to return to England), "Vindiciae Judaeorum" [in English], originally London, 1656, then in the compilation "Phenix," London 1708; in German, "Rettung der Juden," by Marcus Herz, with a preface by Moses Mendelssohn, as supplement to Chr. W. Dohm's "Uber die bürgerliche Verbesserung der Juden," Berlin and Stettin, 1781.—The* OATH OF PURIFICATION *taken by him in the volume mentioned, runs: "If all that has been hitherto said is not even then sufficient to nullify this accusation, I am forced, since the matter on our side is simply one of negation, and therefore is incapable of elucidation by witnesses, to use another kind of proof, which the Eternal has ordained (Exodus xxii.), that of an oath. I therefore swear, without any deception or trickery whatever, by the highest God, the Creator of heaven and earth, who revealed His law to the people of Israel on Mount Sinai, that I have never, even to this day, seen such a practice among the people of Israel, that they have never regarded such a practice as a lawful, divine ordinance, nor as a command or institution of their wise men, and that they have never (as far as I know, as far as I have heard in a credible way, or read in any Jewish author) practised or attempted such a villainy! And if I lie in this, may all the curses mentioned in the books of the Law (Leviticus and Deuteronomy) visit me; may I never see the blessing and the solace of Zion, nor take part in the resurrection of the dead!"*—MOSES MENDELSSOHN *declares himself ready to repeat this oath verbatim; this oath has been uttered by* SALOMON HIRSCHELL, *the London Chief Rabbi, and by* DAVID MELDOLA, *the Chakam of the Portuguese-Israelite community in London, on 30th June, 1840; in the same year the missionary* G. W. PIERITZ *(a Jewish Christian) did the same thing (v. Löwenstein, "Damascia,"[2] 203, 237 sq.).*

ISAAK CANTARINI, *"Vindex sanguinis," Amsterdam, 1680; reprinted as supplement to Wülfer's "Theriaca judaica," Nuremberg, 1681.*

JAKOB EMDEN *(1698-1776, at Altona and Amsterdam) in a missive, which is attached to his edition of the "Seder olam rabba wezutta," Hamburg, 1757; v. D. Hoffmann, "Schulchan-Aruch,"[2] Be., 1894, 26.*

JONATHAN EIBESCHUTZ *(1690-1764), v. supr. p. 151.*

J. TUGENDHOLD *(Censor in Warsaw), "Der alte Wahn vom Blutgebrauch der Israeliten am Osterfeste"* [*written in 1831*]. *Translated from the Polish. Be., 1858 (90).*

ISAAK BAER LEVINSOHN, "*'Ephes Damîm*" [*in Hebrew*], *Wilna, 1837; Englished by* L. LOEWE*:* "*Efés Dammîm. A series of conversations at Jerusalem between a Patriarch of the Greek Church and a Chief Rabbi of the Jews,*" *London, 1841; German by A. Katz:* "*Die Blutlüge,*" *Be., 1892 (102).*

L. ZUNZ, "*Damaskus. Ein Wort zur Abwehr,*" *Be., 1840 (reprinted in* "*Gesammelte Schriften,*" *II., 160-70).*

L. H. LOWENSTEIN, "*Damascia. Die Judenverfolgung zu Damaskus und ihre Wirkungen auf die öffentliche Meinung.*" *Second revised edition. Rödelheim, 1841 (416).—Supplement to it by the same author:* "*Stimmen berühmter Christen* [*J. F. v. Meyer, F. J. Molitor*] *uber den Damaszener Blutprozess,*" *Rödelheim, 1843 (46).*

M. SCHLESINGER, "*Neki Kapajim.*" "*Clean hands.*" *Refutes the accusations levelled against the Jews. (from the Hebrew). Budapesth, 1882 (30).*

M. L. RODKINSSOHN, מַצַּת־מִצְוָה וַעֲלִילַת הַדָּם. "*Das ungesäuerte Brot und Die Anklage des Blutgebrauchs am Passah-Feste.*" [*Hebrew with German preface*]. *Pressburg and Vienna, 1883. (VIII., 32).*

M. H. FRIEDLÄNDER "*Zur Geschichte der Blutbeschuldigungen gegen die Juden im Mittelalter und in der Neuzeit.*" *Brünn, 1883 (32).*

M. DUSCHAK, "*Tôr Estêr*" [*v. Esther ii., 15*] "*Mittel gegen die falschen Blutbeschuldigungen.*" *Cracow, 1883 (66).*

CORRADO GUIDETTI, "*Pro Judaeis. Riflessione e documenti. Turin, 1884 (386).*

GIORGIO A. ZAVIZIANI, "*Un raggio di luce. La persecuzione degli Ebrei nella storia,*" *Corfu, 1891, Tipografia* "*Corai*" *(356).*

The statements which occur in poetry, which is

only intended for Jewish readers, seem to me of a special importance.* Violent outbursts of bitter rancour against their merciless persecutors are not rare, but nowhere is there even a single word which could be applied to the charge here in question; the "blood accusation" is much rather regarded as an abominable slander, as, for instance, in a "Selicha" (prayer of penitents) by Salomo ben Abraham (about 1220), v. Zunz, "Die synagogale Poesie des Mittelalters," Be., 1855, 27.—The Jews, as they say themselves, in the last five hundred years of the Middle Ages, slaughtered, sacrificed children—but their own children, in order to save them from baptism, cf. Zunz 16, 20, 22 sq., and likewise the moving report of Salomo bar Simeon about the persecution of the Jews in Mainz in 1096, v. "Quellen zur Geschichte der Juden in Deutschland," II. (Be., 1892), 9, 12, or 101, 107. Cf. also *Salfeld*, 105 (note 3), 143, 202.—In recent times cf. *G. Dalman*, "Jüdischdeutsche Volkslieder aus Galizien und Russland," 2nd edition, L., 1891, 49.

B. PROSELYTES

Owing to what happened in Fulda (v. supr. p. 178 sq.), the German Emperor Frederick II. set on foot a thorough investigation of the question, whether the Jews used human blood. *R. Höniger* ("Zeitschrift für die Geschichte der Juden in Deutschland," I. [1887], 137-44) has published the golden Bull of July, 1236, from the Cologne municipal archives, in whose second part the Emperor reports as to the result of his researches:

* The contradiction in "Niççaḥôn jashān" (p. 257 of Wagenseil's edition in "Tela ignea Satanae"), was also not intended for Christian readers.

"*Moreover all men now living and going to live should know: As, in consequence of the murder of some boys at Fulda, a grievous accusation was brought against the Jews then living there, and hence a menacing public opinion arose generally against the rest of the Jews in Germany, on account of the sad event, although the traffic in secret crime was not revealed, we, in order to clear up the truth in respect of the before-mentioned accusation, resolved to summon before us from every quarter princes, magnates, and nobles of the Empire, as well as abbots and ecclesiastics, and to question them. Now as these were of divers opinions about the matter, and could not arrive at a satisfactory issue in relation thereto, we came to the conclusion that owing to the secret action taken against the Jews accused of the aforesaid crime, the matter could not be more suitably dealt with than by those who had been Jews, and had been converted to the Christian faith, since these as adversaries would conceal nothing of what they know against those other Jews, or against the Mosaic books, or the whole series of the Old Testament. And although our conscience regarded the innocence of the aforesaid Jews as adequately proved on the ground of several writings, which had been brought to the knowledge of our Majesty, yet for the satisfaction no less of the uneducated populace than of the feeling of justice, according to our sound decision, and with the unanimous consent of the princes, magnates, nobles, abbots, and ecclesiastics, we sent extraordinary ambassadors to all the Kings of the West, by whom accordingly many converts experienced in the Jewish law were sent to our presence from the various kingdoms. We commanded these, who sojourned no short time at our Court, to trace out the truth, so that they might industriously investigate and inform us, whether there was any opinion existing among them [the Jews]* *which would induce them perchance to commit another crime, and which might have induced the Jews themselves to commit the aforesaid crime. Their* ANSWER *ran: 'Neither in the Old nor in the New Testament is it found that the Jews are greedy for human blood. Rather it is expressly stated in complete opposition to such an assertion in the Bible, which is called in Hebrew "Bereschith,"* in the laws given to Moses, in the Jewish ordinances, which are called in Hebrew Talmud, that they must altogether beware of pollution with any blood whatever. We add, and it is an addition which concerns us very closely, that those who are forbidden the blood, even of the animals allowed them, cannot have any thirst for human blood, because of the horror of the thing, because nature forbids it, and because of the relationship of species which connects them also with the Christians . . and that they would not expose their property and life of peril.' We have therefore with the agreement of the Princes declared the Jews of the before-mentioned place to be entirely acquitted of the crime attributed to them, and the rest of the Jews in Germany of so grave an accusation."* . . . †

Paulus, de Santa Maria, 1351-1435 (as a Jew,

* [Bereshîth, "In the beginning," the first word of the Hebrew Bible among the Jews, the ordinary name of Genesis, here signifies the whole Hebrew Bible.]

† The sentence that contains the judgment of the Commission runs verbatim as follows in the copy of the Bull which belongs to the 14th century, but is unhappily not free from mistakes: "Quorum super hoc assercionibus publicatis, quia compertum non est in testamento veteri vel in novo, Judeos avidos esse humani sanguinis hauriendi, immo [add.. quia], quod est predicto prorsus contrarium, quod ab omnis omnino sanguinis fedacione caveant in biblia que dicitur abraice berechet, preceptis Moysi datis, decretis iudaicis que dicuntur ebrayce talmilloht, expressius habeamus, presumentes eciam presumpcione non modica, hiis quibus sanguis prohibitus est et animalium permissorum sitim non posse humani sanguinis superesse, rei horribilitate, nature prohibicione ac speciei comoditate qua Christianos eciam amplectuntur, et quod pro eo quod expositum de animalibus de virorum municionibus [?] habere possent pro nichilo,

Salomo Levi), *Bishop of Burgos*, who was by no means friendly inclined to the Jews, nevertheless writes in his additions to the commentary of Nikolaus von Lyra on Genesis I.: "It is therefore not useful for the conversion of the Jews to ascribe this aberration to them. For they believe that we are inventing lies against them, and that affords us no small impediment in being believed by them." (Ganganelli has already referred to this passage).

Many persons will be influenced less by actual reasons given than by the testimony of *Johannes Pfefferkorn*, the enemy of the Talmud and the Jews, well known through his dispute with Reuchlin (cf. Wolf, "Bibl. Hebr.," No. 1845, in Vols. I. and IV.). In his pamphlet about the Jewish Passover, which appeared in 1509, he says nothing about the Jewish use of Christian blood. And in "Speculum Adhortationis Judaicae ad Christum," Cologne, 1507, he writes: "I should here like to refute a wide-spread, but worthless piece of gossip against the Jews, in order that we Christians may not in consequence become ridiculous. It is commonly said among Christians, that the Jews have need to use Christian blood as a means of cure, and therefore kill little Christian children. Dear Christians! Believe it not! It is contrary to the Holy Scriptures and the law of Nature and reason. Therefore I must defend the Jews in this matter, but with one limitation. It is conceivable that Jews are found, and perhaps may hereafter be found, who secretly persecute Christian children even to their death, nevertheless not on account of any necessity for having their blood, but out of hatred, and in order to revenge themselves on

non exponerent periculo substancias et personas, Judeos loci predicti ab obiecto crimine ac alios Judeos Alemannie a tam gravi infamia dictante sentencia principum pronunciavit [read: "-avimus"] penitus absolutos."

the Christians, even as they once, when they had more power than they have now, publicly persecuted Christ, the Apostles and his pupils, and followers. Therefore do not be disquieted about it! . . . . Flee from and avoid accordingly this ludicrous, mendacious talk which, if you wish to consider it closely, contributes no little to casting contempt on the Christians. Abide by the truth, whilst abandoning such delusions, oh Christians! We do not want to invent anything that is false and brings us no honour!"

Ant. Margaritha, once lecturer in Hebrew in Augsburg, Leipsic, and Vienna, says in "Der gantze Jüdische Glaube" (Augsburg, 1530; I possess the edition of Reineccius, L., 1705), much wicked stuff about the Jews and their blindness, but not a word about the utilisation of Christian, or generally speaking, human blood for superstitious or even ritual purposes.

Julius Morosini (ob. 1687, as Reader of the Hebrew language in Rome), author of the anti-Jew book, "Via della fede nostra mostrata agli Ebrei," Rome, 1683, characterised the assertion of the use of blood as a fiction.

Also the physician, *Paolo Medici*, "Riti e costumi degli Ebrei confutati," Madrid, 1727, and often, said not a word about the blood-accusation. Against the contrary declarations of Rohling and others, v. *J. Kopp*, 32-4; *Bloch*, "Acten," I., 152. Cf. about Paolo Medici, also *A. Fürst*, "Christen und Juden," Strasburg, 1892, 94-6.

FRIEDRICH ALBRECHT CHRISTIANI, *baptized 1674 at Strasburg, "Docent" at the University of Leipsic, a thorough-going expert in Rabbinical literature, says in his work which is by no means friendly to the Jews, "Der Jüden Glaube und Aberglaube," L., 1705, Supplement IV., 181-4, amongst other things:*

"*Although there is indeed a general slander against the Jews, that they follow after Christian children, and when they have got hold of them, stab them horribly, extract the blood from them, using it with certain ceremonies as a remedy, partly in the case of their wives during the severe pangs of labour, and partly for dying persons in their last agonies, I am able, as a born Jew (who without boasting, know well all their customs, having myself practised, or at any rate seen with my eyes, most of them) to asseverate by God, that the whole time I was connected with Judaism, I never heard among them of such dealings with Christian children, much less that they had ever had Christian blood or had ever used it in the aforesaid manner."—So far as concerns the cases reported to have occurred at Trent, Frankfort a. M. and elsewhere in the latter centuries Christiani believes "assuredly and veritably, that some wicked Christians, who were spiteful against the Jews in these places, committed the deeds out of peculiarly bitter hatred to bring disaster upon them.*"

Aloysius von Sonnenfels, "Jüdischer Blut-Eckel, Oder Das von Gebrauch des unschuldigen Christen-Bluts angeklagte, untersuchte und unschuldig-befundene Judenthum, Aus Trieb der Wahrheit An Tag gegeben." Vienna, 1753 (161; Latin title: "Judaica sanguinis nausea.") Cf. especially 20 sq.: "Now if all this as it is narrated were to correspond with truth, Christian authorities would not have to be blamed for persecuting this so villainous inhuman people with fire and sword, and tearing them to pieces with raving dogs, or they might order them to be dismembered by the hangman. I, however, who under guidance of my father as Chief Rabbi at Berlin and of the whole electorate of Brandenburg, got to know, even in my tenderest youth, the most precise and hidden secrets of the whole of Judaism, even to the smallest detail, because at one time he desired to make of me a man of his profession. I can bear witness before God, on my soul and conscience, that this is one of the greatest untruths which has ever been heard in the world."

Joh. Heinr. Raph. Biesenthal (missionary, died 25th June, 1886, in Berlin), "Ueber den Ursprung der wider die Juden erhobenen Beschuldigung, bei der Feier ihrer Ostern sich des Blutes zu bedienen, nebst kurzer Darstellung des jüdischen Rituals in Beziehung auf den Genuss des Blutes. Historisch-kritischer Versuch von Dr. Karl Ignaz Corvé" [pseudonym]. Be., 1840 (66).

Johann Emanuel Veith, Cathedral preacher at St. Stephen in Vienna, baptised 1816, died 1876. F. J. Molitor writes in his professional account (mentioned p. 192): "This pious priest, who was at one time a Jew, uttered [1840] in the pulpit, crucifix in hand, a high and holy oath, that there was no single word of truth in the charge against the Jews."

Since then both Jews and Christians have very often appealed to this testimony, e.g. the Roman Catholic clergyman and Bavarian Landtag Deputy, F. FRANK, "*Die Kirche und die Juden,*" *Regensburg, 1892, 53. But on 14th March, 1892, the Viennese* DEUTSCHE VOLKSBLATT *(and following it, other papers) published an article called* "*Eine millionenmal gedruckte Judenlüge*" *("a million-times-printed Jewish lie,") in which it is observed:* "*The* WIENER KIRCHEN-ZEITUNG, *in 1854 and 1856, at the time when Dr. Veith was a collaborator. . . . . and articles signed by him appeared in that journal, published* AT VEITH'S INSTIGATION *a declaration that the whole story of the oath-taking in the pulpit was a 'contemptible slander,' and that Dr. Veith had never said a word in the pulpit on the subject.*" *On which I remark: (1) The years mentioned in connec-*

nection with the WIENER KIRCHEN-ZEITUNG *show no articles with Veith's signature. (2) The declaration (1854, No. 19; repeated in 1856, No. 80) was* NOT *published at Veith's instigation. (3) The statements, which, as can be easily recognised by the crude manner of expression ("lying in the most contemptible way," "lies thick as your fist," "unparalleled impudence,") were drawn up by Sebastian Brunner, the publisher of the* WIENER KIRCHEN-ZEITUNG, *are* UNTRUE *in substance, and Molitor's statement is far more correct.*

1. *The Israelite religious community in Vienna possesses the following holograph of Dr. med. Joh. Veith, University Professor, a piece of testimony notarially authenticated on 17th June, 1882, which has lain before me in the original: "At the request of Herr L. A. Frankel, I declare that the article contained in the* ILLUSTRIERTES EXTRABLATT *of* [5] *June,* about a statement made at the end of a sermon by my late brother, Canon John Emanuel Veith, regarding the*

* [*Illustriertes Wiener Extrablatt*, Vienna, Monday, 5th June, 1882, no. 153. This is the chief passage in the article, "A timely reminiscence": "It was on Ascension Day of that year [1840; accordingly on 28th May] when the famous pulpit-preacher spoke the following remarkable words at the end of his sermon, in the presence of thousands of pious Christians: 'You all know, my pious hearers, and those, who perhaps do not know it, may learn, that I was born a Jew, and, enlightened by the Grace of God, have become a Christian, further, I have given faithful expression to this conviction attained to by me in Christian mission, and on every occasion have given testimony for the truth' . . . And then the excellent man raised the crucifix, and went on in impassioned tones: 'And so I swear here, in the name of the triune God, whom we all acknowledge, before you and all the world, that the falsehood which has been disseminated by cruel cunning, to the effect that the Jews use the blood of a Christian in the celebration of their Easter festival (Pesach) is a malicious, blasphemous slander, and is contained neither in the books of the Old Testament, nor in the writings of the Talmud, which I know thoroughly and have zealously examined. So may God help me and be a merciful Saviour to me in my last hour!' What a deep impression, what a thrilling effect this solemn testimony produced within and without the cathedral are indescribable."]

absolute untruth of the rumour of the Jewish custom at the Passover feast of using the blood of a Christian child was truly delivered by my late brother, according to my recollection. Vienna, on 12th June, '82. Prof. Veith, m.p." (The uneven structure of the sentences, which is not strange in a man of advanced years, proves that Prof. Veith immediately and readily complied with the request for him to write down what he remembered, that therefore no attempt was perchance made to induce him to sign a declaration he had not himself written).

The Israelite religious community in Vienna possesses the following writing, which DR. EDUARD KAFKA, *the celebrated barrister, addressed to Dr. Alois Müller, the University Librarian at Graz, on 30 August, 1883. (The original has lain before me):*

"It is a NOTORIOUS *fact, and therefore needs no proof, that Dr. Veith said in the [Viennese] City Church am Peter, before a congregation as crowded as usual [and one] of a most highly educated public, as was always the case, at the period when for the first time for centuries the absurdity that the Jews used Christian blood at Easter again cropped up, and was being used as a pretext by the populace for plundering the Jews: Dear Christians! I was myself born a Jew, and have a most thorough knowledge of their laws, and esteem myself happy to have become a Christian, but on my word of honour, and with the clearest conscience, I declare and confirm it to you that Judaism possesses no such law and no such interpretation of law, nor has ever followed such.'—I myself, who never omitted a sermon of Veith, was one of those who heard him say this. He always published his sermons systematically in book form; whether he included this episode in his next book I do not know. . . . So far as I am concerned, I do not go into the question of the Talmud and its interpreters,*

because I do not possess the necessary knowledge for it, but I judge merely according to the course of history, and say: If the need of Christian blood were a command or a custom of Judaism, all orthodox Jews would be bound to know, and to practise it. However, we hear of nothing of the kind either from Jerusalem nor from Poland, where the greatest Jewish fanatics live; only the poor, small ignorant community of Tisza-Eszlar is alleged to have been an exception. Why, Christian blood might be got from America, China, etc., and it would be a very costly article of traffic, of which nobody has ever heard."

So far Dr. Kafka. As the declaration of Veith was only an "episode," it is quite natural that it was not reproduced in the collections of sermons, at least, as far as I have been able to ascertain. According to the three independent testimonies of Prof. Molitor, Prof. Veith, and Dr. Kafka is it nevertheless to be considered certain, that J. E. Veith publicly and solemnly spoke out against the blood-accusation.

Dan. Chwolson (Prof. of Oriental Languages in St. Petersburg), "Die Blutanklage und sonstige mittelalterliche Beschuldigungen der Juden." Frankfort a. M. 1901 (362).

Christ. H. Kalkar, Dr. theol., Pastor (in Copenhagen, ob. 1886), son of a distinguished Rabbi, in a declaration on 22nd October, 1882 (v. "Christliche Zeugnisse gegen die Blutbeschuldigung der Juden," Be., 1882, 23 sq.).

Alex. Mc.Caul, "Reasons," 45 sq., 57 sq., published the following statement signed by 58 *proselytes*: "We, the undersigned, by nation Jews, and having lived to the years of maturity in the faith and practice of modern Judaism, but now by the peace of God members of the Church of Christ, do solemnly protest that we have never directly nor indirectly heard of, much less known amongst the Jews, of the practice of killing Christians or using Christian blood, and that we believe this charge, so often brought against them formerly, and now lately revived, to be a foul and Satanic falsehood."—The first of the signatories, M. S. Alexander, at that time Professor of Hebrew and of Rabbinical Literature, was once Rabbi at Norwich and Plymouth, and became later Anglican Bishop of Jerusalem (d. 23 November, 1845). And also every one acquainted with the history of the mission to the Jews knows about most of the others, that they proved themselves upright Christians in their lives and teaching.

A similar declaration (in the German language) was made on 16th November, 1899, by more than thirty Jewish Christians living in Jerusalem. It lies before me in two despatches attested by the English missionary, A. Hastings Kelk. The chief sentences run: "As born Jews, who are intimate with all the ritual prescriptions, uses, and traditions of the Jews, and all Jewish sects, and as Christians who believe in Him who is the truth and the light, we hereby testify solemnly before the All-knowing Triune God, by the salvation of our souls and by our honour and conscience, that the accusation against the Jews in general or any Jewish sect whatever, that they are either compelled to use or have used at any time Christian blood or human blood for ritual purposes, is an absolutely mistaken, false calumny, lacking in all foundation, and is nothing but a calumny."

The signatures (I put them in alphabetical order) are: Lazar Abramovich, Samuel Alkalay, J. Th. Altaresky, Samuel Amada (?), Hermann Axler, Vitali Behor, Salomon Beinisch, Simon Bortnikoff, Adolph Datzi, Joseph Datzi, Samuel Feldmann, John Morris Goldmann, Nathan Grossmann, J. Haddas, Bernhard Heilpern, Lucas Huff, Peppi John Karp, Johannes Kroiter, Paul Levertoff, J. Lyons, Isidor

Metzger, M. Perahas, Jaca Perahia, P. Reinstein, Joseph J. Silbermann, Josef Stern, S. Wisemann, Franz Zimmermann, Hermann Zimmermann, jr.

C. POPES.

The peculiarly high position of the Popes justifies me in devoting a special section to them. The utterances of the Popes are the more significant, in that they shared the mistaken notions of their age in regard to magic, witchcraft, etc. (Cf. Graf von Hœnsbrœch, "Das Papsttum in seiner sozial-kulturellen Wirksamkeit," vol. i., L. 1900). The anonymously published work, "Die Päpstlichen Bullen über die Blutbeschuldigung," Be., 1893, and Munich (Aug. Schupp), 1900 (151), contains on pp. 1-36 the Bulls of Innocent IV. of 28th May (2) and 5th July, 1247, and of 25th September, 1253; Gregory X.'s of 7th October, 1272, Martin V.'s of 20th February, 1422; and Paul III.'s of 12th May, 1540; and further on pp. 37-133, the expert report of Lor. Ganganelli in 1759 (infr. p. 259.).—Cf. also *Moritz Stern*, "Urkundliche Beiträge über die Stellung der Päpste zu den Juden," 2 vols., Kiel, 1893, 95 (192 and 72 pp., unfortunately not completed).

Besides the Bulls that expressly rebut the blood accusation, there is also importance in the numerous "Bulls of protection," especially those in which the *ritual of the Jews* is also taken *under protection.* The oldest of the "Sicut Judaeis" Bulls that have been preserved is that of Alexander III. (1159-81) who explicitly announces his intention of walking, in this respect, in the footsteps of his predecessors, Calixtus II. (1119-24, and Eugene III. (1145-53) (Mansi, "Conciliorum nova et amplissima collectio," XXII., 355 sq.; *Stern*, "Beiträge," No. 171). Under threat of excommunication, he forbids forcing Jews to be baptized, killing or wounding them without judicial trial, robbing them of their money, disturbing* them in the celebration of their festivals with cudgels or stone-throwing, or damaging their churchyards. Clement III., 1187-91 (Stern, No. 172), Coelestinus III., 1191-8 (No. 173), Innocent III., 1198-1216 (No. 174), Honorius III. 1216-27 (No. 178), Gregory IX., 1227-41 (No. 195), Innocent IV., 1243-54 (Nos. 204, 208, 212), Urban IV., 1261-4, Gregory X. (10th September 1274; Cf. Potthast, "Regesta Romanorum Pontificum," 20915), Nicholas III., 1277-80; Honorius IV., 1285-7; Nicholas IV., 1288-92; Clement VI., 1342-52 (4th July, 1348); Urban V., 1362-70 (7th July, 1365); Boniface IX., 1389-1404 (2nd July, 1389); Martin V., 1417-31 (Stern, No. 11); Eugene IV., 1431-47 (No. 34), renewed this Bull.

Among other Bulls of protection that belong here let the following be mentioned. On 6th April, 1233, Gregory IX. commanded the Archbishops and Bishops of France to take care that the Jews should not be maltreated, despoiled, or banished without proper reason or proved guilt, but they should be let live according to their Law in the customary way (" secundum legem suam vivere in solito statu permittant.") He closes with words worth taking to heart: "The same kindness, however, should be shown Jews by Christians as we wish should be shown to Christians living amongst the heathens" (Stern, No. 192).† In two Bulls of 5th September, 1236, the same Pope demands that compensation be given the persecuted and plundered Jews of France (Nos. 196, 197).—

* "Praesertim in festivitatum suarum celebratione quisquam fustibus vel lapidibus nullatenus perturbet."

† "Est autem Judeis a Christianis exhibenda benignitas, quam Christianis in paganismo existentibus cupimus exhiberi."

Martin V., 1417-31, confirmed on 12th February, 1418, the privileges and marks of favour (No. 9) granted by previous Popes to all Jews in Germany, Savoy, and Bresse, and explains this on 22nd February amongst other thing by the sentence, that they should be troubled by nobody in their synagogues, festivals, houses, books, churchyards, property, on account of their observance of the law ("propter eorum observantiam legis a nemine valeant aggravari," No. 10). Confirmation of the privileges on 1st January, 1421, occasioned by the complaints of some Austrian and Venetian Jews (No. 16). On 13th February, 1429, the Dominican friars are forbidden to incite the populace in Italy against the Jews; the Jews are, in particular, not to be compelled to work on Sabbaths and other days on which they are accustomed to practise their ceremonies and laws, and they must not be prevented by a far-fetched pretext from observing their ceremonies, rites, laws, and ordinances, and rejoicing in them ("quominus eorum ceremonias, ritus, leges, et statuta observare illisque uti et gaudere valeant," No. 31). This prohibition was repeated, in great part verbatim (v. infr. p. 257 sq.), by Nicholas V., on 2nd November, 1447.—Julius III., 1550-5, expressly mentions in his confirmation of the privileges of the Jews at Ancona the liberty to live according to their ritual ("ritu vivendi," No. 106).

Pius II., 1458-64, wrote, shortly before his elevation to the Papacy, whilst he was Enea Silvio de' Piccolomini, the history of Bohemia. In that book he expresses himself about the persecution of the Jews, which took place in Prague in 1389, as follows "Historia Bohemica," Ch. 34; Works, Helmstädt, 1699, 48: "Inter haec Pragenses populari tumultu incitati atque in furorem acti Judaeorum domus invadunt, bona eorum diripiunt, domos incendunt atque inter duas horas non sexui non aetati parcentes *infelicem gentem gladio caedunt. Periisse aliquot milia feruntur, servati complurimi infantes misericordia bonorum civium baptismi gratiam acceperunt.* CALAMITOSUM GENUS HOMINUM *Judaei inter Christianos agentes, qui ubi paululum abundare creduntur mox, tamquam Jesu Christi Dei nostri majestatem contempserunt aut religioni illuserunt, non fortunas tantum sed vitam quoque amittunt. Impune apud Pragenses* FLAGITIUM *fuit, tum quia populi haud facile corriguntur scelera, tum quia Venceslaus desidia corruptus praesenti rerum statu contentus neque praeterita corrigere neque futura curavit. Fuit enim Venceslaus longe patri absimilis, voluptatum sequax ac laboribus refugiens, vini prorsus quam regni curiosior.*"*

Bulls printed directly against the "*blood-charge.*"

Innocent IV. The two Bulls of 28th May, 1247, resulting from the "Valréas case" (v. supr. pp. 179 sq.) are printed: Bulls 2-9; Stern, Nos. 206, 207. The Bull of 5th July is represented by: Bulls 10-13; Stern, No. 210; the single despatch of 18th August for Vienne, Stern, No. 211. The beginning of this original document of 5 July, 1247, repeats in detail the complaint of the Jews, "that certain spiritual and temporal princes, in order unjustly to appropriate their belongings, are meditating godless attacks on them, and inventing manifold occasions. . . . . Although the Holy Scriptures say, 'Thou shalt not kill,' and forbids them to touch anything dead at their Passover festival, they are falsely accused of dividing among themselves, precisely at the Passover festival, the heart of a murdered boy. . . . . And they are

* About this persecution, Cf. F. Palacky, "Geschichte von Böhmen," III., 54; Pelzel, "Lebensgeschichte Wenzel's I." 214 sq.; Grätz, "Gesch. der Juden[2]," VIII., 50, and the "Passio Judeorum Pragensium secundum Johannem Rusticum Quadratum," published by Tomek, in "Sitzungsberichte der Kgl. Böhm. Gesellschaft der Wissenschaften," 1877 [Prague, 1878].

malevolently charged with murder, when a dead boy is found anywhere." The judgment then runs: "We do not wish the aforesaid Jews to be unjustly tormented ('injuste vexari,') and therefore command you, that showing yourselves kindly and affable to them, you restore legal conditions whenever any thoughtless action has been taken against the Jews by the aforesaid prelates, nobles, and magnates, and do not tolerate that the Jews should be further unduly molested ('indebite molestari') on account of these or similar points."—Several persons have inferred from the words "injuste" and "indebite" that this Pope did not discountenance the blood-accusation in itself, but only when it was unjustified, and made without proof. This conclusion, however, is shown to be false, firstly, by the context of the three Bulls sent to France in 1247, secondly, by the despatch at least three times of a "Sicut Judaeis" Bull, thirdly by the Bull of the same Pope of 25th September, 1253, v. *Rössler*, "Deutsche Rechtsdenkmäler aus Böhmen undMähren," I. (Prague, 1845), 178 sq.; Bulls 14-17; Stern, No. 212. The chief sentence of the Bull of September, 1253, runs:

"*Ad haec malorum hominum pravitati [et]* avaritiae obviantes decrevimus ut nemo cimiterium Judaeorum inutilitare vel minuere audeat seu obtentu pecuniae corpora humata effodere,* NEC ETIAM ALIQUIS EIS OBIICIAT, QUOD IN RITU SUO HUMANO UTANTUR SANGUINE, *cum tamen in veteri testamento praeceptum sit eis, ut de humano sanguine taceamus, quod quolibet sanguine non utantur, cum apud Fuldam [v. supr. p. 178 sq.] et in pluribus aliis locis propter hujusmodi* SUSPICIONEM *multi Judaei sint occisi, quod auctoritate praesentium, ne deinde fiat, districtius inhibemus.*"

* "Et" is wanting in the MS.

The attitude of Innocent IV. deserves the more consideration, because that Pope was by no means well-disposed towards the Jews, Cf. his ordinances of 23rd October, 1245, on the imposition of the Jewish mark, and 7th July, 1248, about the burning of the Talmud, dated 8th May, 1244, and the Bull of 5th January, 1245, directed against the Jews.

Gregory X., 1271-6. Dr. Moritz Stern was, so far as I know, the first to call attention to his Bull of 7th October, 1272. I owe my knowledge of its wording to the courtesy of Prof. M. Flunk, S.J., of Innsbruck (now also in Stern, "Beiträge," No. 1; Bulls 18-23). The original document, preserved in a 15th century copy, is at the present moment in the Government archives at Innsbruck; in the margin are three notes by the hand of Bishop Hinderbach, well-known through the proceedings in respect to Simon of Trent (v. supr. p. 193). The substance of the older Bulls of protection is renewed at the beginning and end; between them occurs the following pronouncement:

"*Statuimus eciam, ut testimonium Christianorum contra Judeos non valeat, nisi sit Judeus aliquis inter eos Christianos ad testimonium* perhibendum, cum Judei non possint contra Christianos† testimonium perhibere, quia contingit interdum, quod aliqui Christiani perdunt eorum pueros christianos et impingitur in Judeos ipsos per inimicos eorum, ut pueros ipsos christianos furtim subtrahant et occidant, et quod de corde et sanguine sacrificent eorundem, ac* PATRES EORUNDEM PUERORUM VEL CHRISTIANI ALII JUDEORUM IPSORUM EMULI CLAM ABSCONDUNT IPSOS PUEROS, UT POSSINT JUDEOS IPSOS OFFENDERE *et pro eorum vexacionibus redimendis*

* Hinderbach says indignantly in the margin: "Istud videtur esse iniquum et non servatum."

The manuscript has "Judeos"; Hinderbach correctly: "Christianos vult dicere, ut credimus."

possint a Judeis ipsis extorquere aliquam pecunie quantitatem ASSERANTQUE FALSISSIME, QUOD JUDEI IPSI PUEROS *ipsos clam et furtim* SUBTRAXERUNT ET OCCIDERUNT ET QUOD JUDEI EX CORDE ET SANGUINE EORUM SACRIFICENT PUERORUM, *cum lex eorum hoc precise inhibeat et expresse, quod Judei ipsi tangant* non sacrificent, non comedant sanguinem neque bibant nec eciam comedant de carnibus animalium habentium ungues scissas, et hoc per Judeos ad christianam fidem conversos in nostra curia pluries probatum,* HAC OCCASIONE HUIUSMODI JUDEI PLURIMI PLURIES CONTRA IUSTITIAM CAPTI FUERUNT ET DETENTI. STATUIMUS, *quod Christiani in casu [et]† huiusmodi occasione contra Judeos audiri non debeant et mandamus,* QUOD JUDEI CAPTI HUIUSMODI OCCASIONE FRIVOLA A CARCERE LIBERENTUR NEC DEINCEPS HUIUSMODI OCCASIONE FRIVOLA CAPIANTUR, *nisi forte, quod non credimus,‡ in flagranti crimine caperentur. . . . . . .*"

The Bull issued by *Martin V.*, 1417-31, on 20th February, 1422, repeats much out of the old protective Bulls, to which reference is expressly made at the beginning. Here the following may find room, according to the "Analecta juris pontificii," XII. (1873), column 387 sq. (now also in Bulls 24-9, Stern, No. 21):

"*Sane querelam quorundam Judaeorum nuper accepimus continentem quod nonnulli praedicatores verbi Dei tam mendicantium ordinum quam aliorum ad populum praedicantes inter alia Christianis exhibent per expressum (praeceptum) ut fugiant et evitent consortia Judaeorum nec cum eis quoquo modo participent nec coquere aut ignem vel aliquid ad laborandum ministrare seu ab illis recipere seu Judaeorum pueros*

* Dele "tangant," or read "non tangant."

† The word "et" is wanting in the manuscript.

‡ Hinderbach: "Prout est compertum hic in civitate Tridentina."

lactare et alere audeant vel praesumant quodque facientes contra sint jure ipso gravibus excommunicationis sententiis et censuris ecclesiasticis innodati. Propter quae nonnunquam inter eos et Christianos dissensiones et scandala oriuntur daturque materia ipsis Judaeis, qui forte ad christianam fidem converterentur, si pie et humane tractarentur, in eorundem perfidia perdurandi. Nonnumquam etiam plurimi Christiani, ut dictos Judaeos redimi facere et eos bonis et substantiis spoliare et lapidibus caedere possint, FICTIS OCCASIONIBUS ET COLORIBUS ASSERUNT *mortalitatum et aliarum calamitatum temporibus* JUDAEOS *ipsos* VENENUM IN FONTIBUS INJECISSE ET *eorum* AZYMIS HUMANUM SANGUINEM IMMISCUISSE; *ob quae scelera eis sic* INJUSTE *objecta talia asserunt ad perniciem hominum pervenire. Ex quibus occasionibus populi commoventur contra Judaeos ipsosque caedunt et variis persecutionibus et maleficiis afficiunt et affligunt.*"

Nicholas V., 1447-55, in consequence of a complaint of the Jews in Spain, repeated on 2nd November, 1447, the substance of the old Bull "Sicut Judaeis," and added: "In order to make the Jews more readily hateful to the Christians, some persons have presumed, and daily presume to assert falsely, and persuade Christians, that the Jews are unable to celebrate and do not celebrate certain festivals without the liver and heart of a Christian. . . . We forbid in the strictest way by this permanent and immutable ordinance. . . . all believers in Christ, in the future, either themselves or through others, publicly or privately, directly or indirectly, to take such action against the Jews or against any one of them."* The

* "Nonnulli . . . . ut facilius Judeos ipsos ad Christianorum odium deducere possint, eisdem Christianis quod dicti Judei aliquas festivitates absque iecore seu corde alicujus Christiani celebrare nequeunt neque celebrant falso asscrere illisque persuadere presumpserunt et dietim presumunt."

prohibitions issued by Martin V. on 13th February, 1429, are then repeated (v. supr. p. 252 sq.). The wording of this Bull was first made public in the *Israelitische Monatschrift*, 1893, No. 6 sq. (supplement to the *Jüd. Presse*, 1893, Nos. 22, 77), "Regest," Stern, No. 39.

Paul III., 1534-49, says in the protective Bull of 12th May, 1540, in which he alludes to Martin V., and many other predecessors, and confirms and declares permanent all the privileges granted to the Jews (v. Bulls 30-36. In the *Evangel. Kirchen-Zeitung*, 1900, No. 50, the wording is copied from the draft preserved in the Vatican archives):

"*Sane universorum Judeorum in partibus istis commorantium conquestionem displicenter accepimus, quod a nonnullis annis citra certi oppidorum domini ac nonnulle universitates et alii potentiores quidam in eisdem partibus degentes* :*emuli capitalesque ut ajunt eorundem Judeorum inimici odio et invidia aut quod verisimilius videtur* AVARICIA OBCECATI UT IPSORUM HEBRAEORUM BONA CUM ALIQUO COLORE USURPARE VALEANT, QUOD PARVULOS INFANTES OCCIDUNT UT EORUM SANGUINEM BIBANT ET ALIA VARIA ET DIVERSA ENORMIA CRIMINA *praesertim contra dictam fidem nostram tendentia eis* FALSO IMPINGUNT *sicque conantur simplicium Christianorum animos contra eos irritare, quo fit ut saepe non solum bonis sed propria vita injuste priventur.*"

Clement XIII., 1758-69, the "unchangeable friend of the Jesuits," spoke out twice, 9th February, 1760, and 21st March, 1763, against the blood-accusation (Bulls 144-151). On the former date he made Cardinal Corsini write to the Nuncio of the Apostolic See in Warsaw: "The Jews have often been accused of murder because of the ill-founded popular conviction ('sulla mal fondata persuazione del volgo,') that they mix human blood, especially that of Christians, in the dough of the unleavened loaves."

Lorenzo Ganganelli (as Pope Clement XIV., 1769-74), when he was adviser to the Holy Office in Rome, had, as the result of a petition by a Jew, Jacob Selek, to express himself professionally about the "blood-accusations." It is true he holds two cases of murder from hatred of the Christian faith to be historical (Simon of Trent, 1475, and Andreas, of Rinn, 1462, v. supr. pp. 193 sq., 191 sq.), but states that no general conclusion can be drawn from these particular cases, and very decisively opposes the assertion of the use of Christian blood for Jewish ritual purposes. He makes the excellent point that no single Pope has regarded the "blood-accusation" as justified. This fact seems to me significant because not a few Popes, in the matter of belief in *witches*, were not superior to the delusions of their contemporaries, e.g. the five Popes between 1484 and 1523: Innocent VIII., Alexander VI., Julius II., Leo X., Adrian VI.

The original Italian text of the report, which was completed in 1759, was first published by IS. LOEB *in the* "REVUE DES ÉTUDES JUIVES," *XVIII. (Paris, 1889), 185-211. A German translation was first given by* A. BERLINER, "*Gutachten Ganganelli's—Clemens XIV —in Angelegenheit der Blutbeschuldigung der Juden,*" *Berlin, 1888 (48).* M. STERN *discovered a better copy at Mantua, and at Verona the supplements as well, which till then were not known, and in 1893 he published it all, with valuable notes and a new translation, in "Die Päpstlichen Bullen über die Blutbeschuldigung," Be., 1893, and Munich (Aug. Schupp), 1900, 37-143.*

D. TEMPORAL PRINCES.

German Emperors, too, have declared themselves against the "blood-accusation," as well as Bohemian, Polish, Silesian, French, English, Italian, Hungarian, Russian, Turkish, and other rulers. I consider these declarations extremely significant; for nothing was easier then, by stating this accusation, to inaugurate persecutions of the Jews and lucrative confiscations of Jewish property. So I give here at any rate a selection, referring the reader for yet further material to *H. Hildesheimer's* essay in the *Jüd. Presse*, 1892, Nos. 16-19, 21.

1. *German Rulers.* Emperor Frederick II., v. supr. p. 239 sq.

Rudolph I. of Habsburg, 1273-91, confirmed on 4th July, 1275, the Bull of Innocent IV. of 5th July, 1247, and its renewal by Gregory X. on 7th July, 1274, v. *Ennen and Eckertz*, "Quellen zur Geschichte der Stadt Köln," III. (Cologne, 1867), No. 107. He added that Jews must and should altogether only be punished for a charge of the kind, if they are convicted by the legal evidence of Jews and Christians.* Rudolph's decrees in connection with the "good Werner" are in harmony with this, v. supr. p. 184.

Frederick III., 1440-93, owing to the Endingen trial, forbade in 1470 the accusation that Jews must have Christian blood, v. *J. Ch. Wagenseil*, "Widerlegung," L., 1705, 169-72; *J. Kracauer*, "L'affaire des Juifs d'Endingen de 1470," in "Revue des Études juives," xvi (Paris, 1888), 236-45.

Charles V., 1519-56. In the edict issued at Speyer on 3rd April, 1544, it is stated (Limnaeus, "Juris

* "Adicimus ut nulla omnino causa dampnari possint vel debeant, nisi legitimo Judeorum et Christianorum testimonio convincantur." Cf. the Jewish ordinance of Ottokar II. of Bohemia, infr. p. 262.

publici Imperii Romano-Germanici, Vol. I., additiones al libr. III., cap. 2;" *Jüd. Presse*, 1892, No. 17): "*After the Jewish community inform us how that they are frequently accused by their adversaries that they must have Christian blood for their needs, and are therefore said for their purposes to procure it from Christian beings, not (being accused) because of public or known deeds, or because of sufficient proof and information, but because of imaginary causes and suspicions, on the mere charge of their haters (not considering that our Holy Fathers, the Popes, have made declarations about this, and have forbidden it to be believed, and likewise our dear lord and ancestor, the Empreror Frederick, of most famous memory, in consequence of such Papal declaration, despatched grave letters of instruction to all ranks of the Holy Empire, addressing some of them in particular command that they should abstain from such actions, also prevent others from doing them, and not allow such things, but gravely commanded that, where such things happened the same should be communicated to His Majesty as supreme lord and judge, to whom the Jewish community are directly attached. Also, again, that the liberties and ancient traditions of the Jews are in the highest degree oppressed; they are imprisoned, tortured, brought from life to death, and their goods and property are ravished from them by force, and yet we learn from such Papal declarations, and the decrees pronounced by our ancestor, the late Emperor Frederick, so much information that such treatment must not be accorded to the Jews; therefore, and also because of other causes and motives, we resolve and will that in future no one, whatsoever his standing be, shall commit such actions against any Jew or Jewess, and without previous sufficient information or proof of credible witnesses, or discovery of the deed, punish and torture them, or sentence them from life to death; but when such complaint or conduct occurs the same must be communicated first of all to us or our posterity, Roman Emperors and Kings, as the supreme authority over the Jewish community in the Empire, and must there await decision.*"

This document was renewed by Maximilian II. (8th March, 1566), Rudolph II. (15th June, 1577), Matthias (13th November, 1612), Ferdinand II. (2nd March, 1621), Ferdinand III. (12th January, 1645), Leopold I. (22nd September, 1665).

2. *Bohemia.* Ottokar II., the rival of Rudolph of Habsburg, issued on 29th March, 1254, a decree about the Jews, whose 31st article runs:

"*In accordance with the ordinances of the Pope [Innocent IV., Bull of 25th September, 1253, v. supr. p. 253 sq.] in the name of our Holy Father, we most strictly prohibit that Jews dwelling in our dominions should further be accused of using human blood, since, according to the prescription of their law, all Jews must absolutely refrain from any blood whatever. When, however, a Jew is accused by a Christian of the murder of a Christian child, he must be convicted by three Christians and an equal number of Jews; and after he has been convicted, the Jew in question must himself be punished, and then only with the punishment established for the crime committed. But if the aforesaid witnesses do not convict him, and his innocence comes to light, the punishment shall deservedly be meted out to the Christian which the Jew would have had to suffer.*"*

* "Item iuxta constitutiones Pape in nomine sancti Patris nostri districtius prohibemus, ne de cetero Judaei singuli in nostro dominio constituti culpari debeant, quod humano utantur sanguine, cum iuxta preceptum legis ab omni prorsus sanguine se Judaei contineant universi. Sed si aliquis Judaeus de occisione alicuius pueri christiani per Christianum fuerit inculpatus, tribus Christianis et totidem Judaeis convinci debet; et postquam convictus fuerit, tunc ipse Judaeus tantummodo poena, quae sequitur, puniatur crimine pro commisso. Si vero ipsum testes supradicti [non convincant] et

The main sentence of this decree (up to "any blood whatever,") was renewed on 23rd August, 1268. Wencelaus II. confirmed this briefer version about 1300; John of Luxemburg, Charles I., on 30th September, 1356 (as German Emperor Charles IV.), and Wladislaw IV., on 14th May, 1454, renewed the version of 1254.

3. *Poland.* Boleslaus V. Pius, Duke of Kalisch, repeated verbatim the 31st article of Ottokar's Jewish decree in the "Privilegium libertatis," issued in 1264 for the Jews of Great Poland. Renewal by Casimir III. the Great on 9th October, 1334. Casimir IV. on 14th August, 1453, added to it, that, if a Christian in his audacity accused a Jew of the use of Christian blood, he must prove the charge by three trustworthy Jewish witnesses living in the kingdom [and four Christians of the same kind (thus the Codex Bandtkianus)]. If nobles or burghers do violence to Jews in such matter, their property shall be sequestrated, the omission of the death penalty depend on especial royal mercy. Confirmation of this severer version by eleven later kings, e.g. by Stephen Bathory on 5th July, 1576, and the last King of Poland, Stanislaus Augustus, on 24th April, 1765. Cf. *Bandtkie*, "Jus Polonicum," Warsaw, 1831; Tugendhold, "Wahn," 57-9; *H. Sternberg*, "Geschichte der Juden in Polen unter den Piasten und Jagiellonen," L., 1878 (191).

4. SILESIA. Of the ancient Jewish "Privilegia," that of Duke Henry III. of Glogau, in 1299, and that of Duke Bolko II. of Schweidnitz, on 6th December, 1328, are preserved (reproduced in Sommersberg, "Silesiorum rei historicae et genealogicae accessiones," L., 1732, 105 sq. and 91 sq.); they are derived from the protective letters of Henry IV. and Henry V. of Bres-

sua innocentia expurgabit, poenam Christianus, quam Judaeus pati debuerat, non immerito sustinebit." Cf. *Rössler*, "Deutsche Rechtsdenkmäler aus Böhmen und Mähren" I. (Prague 1845), 180 sq.; *H. Jireček*, "Codex juris Bohemiae" I. (Prague 1867), 134; *J. Emler*, "Regesta diplomatica nec non epistolaria Bohemiae et Moraviae," Part II., 9 (Prague 1882), no. 17.

lau, the latter from the Jew ordinance of Ottokar IV. of Bohemia, using at the same time the penal ordinances in Boleslaus V.'s "Privilegium" (v. M. BRANN, "Geschichte der Juden in Schlesien I." Supplement I, in the JAHRESBERICHT DES JÜDISCH-THEOLOG. SEMINARS IN BRESLAU, 1896).

5. *France.* Philip IV., the Fair, 1285-1314, was certainly very hostile to the Jews, but did not consider the blood-charge had any foundation. For, three weeks after thirteen Jews had been burnt, on 24th April, 1288, by the Inquisition at Troyes, in Champagne, owing to the alleged murder of a Christian, he prohibited the persons of the Order in the strictest way from arresting Jews without previous information to the judicial authorities. Cf. *A. Darmesteter*, "Deux élégies du Vatican," in "Romania," III. (1874), 443-86, and "L'autodafé de Troyes," in "Revue des Études juives," II. (1881), 199-247; *S. Salfeld*, 162 sq. Moreover, in the edict of 21st January, 1306, by which he ordered the expulsion of all Jews from France, neither the murder of Christians nor the use of blood is given as a reason.

Louis XIV. decreed, in consequence of the proceedings against Raphael Levi (Glatigny, between Metz and Boulay), who had been burnt January, 1670, that such charges against Jews should always be submitted to the King's High Council, v. *Grätz*, "Geschichte,"[2] X., 271.

6. *England.* Henry III., 1216-72, said in answer to the request of the German Emperor Frederick II., to send him some proselytes for the purpose of testing thoroughly the blood-accusation (Cf. supr. p. 260): he would gladly send two of his most trustworthy converts ("duo de discretioribus neophytis qui reperiri potuerunt in regno nostro,") but a case like that of Fulda was unheard of in England ("casum a nobis inauditum.") Cf. *Huillard-Bréholles*, "Historia diplomatica Friderici II." (Paris, 1852), IV., 809.

7. *Italy.* The documentary record of Count

Edward of Savoy of 20th July, 1329 (Cf. supr. p. 190 sq.) was first called attention to in Germany by *H. Hildesheimer* (*Jüd. Presse*, 1892, No. 18, p. 211); the complete wording is to be seen in *M. Stern*, "Beiträge," I., No. 2. The Jews are not only declared not guilty of the employment of human blood for ritual objects in the particular case, but also in general; for the corroboration of this judgment reference is made also to the Bulls of Innocent IV., of 5th July, 1247, and Gregory X., of 7th October, 1272.

Decree of the Doge of Venice, Petrus Mocenigo, 22nd April, 1475; decree of the Dukes of Milan, Bona and Johannes Galleazzo Sforza, 19th May, 1479; judgment of the Podestà of Verona, Justinian Contareno, 28th February, 1603; prohibition of the Duke of Mantua and Montferrat, 26th July, 1603; decree of the Senate of Venice, 8th April, 1705; v. GUIDETTI, "Pro Judaeis"; JUD. PRESSE, 1892, No. 18, p. 211 sq., and No. 19, pp. 224-6; GANGANELLI (ed. Stern), 96-100.

8. *Hungary.* The Royal Constitution of 1791 says in article 38: "The Royal Government has. . . . to enjoin it upon all the counties, that a point should be made of extirpating from the minds of the people the prejudice that human blood is sacrificed at the religious service of the Jews, in the way best suited to local circumstances. . . . and of teaching the people that this revolting offence . . . . is contrary to the Mosaic law; consequently, in the case of a murder, which has been committed by some Jew or other, even if it was shown that it was committed from superstitious intention, it could with as little justice be imputed to the whole Jewish religion, as the whole of Christendom could not be accused on account of such cases, when they happen among Christians. (*Jüd. Presse*, 1892, No. 19, p. 226, following Wertheimer's *Jahrbuch für Israeliten*, Vienna, 1862, 37 sq.)

9. *Russia.* At the behest of the Emperor Alexander I., Prince Alexander Galizyn, Head of the Department of the Religious Affairs of Foreign Con-

fessions in Russia, sent an edict to the Governor of Grodno, in which it is stated: "On the ground of the suspicion that they use Christian blood for their Pesach (Passover) cakes, the Jews, at the time of the Polish Dominion, were repeatedly accused of the murder of Christian children. Investigations have not corroborated the charge. . . . In consequence of accusations, which are now being raised against the Jews in some formerly Polish, now Russian, Governments, that murders of Christian children have happened for this object, and considering that such accusations have already been refuted before by unbiassed investigations and Royal decrees, His Imperial Majesty is pleased to command me to make known to all Governors as his will: that the Jews must no longer be accused without proofs, and merely owing to prejudice, of wanting Christian blood; should, however, a murder occur, and suspicion fall on Jews, apart from the prejudice that they employ Christian blood for ritual purposes, the inquiry must take place on a legal basis according to the same ordinances as hold good for persons belonging to other beliefs when they are charged with murder." 6th March, 1817. (*Tugendhold*, 89 sq.; *J. B. Levinstein*, "Blutlüge," 101 sq.)

10. *Turkey.* Sultan Soliman II. (1520-66), in consequence of an accusation, admitted to be false, gave orders that henceforth any accusation that the Jews use blood for their mazzoth should not be tried before any Judge, but before the Divan (i.e. the Sultan himself).

Abdul Medjîd issued on 6th November, 1840, the following firman: "An ancient prejudice has prevailed against the Jews. Ignorant people believed the Jews were accustomed to sacrifice a human being in order to employ the blood in the celebration of their Passover. Owing to this prejudice, the Jews of

Damascus [v. supr. p. 207] and Rhodes. . . . have been persecuted. . . . The charges levelled against them and their religion are sheer calumnies. . . . We forbid that the Jewish nation, whose innocence has been acknowledged, should be disturbed or tortured on account of a baseless accusation of the kind; rather should . . . indivduals of that religion enjoy equal rights with all the members of other nations subject to our power." (*Jüd. Presse*, 1892, No. 19, p. 227).

E. OTHER BORN-CHRISTIANS (SCHOLARS AND ECCLESIASTICS).

Andreas Osiander [a clergyman in Nuremberg] "Ob es war und glaublich sey, dass die Juden der Christen Kinder heymlich erwürgen und ir blut gebrauchen [appeared anonymously 1540, caused by the Pösing case in 1529, v. supr. p. 204 sq.] "Andreas Osianders Schrift über die Blutbeschuldigung, wieder aufgefunden, im Neudruck herausgegeben und erläutert von Moritz Stern," Kiel, 1900 (66).

The General of Dominicans, *John Baptist de Marinis* writes from Rome on 9th February, 1664, to the Provincial of the Order at Cracow, in order to protect the Jews against the charge of employing Christian blood for their unleavened bread:

> Moved by just sympathy, we enjoin on your Reverence that you and yours should come to the help of so unhappy a people against all slanders. . . Especially may Your Reverence command all preachers of the Divine Word to admonish the people not to persecute this unfortunate people by unallowable hatred, false accusations, fictitious rumours, and thereby to insult God, who is our and their (the Jews') Legislator, by foolishly thinking thereby to show the Supreme Being welcome obedience, although the Christian law and natural ethics teach otherwise. . . We trust to your insight . . that the Jews shall learn by your action that we do not desire their destruction, but their salvation."

Johann Christoph Wagenseil, 1633-1705, Professor of Jurisprudence and Oriental languages at Altdorf, near Nuremberg, a thorough scholar in Jewish writings and customs, who published several works written by Jews against Christianity under the title "Tela ignea satanae" (Altdorf, 1681), and therefore cannot be reproached with partisanship in favour of the Jews, wrote a book whose title runs: "Der Denen Juden fälschlich beygemessene Gebrauch des Christen-Bluts. Das ist Unwidersprechliche Widerlegung der entsetzlichen Unwarheit, Dass die Juden zu ihrer Bedürffnis Christen-Blut haben müssen, Welche so viel tausend dieser unschuldigen Leute um Haab, Gut, Leib und Leben gebracht" (in W.'s "Benachrichtigungen Wegen einiger die Judenschafft angehenden wichtigen Sachen," 1st Part, L., 1705, 126-206; also in "Hofnung der Erlösung Israelis, editio altera," Nuremberg and Altdorf, 1707. Supplement, 45-140).

Johann J Schudt, who was far from friendly disposed to the Jews, co-Rector of the Gymnasium at Frankfort a. M., in several passages of his thick volumes, "Jüdische Merckwürdigkeiten," Frankfort and L., 1714 sq., e.g. Bk. VI. Ch. 36, § 4, decisively declared the assertion false that Christian blood is required for any object of the Jewish ritual.

The professional opinion of the *Theological Faculty at Leipsic, of 8th May, 1714 (author G. Olearius)*, is printed in Ch. F. Börner's "Auserlesene Bedenken der theologischen Facultät zu Leipzig," L., 1751, 613-22, also in Löwenstein's "Damascia,"[2] 352-62.

F. HASELBAUER, 1736 (v. supr. p. 152): "Since I, the undersigned, have been entreated by Jonathan Eybeschütz, the Jewish preacher of Prague, in the name of the whole Jewish community, to give an answer in the form of testimony to the question: Whether the Jews have need of Christian blood according to their Talmud and Rabbinical customs? I herewith declare that I have found neither in any of the Jewish or Rabbinical writings, nor in other Hebrew books that have been printed, that such a thing is enjoined on the Jews therein; rather is all use of blood absolutely forbidden them as an abomination; likewise in the writing of Christians learned in

Judaism, such as Buxdorffer,* Eisenmenger,† and others, who have examined closely the errors and superstitions of the Jews and brought them to light, there is no reason to be found for this accusation, and, lastly, the whole body of Jews who entered the Christian faith before, as well as since the twenty-six years of my professorship, and have frankly revealed the weakness of their nation, have unanimously affirmed that this accusation of Christian blood being needed is a purely invented charge, which I herewith attest as a contribution to truth, and corroborate by signing my name and the printed seal of Tessers Collegium. Prague, the 20th October, 1736. FRANCISCUS HASELBAUER e Societate Jesu Librorum Hebr. Censor mpa."—The copy in the possession of the Israelite Religious Community in Vienna is authenticated by the Imperial-Royal book-controller and censor, Karl Fischer. The document was read by the Deputy Dr. Jos. Bloch in the Austrian Reichsrat at Vienna on 11th February, 1890, v. OESTERREICH. WOCHENSCHRIFT, 180, No. 18.

Christian Benedikt Michaelis (1680-1764) and *Johann Salomo Semler* (1725-91) on 21st February, 1760, v. supr. p. 152.—Semler's report is first printed in S.'s "Historisch-theologische Abhandlungen," 2nd series, 2nd part, Halle, 1762.

Joh. Friedr. von Meyer, "Erklärung über den angeblichen Blutgebrauch der Juden" (1841), in Löwenstein's "Damascia,"[2] appendix pp. 5-10; also in "Neuer Pitaval," II. (1842), pp. xxv. sq.

Franz Joseph Molitor (a learned Catholic, author of the "Philosophie der Geschichte"), "Erklärung über die Blutfrage im Judentum" (1841), in Löwenstein's "Damascia,"[2] Appendix pp. 11-16; also in "Neuer Pitaval," II. (1842), pp. xxx. sq.

BINTERIM [*a Catholic priest*], "*Über den Gebrauch des Christenblutes bei den Juden,*" *Düsseldorf, 1834 (29) and 1891 (20).*

WIEDENFELD [*an Evangelical pastor*], "*Was von der Behauptung, 'dass die Juden Christenblut. geniessen' zu halten sei? Ein Wort der Belehrung und*

* There is probably especial reference to Joh. Buxtorff, senior's (1564 to 1629) "Synagoga Judaica," Bâle 1603 and frequently.

† [Cf. however supr. p. 169 note.]

Warnung," *Elberfeld, 1834 (29).* *Cf. supr. p. 206 sq.*

Alexander McCaul, who is proved by his work "The Old Paths" [N^{e}thibôth'ôlām," or "The True Israelite"] to be not only thoroughly acquainted with Pharisaic Judaism, but also to be a penetrating, even too incisive a critic of it, published in 1840: "Reasons for believing that the charge lately revived against the Jewish people is a baseless falsehood," London (58).

Franz Delitzsch (ob. 4th March, 1890). Cf. supr. p. 157, and "Christliche Zeugnisse," etc., 12-18.

H. Oort, "Der Ursprung der Blutbeschuldigung gegen die Juden," Leyden and L., 1883 (31).

Alois Müller (Catholic), "Brauchen die Juden Christenblut?" Vienna, 1884 (16).

Gustaf H. Dalman, "Die Tötung Ungläubiger nach talmudisch-rabbinischem Recht.," L., 1885 (48).

J. J. J. v. DÖLLINGER *in his speech delivered at the Munich Academy on 25th July, 1881, v. "Akademische Vorträge,"*[2] *I. (Munich, 1890), 208 sq.: "Accustomed to the idea that every Jew was the born enemy and debtor of the Christian, the nations, at a time which, moreover, credulously grasped at the horrible and unnatural by preference, nay, even with greediness, held the Jews capable of any crime, even the most improbable or impossible. . . . If there was a corpse anywhere, on which there appeared traces of violence, or a dead child was found, a Jew was bound to be the murderer; as a rule it was assumed the crime was committed by several people together, and torture was continued until they made confession. Then followed horrible executions, and in many cases a killing of the whole Jewish population in town and country en masse. An orderly, unprejudiced trial was not to be imagined. The judge or magistrate themselves trembled at the rage of the populace, who were convinced beforehand, for it was now an estab-*

lished presumption that the worst villainous deeds were to be expected from each member of the murderous nation."

DIONYSIUS LATAS, *Greek Archbishop of Zante, at the International Congress of Religions at Chicago, made the following statement on 23rd September, 1893, v.* OESTERR. WOCHENSCHR., *1893, No. 44, p. 864: "The belief is widespread in the Orient among the ignorant masses of the population that Jews use the blood of Christian children for the objects of their religious ritual, and, in order to procure such, do not shrink from committing murders. Persecutions of the Jews frequently break out because of this belief, and the innocent victims are exposed to many deeds of violence and dangers. Considering the fact that such erroneous ideas are also widespread among the ignorant masses of other countries and that in the last decade Germany and Austria were the scene of maltreatment of innocent Jews, who were charged with having perpetrated such ritual murders, I, as a Christian priest, demand of this Congress that we record our conviction that Judaism forbids murder of any kind, and that none of its sacred authorities or books commands or permits murder or the use of human blood for ritual purposes or religious ceremonies. The spread of such a* CALUMNY *against the believers in a monotheistic religion is* UNCHRISTIAN. *It is irreconcilable with a Christian's duty to leave so terrible an accusation uncontradicted, and the good name of Christendom requires that I should beg this parliament to declare that Judaism and the Jews are as guiltless of the crime imputed to them as were the Christians of the first centuries."*

NATHANAEL, *Greek Archbishop of Brussa, Pastoral Letter of 15th April, 1893. "A few days before Easter a young man of Ghemlek, by name Charalambos Spanon, was found dead near the village of*

Cazikli, near Brussa. . . . The doctor examined the body, and after finding neither wounds nor other marks of violence, came to the conclusion that the young man, who was not normal mentally, had spent the night at the spot, and finally been frozen to death. . . . We do not understand how his death can be attributed to the Jews. This absurd assertion, which was disseminated by malicious persons, provoked the inhabitants of Ghemlek against the Jews, several of whom were maltreated. These deeds of violence have been repeated in other places in our diocese. . . . These barbaric actions have filled us with great pain and sorrow. . . . Nothing is less in consonance with the spirit of our holy religion than the racial hatred and the blind fanaticism which provoke the lower passions of the populace. Therefore, and because we consider absurd and mad the belief that the Jews slaughter Christian children in order to use them for secret rituals, we advise you herewith paternally to refrain from any deed of violence against the Jews. Those who act contrarily will incur censure from us and punishment from the Imperial [Turkish] Government. . . . We beg you to live in freedom and accord with all your fellow-burghers, as the Holy Scriptures prescribe in the words: 'Blessed are the peace-makers: for they shall be called the children of God.' We also entreat for you the mercy of our Saviour, and give you our Archiepiscopal blessing." *Cf.* OESTERR. WOCHENSCHRIFT, *1893, No. 30, p. 563 sq.*

Fr. Frank [a Catholic priest], "Der Ritualmord vor den Gerichtshöfen der Wahrheit und der Gerechtigkeit," Regensburg, 1901 (327), "Nachträge," 1902 (100).

"Christliche Zeugnisse gegen die Blutbeschuldigung der Juden," Be., 1882 (58) [22 declarations and professional reports by Faculties (Amsterdam,

Utrecht, Copenhagen, Upsala, Christiania), bishops, and scholars, among others by Franz Delitzsch, Paul de Lagarde, Ad. Merx, Th. Nöldeke, C. Siegfried of Jena, H. L. Strack and A. Wünsche of Dresden, drawn up apropos of the Tisza-Eszlar proceedings].

A similar compilation, which, however, also goes back to former times, is, "Die Blutbeschuldigung gegen die Juden. Von christlicher Seite beurtheilt," Vienna (Steyrermühl), 1883.

The International Orientalist Congresses at Leiden, 1883, and Rome, 1899, also declared themselves against the blood accusation.

XX. ABOUT THE ORIGIN OF THE "BLOOD-ACCUSATION"

The blood-accusation in its narrower sense, i.e., the assertion that the Jews need Christian blood, is not yet seven centuries old. The monk Rudolph of Mainz, who incited against the Jews in 1146, certainly described them as enemies of the Christian religion, but without mentioning the blood-accusation. And it is as little mentioned by Bernhard of Clairvaux (1091-1153), who, contrary to this Rudolph, warned against murder of the Jews. Agobard, Archbishop of Lyons (ob. 840), made the most violent attacks on the Jews in his works "De Insolentia Judaeorum" and "De Judaicis superstitionibus," in order to keep the Christians as far as possible away from the Jews. He, however, makes not the slightest allusion to the employment of Christian blood by Jews; he does not even say that Jews had committed murders of Christians. His silence is therefore a strong proof that he knew nothing whatever about the "blood-accusation." Aug. Rohling accordingly uttered a gross untruth when he wrote in "Meine Antworten an die Rabbiner," p. 56, that Agobard had, in the two above-named works, "published the more ancient facts of the case."

1. The most ancient accusation against the Jews connected with our work is that out of hatred against Christianity and the Christians they crucify Christian children at the time of the Christian Easter (Inmestar 416, William of Norwich 1144, v. supr. p. 176 sq.).

2. On a line with this and connected with it we find the blood-superstition operative, i.e., the conviction that an especial magical and cure-working power is a quality peculiar to the human blood. It is easy to assume that one's fellow-man also shares a superstition in which one is oneself entangled; one is particularly disposed thereto in the case of those with whom one lives in the same country, but whose language, religion and custom one does not know. Now, there can scarcely be any doubt that the Jews, on the average, knew more about the people in whose midst they lived than the latter about the Jews.* It is therefore, on the whole, easier to assume a transference of folklorist (popular-medical, superstitious, etc.) notions from the ruling peoples to the Jews than the inverse. We have now seen that the belief in the efficacy of the blood, apart from the purely religious offering, was widespread almost universally since very ancient times, but is relatively very rare precisely in the case of the Jews. Accordingly it is probable that the view which was first expressed in the thirteenth century, that the Jews make use of Christian blood as a means of cure (Fulda 1235, Thomas of Cantimpré, v. supr. p. 178 sq.), springs from the belief which was widespread among the Jews in the Middle Ages in the great effectiveness of blood. So far as a judgment is possible after a critical testing of the tradition, this belief has only been imputed to the Jews of the Middle Ages and of later times, but they did not themselves possess it.

* *Thence*, it is also explained, that the Jews became in many ways the *object of superstitious ideas*, Cf. supr. p. 23, 25 sq.; p. 33 sq.; p. 75, 76; p. 94, 8 sq. and 18; p. 101, 22 sq. and 102, 22. Likewise, *Wuttke*[2] (v. index); *Ur-Quell* 1892, 51, 53, 54, 126-8, 150, 151, and 1897, 52. According to *Grimm*, "Mythologie," Supplement p. lxx., lxxxii., lxxxv., no. 473, there is a ghost dangerous to children called "Judel." In essentially evangelical country places, the Catholic priest is not seldom regarded as a wonderworker, or vice versa.

3. *Blood-ritual.* The Alexandrine grammarian Apion (first half of the first century A.D.) accused the Jews according to Josephus ("Contra Apionem," II., 8), that every year they fattened up a Greek in the temple, and then made of him a victim for sacrifice, and consumed part of his entrails, whilst they swore to be enemies of the Greeks ("occidere hominem et ejus corpus sacrificare secundum suas sollemnitates etgustare ex ejus visceribus et jusjurandum facere in immolatione Graeci, ut inimicitias contra Graecos haberent"). According to Suidas ("Lexicon," s.v. *Δαμόκριτος*) a certain Damocritos asserted that the Jews "*κατὰ ἐπταετίαν ξένον ἀγρεύοντες προσέφερον καὶ κατὰ λεπτὰ τὰς σάρκας διέξαινον καὶ οὕτως ἀνῄρουν.*"

We read nothing about a Jewish blood-ritual for much longer than a thousand years, till right into the thirteenth century. It is mentioned for the first time in 1236 on the occasion of the Fulda case (v. pp. 178, 239, 276), but then already as being generally believed in Germany. The Emperor Frederick II. asks "utrum, sicut fama communis habet, Judei christianum sanguinem in parasceve necessarium haberent." King Henry III. of England writes in regard to the question put him by the Emperor: "Casum a nobis inauditum." Whence came this "fama communis?" I think it very probable that it was due to such notions as Thomas Cantimpré put forward (v. supr. pp. 178, 239), partly on the authority of a proselyte who was hostile to the Jews.—The Christian Easter festival is almost simultaneously mentioned.

In 1247 the Jews tortured at Valréas (v. p. 179), "confessed" on 4th April, after sufficiently long torturing, especially the following (a) Bendig: Out of fear of the populace, the blood had been poured into the privy.* With part of the blood they wanted to hold communion on the Saturday in Passion Week, because they believed they would thereby be relieved of sin. That was a custom among the Jews, and where there many of them it took place yearly, especially in Spain, and if no Christian could be procured, they bought a Saracen.† (b) Burcellas, in answer to the question what they wanted to do with the blood, said: That in olden times the high priest had sprinkled the altar with the blood. (c) Lucius: That if a child could be got, they wanted to make out of the blood a sacrifice as it were,‡ and that they were under obligation to send some of the blood to other Jews, and that the child ought really to have been crucified on Good Friday (v. supr. p. 178), but they had not been able to conceal it so long, and therefore already killed it on the Wednesday night. All had touched the girl, in order to obtain atonement.§—In the same year,

* He who wants blood and is accustomed ("consuetudo") to murder for the sake of blood, is sure (there can be no doubt about it) to think *before* every murder about a safe place for keeping the costly stuff, and will not be ready to throw away the blood from fear of discovery.

† "Quod de dicto sanguine debebant communicare die sabbati sancto [30th March] nuper preterito et credebant salvari. Item dixit idem Bendig, quod consuetudo est inter Judeos et ubicunque maxima sit multitudo Judeorum, facere factum simile annuatim et maxime in partibus Yspanie quia ibi est maxima multitudo Judeorum, et quando non possunt habere Christianum, emunt Saracenum." The absurdity of the "confessions" is here, too, a proof, that the martyred men finally said everything that was expected to be heard from them. Rightly does Stern remark, "Beiträge" II., 50, on Bendig's statement: "But in Valréas there was precisely a quite small Jewish community. So, how many Christian children must have been killed at Easter every year! In spite of zealous examination of authoritative sources no case of such an accusation has yet come to light before 1247. Neither in Spain, nor in the countries of Islam, did even a single accusation of a ritual murder of a Saracen occur during the whole of the Middle Ages."

‡ "Quasi sacrificium." This phrase is explained by L. by the additional statement that the Jews could not offer a real sacrifice, because they had no temple.

§ Cf. the laying-on of hands at the sin-offering, Leviticus IV., 15. Copy of the protocol in *Stern*, "Beiträge," no. 205.

1247, the Jews of Germany and France complain to Pope Innocent IV. that they are accused of communicating at the Passover Feast with the heart of a slaughtered child.*

It is extremely probable also that several factors were operative in the swift dissemination of the charge, and no doubt in different ways in different places and times. At any rate, hatred and envy co-operated everywhere, even as they were the principal motives for the accusation that the Jews poisoned the wells.† The general imagination excited in some way (e.g., by the Crusades, by the Black Death) may also have received an impulse from the following facts:—(1) The circumstance that the Easter loaves (Maççoth) were produced with special solemnities, unintelligible to the Christians.—(2) The superstitious value once set upon the Easter loaves by many Jews, and still set upon them.—(3) The Jews remembered in their Easter Festival the Israelite children destroyed, according to the legend (supr. p.

* "Quod in ipsa solempnitate se corde pueri communicant interfecti." Bull of 5th July, 1247, v. supr. p. 253.

† This accusation occurs in 12th century in Bohemia, 1308 in the Waadt, 1321 in France, 1348 and 1349 in Germany. It was said the poison was prepared out of poisonous plants, human blood, urine, and a consecrated wafer [cf. supr. p. 58] and then thrown in a bag into the well. Cf. Grätz, "Geschichte" VII., 369 sq.—Konrad von Megenberg writes in his "Buch der Natur," p. 112: "Veritably whether some Jews did it, I know not . But I know well, that there were more of them in Vienna than any other city that I knew in German lands, and that they died there in such large numbers that they had greatly to enlarge their churchyard there, and had to buy two houses. Now if they had poisoned themselves, it would have been a foolishness."—Clement VI., 1342-52 declared in his Bull of 20th September, 1348, that the Jews were unjustly reproached with well-poisoning, since they were carried off by the plague just like Christians; he therefore forbade, under penalty of excommunication, the persecution of the Jews under this pretext, v. Raynaldus, "Annalen" 1348, no. 33. Martin V. v. supr. p. 256 sq.—It is curious that this accusation was also levelled against foreigners during the disturbances in China, v. "Globus" 1890, p. 384.

62 sq.), by the leprous Pharaoh, and likewise the other murdered Jews, and they therefore liked to choose red wine for the "four cups," "arbaa' kosôth," which were commanded to be drunk on the two commencing evenings. That ignorance has actually made out of this the consumption of blood is testified by the Polish Rabbi David ha-Levi ben Samuel (born c. 1600) in his highly-prized commentary, "Ṭurê Zahāb," on the "Shulḥan 'Arukh, Oraḥ Ḥajjim," 472, 8, and he asks that this usage should be given up on account of the lies connected with it.—(4) The want of knowledge of the "Drachenblut,"* which is used for the healing of the wound of circumcision, has also given rise to the "blood-accusation."—(5) It is possible that in single cases the Hebrew word "Damîm" (plural only), "money," has been confounded with "Dām," also often in the plural, "Damîm," "blood," and thereby the gaining of money has been converted into thirst for blood (Cf. Schudt, "Jüd. Merckwürdigkeiten," I., 468.)—Cf. also supr. p. 178, and *H. Oort*, "Ursprung der Blutbeschuldigung gegen die Juden," Leiden, 1883.

A serious warning as to the bringing forward of the imputation that Christian blood is employed for a rite of the Jewish religion is also afforded by history. History shows that imputations of the kind have repeatedly been a terrible weapon against innocent persons (innocent, at least, in that connection). The Christians of the second and third centuries suffered

* "Drachenblut" ("dragon's blood") is the dark, blood-red resin, e.g., of the Calamus Draco (Willd.), a palm native of Central India, also of the Pterocarpus Draco (L.), native of the West Indies, the Dracaena Draco (L.), etc. Cf. *H. Lojander*, "Beiträge zur Kenntniss des Drachenblutes," Strassburg i. E. 1887 (73).

severely under them. The celebration of Holy Communion, the mention of partaking of the body and the blood of the Lord afforded a point of connection.* Already the younger *Pliny*, 111 sq., Pro-consul of the province of Bithynia in Asia Minor, appears to have cherished suspicion and to have started an inquiry.† At any rate, he writes ("Epist," X. 97 to the Emperor Trajan) that the persons accused of belonging to the Christian belief, and therefore summoned by him for inquiry, had assured him that they had bound themselves by an oath, not indeed for any vicious purpose, but not to commit theft or adultery, to keep their promises, and not to disown what was entrusted to them. At their meetings they had enjoyed

* The 13th Fragment of Irenaeus in Stieren's edition (I., 832) relates that the heathens had forced heathen slaves, serving in Christian houses, to give evidence about the Christians. In their fear, these slaves, who had heard of the receiving of the body and blood in the holy communion, had given information about this, "αὐτοὶ νομίσαντες τῷ ὄντι αἷμα καὶ σάρκα εἶναι, τοῦτο ἐξεῖπον τοῖς ἐκζητοῦσιν." Cf. Justin, "Apol." ii. 12 (v. p. 282).

† Who or what aroused this suspicion in him is not known to us. But we know well that the Jews were not guiltless of the spreading-abroad of this untrue "blood-accusation." *Origen*, "Contra Celsum, VI., 27, writes "ἐβουλήθη γὰρ [ὁ Κέλσος] τοὺς ἀπείρους τῶν ἡμετέρων ἐντυχόντας αὐτοῦ τῇ γραφῇ πολεμῶσαι πρὸς ἡμᾶς ὡς θεὸν κατηραμένον λέγοντας τὸν τοῦδε τοῦ κόσμου καλὸν δημιουργόν. Καὶ δοκεῖ μοι παραπλήσιον Ἰουδαίοις πεποιηκέναι, τοῖς κατὰ τὴν ἀρχὴν τῆς τοῦ χριστιανισμοῦ διδασκαλίας κατασκεδάσασι δυσφημίαν τοῦ λόγου, ὡς ἄρα καταθύσαντες παιδίον μεταλαμβάνουσιν αὐτοῦ τῶν σαρκῶν, καὶ πάλιν ὅτι οἱ ἀπὸ τοῦ λόγου τὰ τοῦ σκότου πράττειν βουλόμενοι σβεννύουσι μὲν τὸ φῶς, ἕκαστος δὲ τῇ παρατυχούσῃ μίγνυται· ἥτις δυσφημία παραλόγως πάλαι μὲν πλείστων ὅσων ἐκράτει πείθουσα τοὺς ἀλλοτρίους τοῦ λόγου ὅτι τοιοῦτοί εἰσι Χριστιανοί, καὶ νῦν δὲ ἔτι ἀπατᾷ τινας ἀποτρεπομένους διὰ τὰ τοιαῦτα κἂν εἰς κοινωνίαν ἁπλουστέραν λόγων ἥκειν πρὸς Χριστιανούς."

About the attitude of the Jews towards Jewish Christians and Christians in the first two centuries, Cf. Acts of Apostles IV. sq.; Justin, "Dialogue with Trypho," 17 and 108 (the Christians were a "αἵρεσις ἄθεος καὶ ἄνομος"); "First Apologia," 31, 36; "The Martyrdom of Polycarp" XIII., 1, and XVII., 2; Tertullian, "Ad nationes," 1, 17. But the Christians had no right to disregard the warning of the Apostle, I. Thessal., V. 15.

ordinary and innocent meals together; even this they had omitted after my edict in which I had forbidden all public gatherings.—*Justin Martyr* (150-60) was obliged thus to depend his fellow-believers in the so-called "Second Apologia," Ch. 12: "What man, greedy of pleasure or intemperate, and finding satisfaction in the eating of human flesh, would call indeed death welcome and would not sacrifice everything in order to continue his usual mode of life unobserved and as long as possible? If you have extorted by means of tortures some single confessions from our slaves, wives and children, they are no proofs of our guilt. It is not we who do that which is laid to our charge; but you who did it, and yet worse do ye. We therefore needed not at all to deny it, if we did such things. We might term our meetings mysteries of Cronos; we might, if we filled ourselves with blood, as the talk goes, declare it to be a worship after the manner of your Juppiter Latiaris, and would be justified in your eyes." Cf. also "First Apologia," Ch. 26; "Dialogue with Trypho," Ch. 10. *Athenagoras* (177) writes in his "Apology" for the Christians addressed to Marcus Aurelius, Ch. 3: "Three main reproaches are levelled at us: atheism, Thyestean meals, and Oedipodean intercourse. . . . And yet even animals do not touch animals of the same family," and he then proceeds to confute these reproaches in detail (the second in Ch. 35 sq.). Theophilus of Antioch (180 sq.), "To Autolycus," Book III., 4 sq. In the letter of the Christians at Lyons and Vienne, preserved by Eusebius, "History of the Church," V., 1, the same accusations are mentioned. The following phrase is attributed to the woman martyr Byblias: "How could children be eaten by such people, who are not allowed to eat even the blood of senseless animals!" The theme is handled in especial detail in the "Octavius" (written perhaps in 180 A.D.) of Minucius Felix ("The heathen Caecilius," Chs., 9, 30, 31). Tertullian, too, is obliged to defend the Christians as compared with the heathens, who in reality do worse than they falsely assert about the Christians. I quote these words, worth taking to heart, from the beginning of the 7th Ch. of the "Apologeticum" (c. 200): "We are called the most villainous of mortals because of the secret practice of killing and eating children. . . . We are called thus; but you do not seek to prove it. *Prove it then, if you believe it, or believe it not, as you have not proved it.*" Likewise *Origen*, "Contra Celsum," VI., 40. Cf. further: *K. Semisch*, "Justin der Märtyrer," II. (Breslau, 1842), 105-13, and *Kortholt*, "De calumniis paganorum in veteres Christianos sparsis," Kiel, 1668, 157 sq.

Unfortunately Christians, after the Christian religion had become dominant, directed against others the calumny once directed against themselves; firstly against the Montanists, in the latter Middle Ages frequently against heretics, and, as is here shown in Ch. 18, since the 13th century against the Jews. Sectarians, who separated from the Church, were altogether thought capable of any shameful deed.

In regard to the *Montanists* cf. St. Jerome, "Epist." xli. 4: "Praetermitto scelerata mysteria quae dicuntur de lactente puero et victuro martyre confarrata. Malo inquam non credere; sit falsum omne quod sanguinis est." Augustine, "De haeres." 26: "Sacramenta perhibentur habere funesta. Nam de infantis anniculi sanguine quem de toto ejus corpore minutis punctionum vulneribus extorquent quasi eucharistiam suam conficere perhibentur, miscentes eum farinae panemque inde facientes: qui puer si mortuus fuerit, habetur apud eos pro martyre; si autem vixerit, pro magno sacerdote" (Cf. ibid. Ch.

27). In his book on predestination Augustine observes that Tertullian, in the lost work against Apollonius about ecstasy, defended the Montanists against the accusation "de sanguine infantis."—Epiphanius, "Haeres." xlviii. 14, also charges the Montanists with using the blood of a child for their sacrifices, whose body they had stabbed with needles. —Respecting the Gnóstics and the Manichaeans, v. supr. pp. 34-7.

Concerning the later Middle Ages, as at present leisure fails me to compile the facts myself, I refer the reader to Chr. U. Hahn, "Geschichte der Ketzer im Mittelalter," 3 vols., Stuttgart, 1845-50. He quotes III., 382 (following the "Brevis notitia" in "Bibliotheca maxima veterum patrum et antiquorum scriptorum," XXV., 308 (Lugdun. 1677), that the Catharians were upbraided because "Adorant Luciferum," and "pueros eorum ei immolant."—About religious concubitus ("omnibusexstinctis luminaribus, quam quisque primam poterat mulierem quae ad manum sibi veniebat ad abutendum arripiebat," following D'Achery "Spicilegium," I. [Paris, 1724], 605), ibid. III., 380, Cf. also 384, and I., 89 sq. Just the same accusation was brought against the Waldenses in Piedmont, v. J. P. Perrin, "Histoire des Vaudois," Geneva, 1619, 10 sq., in Hahn II., 148.

The last proceedings taken in the Middle Ages against Christian heretics on the ground of the "blood-accusation" is, so far as I know, the "Processus contra haereticos de opinione dampnata," against the "Fraticelli de opinione" existing in the march of Ancona and the neighbouring Romagna in 1466, cf. "Vier Documente aus römischen Archiven," L., 1843 (130), 1-48. Partly owing to the tortures applied, partly from fear of them, the majority of those brought up for examination confess, apart from deviations from the Church doctrine (e.g., the authority of the Pope), the following:—"In fine dictarum missarum lumina extinxerunt et dixerunt: Alleluja, Alleluja, Ciascuno se pigli la sua [quilibet capiat suam!]; et quod his verbis dictis quilibet eorum unam accipiebat mulierem. . . Quod . . . in unum coadunati . . . magnum ignem aliquando accenderunt . . et unum puerum inter eos natum in adulteriis praedictis genitum ceperunt et circum dictum ignem de uno ad alium duxerunt, usque quo mortuus et desecatus [read "desiccatus"] extitit. Et deinde ex illo pulveres fecerunt et in uno flascone vini posuerunt et . . . de hujusmodi vino, loco sacratissimi Christi corporis et verae communionis, ad bibendum semet praebuerunt et dederunt praebereque et dare consueverunt." Cf. too, the "Octavius" of Minucius Felix, Ch. 9, and Origen "Contra Celsum," VI., 27 (supr. p. 281 note).

Lastly, it may be mentioned that such accusations have often been directed not only against hated religious parties, but also against political foes.—ELIOT WARBURTON, *in the "Memoirs of Prince Rupert and the Cavaliers" (London, 1849), I., 17, II., 89, relates that the Puritans had spread the rumour that Charles I.'s cavaliers butchered and ate little children, and in consequence mothers used to overawe their children with the terror of the name of Rupert of the Palatinate.*—THACKERAY, *in "The Four Georges" ("Works," London, 1876, Vol. X., 329): "I came from India as a child, and our ship touched at an island on the way home, where my black servant took me a long walk, over rocks and hills, until we reached a garden, where we saw a man walking. 'That is he,' said the black man, 'that is Bonaparte! He eats three sheep every day, and all the little children he can lay hands on!'"*—LEO TAXIL'S *(the notorious inventor of the devil Bitru) pamphlet, "Der Meuchelmord in der Freimaurerei" (Paris), is known to me only through a review; according to it, he makes the stabbing of the traitor Ritus take place upon his elevation to the grade of a Kadosch-Knight. —For China and Madagascar, v. supr. p. 83 sq.*

INDEX

OF THE MOST IMPORTANT NAMES AND SUBJECTS

(An asterisk attached to the page-number signifies that a bibliography is to be found on that page. The important dates are added in the parentheses.)